LLLAM

BI 3392538 0

REPA

BIRMINGHAM CITY
UNIVERSITY
DISCARDED

CLARENDON STUDIES IN CRIMINOLOGY

Published under the auspices of the Institute of Criminology, University of Cambridge, the Mannheim Centre, London School of Economics, and the Centre for Criminological Research, University of Oxford.

GENERAL EDITOR: PER-OLOF WIKSTRÖM (*University of Cambridge*)

EDITORS: ALISON LIEBLING and MANUEL EISNER
(*University of Cambridge*)

DAVID DOWNES and PAUL ROCK
(*London School of Economics*)

ROGER HOOD, LUCIA ZEDNER, and RICHARD YOUNG
(*University of Oxford*)

Recent titles in this series:

Crime and Markets: Essays in Anti-Criminology
Ruggiero

Parliamentary Imprisonment in Northern Ireland: Resistance, Management, and Release
McEvoy

Policing World Society: Historical Foundations of International Police Cooperation
Deflem

Forthcoming titles:

Accountability in Restorative Justice
Roche

Investigating Murder
Innes

Repair
or
Revenge

Victims and Restorative Justice

HEATHER STRANG

CLARENDON PRESS · OXFORD
2002

UNIVERSITY OF
CENTRAL ENGLAND

UNIVERSITY OF
LIBRARY
SERVICES
CENTRAL ENGLAND

OXFORD
UNIVERSITY PRESS

Great Clarendon Street, Oxford OX2 6DP

Oxford University Press is a department of the University of Oxford.
It furthers the University's objective of excellence in research, scholarship,
and education by publishing worldwide in

Oxford New York

Auckland Bangkok Buenos Aires Cape Town Chennai
Dar es Salaam Delhi Hong Kong Istanbul Karachi Kolkata
Kuala Lumpur Madrid Melbourne Mexico City Mumbai Nairobi
São Paulo Shanghai Taipei Tokyo Toronto

Oxford is a registered trade mark of Oxford University Press
in the UK and in certain other countries

Published in the United States
by Oxford University Press Inc., New York

© Heather Strang 2002

The moral rights of the author have been asserted
Database right Oxford University Press (maker)

First published 2002
Published new in paperback 2004

All rights reserved. No part of this publication may be reproduced,
stored in a retrieval system, or transmitted, in any form or by any means,
without the prior permission in writing of Oxford University Press,
or as expressly permitted by law, or under terms agreed with the appropriate
reprographics rights organization. Enquiries concerning reproduction
outside the scope of the above should be sent to the Rights Department,
Oxford University Press, at the address above

You must not circulate this book in any other binding or cover
and you must impose this same condition on any acquirer

British Library Cataloguing in Publication Data

Data available

Library of Congress Cataloging in Publication Data

Data available

ISBN 0-19-925164-9 (hbk.)
ISBN 0-19-927429-0 (pbk.)

3 5 7 9 10 8 6 4 2

Typeset in Sabon by
Cambrian Typesetters, Frimley, Surrey

Printed in Great Britain
on acid-free paper by
Biddles Ltd., King's Lynn

UNIVERSITY OF
CENTRAL ENGLAND

Book no. 33925380

Subject no. 364.68 Sta

LIBRARY SERVICES

To my parents
Jim and Joan Preece

Acknowledgements

There are so many people who have contributed towards making this book a reality. First, I must thank my family for their generous patience and support. Then there are the many colleagues who have contributed to the research project of which this victim study is one part: these include Geoffrey Barnes, Nova Inkpen, and Malcolm Mearns, all of whom, I am happy to say, I continue to work with on new projects. I would particularly like to mention Dan Woods who has helped me with the data analysis throughout the book, especially in Chapter 7, where he is my co-author. I would also like to pay tribute to the skill of the Australian Federal Police officers who conducted sometimes extraordinary restorative justice conferences. My colleagues in the Research School of Social Sciences at the Australian National University have given me a wonderfully stimulating and encouraging environment in which to work. Finally, John Braithwaite and Larry Sherman have been inspirations and to each of them I owe so much. My grateful thanks to all of you.

Heather Strang
August 2002

General Editor's Introduction

The *Clarendon Studies in Criminology* was inaugurated in 1994 under the auspices of the centres of criminology at the Universities of Cambridge and Oxford and the London School of Economics. It was the successor to *Cambridge Studies in Criminology*, founded by Sir Leon Radzinowicz and J.W.C Turner almost sixty years ago.

Criminology is a field of study that covers everything from research into the causes of crime to the politics of the operations of the criminal justice system. Researchers in different social and behavioural sciences, criminal justice and law, all make important contributions to our understanding of the phenomena of crime. The *Clarendon Studies in Criminology* series tries to reflect this diversity by publishing high-quality theory and research monographs by established scholars as well as by young scholars of great promise from all different kinds of academic backgrounds. We especially welcome manuscripts representing theory-driven empirical research. The inter-disciplinary nature of criminology makes it apt for research that crosses disciplinary boundaries. We therefore also particularly welcome manuscripts that draw upon or integrate knowledge from different disciplines, for example, cross-level analyses of causes of crime or integrative approaches to criminal justice and crime prevention. Much criminological research is parochial in nature. There is a great need for more high-quality historic and cross-national comparative research that addresses, for example, the generality of criminological knowledge and the role of systemic factors for the patterns of crime and criminal justice. We welcome such contributions to the series.

Restorative justice is one of the hottest topics in current criminal justice debates. Academics and policy-makers differ as to the value of restorative justice as an alternative or complementary approach to criminal justice. One important aspect of this debate is the role of the victim in restorative justice. Heather Strang's book *Repair or Revenge: Victims and Restorative Justice* takes on this important question. Her aim is to explore what victims think about restorative justice. The book includes informative discussions of victimological research, the concept of restorative justice and previous research on restorative justice. The major empirical part of the book is the analysis of victim satisfaction using data from the Reintegrative Shaming Experiments in Canberra, Australia. This study compares court and restorative justice alternatives. Strang concludes her book with the argument that her research 'gives grounds for optimism for a better deal for victims through the restorative alternative'. It is my anticipation that Strang's book will be important for and central to the debate on the value of restorative justice for years to come.

Per-Olof H Wikström,
University of Cambridge and Centre for Advanced Studies
in the Social and Behavioral Sciences, Stanford (2002–3)
September 2002

Contents

List of Figures

List of Tables

1

The Victim in Criminal Justice

1.1 Introduction

Imagine a criminal justice system in a democratic state which has evolved over hundreds of years. Imagine those accused of crime in that state acknowledging their legal guilt despite a deep-seated sense of grievance, while advocates on their behalf minimize culpability on grounds their clients scarcely recognize. Imagine the victims of crime in that state having no chance to explain the consequences of the crime, their views seen as irrelevant and even dangerously distracting in the pursuit of justice. Imagine further a criminal justice system in which the guilty parties, having distanced themselves entirely from the consequences of their actions, are punished by the only means available—financial penalty, community service, or loss of liberty—all of them characterized by unconnectedness to the crime, and meaningless to victims except in terms of their desire for revenge.

Is this the best we can do?

The purpose of this book is to explore from the victim's perspective the possibilities of another way of 'doing justice'; one that, while preserving the rights of offenders, seeks to reintroduce into our justice system the voice of those most directly harmed by the crime. And a 'reintroduction' is what it would be, for this voice is one that was strong in former times but that has been progressively silenced in modern democracies, rightly concerned with issues of equity and proportionality in addressing wrongdoers, but progressively less concerned with those who have suffered most directly from the crime.

But there are many who believe that the virtues of the present system far outweigh its shortcomings. For example, in its editorial of 8 March 1998, a major Australian newspaper stated:

One of the greatest achievements of modern criminal law and jurisprudence is that it regards crime as an offence against society, against social order, rather than against the individual. (*The Canberra Times*: 8)

Of course, the segment of 'society' least likely to share this view is the one with more experience than most of 'modern criminal law and jurisprudence', namely victims of crime. We know this, if only because over the past two decades the voice of dissatisfied, even outraged, victims has increasingly been heard, expressing loud and clear the shortcomings from their point of view of traditional criminal justice processing.

The term 'crime victim' formally refers to one who has experienced harm as a result of an offence; it is invariably a term of moral approbation suggesting undeserved suffering (Ziegenhagen 1977). But the experience of victimisation might best be described in more personal terms as being treated

without the respect that we assume to be part of the working principles of daily human relationships, which find protection in the law. . . . [A]t its heart, victimization means that the autonomy and moral person has been robbed and denigrated. Victimization, therefore, is part and parcel of the experience of being dehumanized, in the deepest sense of the word. (Weisstub 1986: 193–5)

Victim status may be intuitively understood and recognized, but victim role has altered over time with changes in the surrounding economy and society (Hagan 1983). So as to understand these changes and the forces which have determined the weight given to the sometimes conflicting consideration of private harm and public harm in the way crime is addressed, I first review the rights and role of victims from a historical perspective. I then discuss the contemporary role of victims, for it was not until the second half of the twentieth century that victims' rights began to be asserted once more. I will also discuss the reasons behind the revival of interest in victims, including the social and demographic changes of the 1970s, improved measurement of victimization, the influence of the women's movement, and the development of victim advocacy and victim support groups. I then address a central theme of this book: what is it that victims want? I identify six concerns which emerge through a review of the victimology literature. These are:

- victims want a less formal process where their views count;
- victims want more information about both the processing and outcome of their cases;

- victims want to participate in their cases;
- victims want to be treated respectfully and fairly;
- victims want material restoration;
- victims want emotional restoration, especially an apology.

I conclude that victims are usually given little attention by our criminal justice system, with scant regard paid to their needs or their wish to participate in, or at least be informed about, the processing of their cases. Despite the successes of the victim movement from the mid-1970s in drawing attention to these concerns and the development of a range of services aimed at improving the lot of victims, I observe that many believe that it is only through a radical restructuring of criminal justice processing based on restorative justice principles that victims can be given what they see as being their due.

1.2   The Role of the Victim in Historical Perspective

Only with the rise of the modern state has responsibility for the investigation, prosecution, and disposition of a criminal offence ceased to be the responsibility of the victim of the crime. Early medieval communities had no organized systems of criminal justice and victims could turn only to their kinship group or their lord to support them in resolving the harm they had experienced. Blood feuds were frequently the outcome, that is continuing conflict based on blood-allegiance (Hagan 1983).

Traditionally, in most places throughout the world restorative justice measures of compensation and restitution have been the dominant model of conflict resolution (Braithwaite 1999), though the implementation of victim rights depended ultimately upon the threat of the kinship feud (Walklate 1989). Greek, Roman, and Arab systems of law accepted the principle of restoration even in homicide (Van Ness 1986), and right to compensation was a feature of Babylonian law (Mawby & Gill 1987). In Saxon England, an offender could 'buy back the peace he had broken' by payment to the victim or his family according to a detailed schedule of injury payments (Harding 1982). In addition the offender was obliged to make a payment to the lord or king, which was regarded as a fee for negotiating the settlement. By the seventh century these payments had been codified in written laws (Jeffrey

1957), the primary purpose of which was to avoid blood feuds (Weitekamp 1997). The Church too played a role in this emerging system. Between 700 and 1066 the share of payment to lords and bishops gradually increased, along with their power and influence.

By the late twelfth century in England, as the institution of the monarchy grew more powerful the king was able to move to a judicial role with a system for imposing his jurisdiction, and the needs of victims were replaced progressively by the interests of the state (Schafer 1968). Private settlement of serious criminal cases was no longer permitted; nor was the Church any longer entitled to punish crime through the use of force (Hagan 1983). The adjudication of serious criminal matters became henceforth a matter for the Crown (Wright 1991). By this time as well, the Crown had replaced victims and their kinship group as the recipient of compensation (Walklate 1989). Further, through the course of the Middle Ages fines to the state in place of compensatory payments to victims in turn gave way to retribution in the form of state punishment (Hibbert 1966).

A similar trend was taking place in Continental Europe at this time, with the state beginning to take a larger role in the administration of justice. Zehr (1985) suggests that this was due at least in part to a revival of Roman law, with its emphasis on a more powerful role for the central authority. Zehr further suggests that this trend may have been in part the consequence of 'the needs of an emerging capitalist order ... [and] the dynamics of emerging nation states' (p. 9). But Weitekamp (1997) argues that it was only through the violent conquest of much of Europe that the central role of the state was reluctantly accepted at this time.

The philosophical justification for these developments was that 'the wrong done to an individual extends beyond his own family; it is a wrong done to the community of which he is a member, and thus the wrongdoer may be regarded as a public enemy' (Pollock & Maitland 1898, quoted by Wright 1991: 5). This justification reflected a change in the way that civil society was being organized, as society as a whole came to be personified by the Crown: 'the king, in whom centres the majesty of the whole community, is supposed by the law to be the person injured by every infraction of the public rights belonging to that community' (Blackstone 1778/1973: 187).

Although the adjudication of serious criminal matters became a matter for the Crown in England from the twelfth century, the right to bring prosecutions in the name of the king continued to rest with individual citizens until the beginning of the nineteenth century. Indeed, victims were often viewed as having a duty to prosecute their cases, even though the involvement of the Crown meant that it was no longer a trial between two private litigants (Maitland 1885: 140), and despite declining prospects of benefit in outcome.

Prosecution could be an expensive business for the victim, and in the seventeenth century there were cases of mediation recorded which saved the victim from what could be considerable trouble and cost. Sharpe (1980) reports that local communities often had a figure seen as an appropriate mediator and outcomes in these cases might include physical chastisement, humiliation, or ostracism.

By the early years of the nineteenth century it became increasingly apparent that offenders were escaping prosecution entirely because of the costs to victims of exercising their legal rights. This was a major reason for the establishment of police constabularies in England during the period 1820–50 (Shapland et al. 1985). Eventually the office of the Director of Public Prosecutions was established in England in 1879 (Hagan 1983), the effect of which was in large measure to remove victims from any meaningful role in the criminal justice system. This state of affairs was replicated through all common law countries where British traditions of jurisprudence has been adopted, and the victim became the ignored party in criminal proceedings (Hudson & Galaway 1975). The victim had become just another witness.

1.3 The Contemporary Role of the Victim

Inevitably the victim and the state hold different perspectives about the nature of the offence and the way it should be dealt with. To the victim, the offence is a personal matter requiring repair of the harm suffered, material and emotional. To the state it is a violation of criminal law, requiring a consistent, predictable, and equitable response under the law (Joutsen 1994).

A major theme of this book will be that deciding what should be done about a crime calls for a balance between the personal and the public aspects of the crime. The reality in the recent past has been that the state has been overwhelmingly favoured in this equation. Indeed, the idea that a victim should have an active role in criminal proceedings came to be regarded with alarm and distaste.

So comprehensively forgotten had victims become in the criminal justice system that it was not until the 1940s with the work of Beniamin Mendelsohn and Hans Hentig that there was any academic interest in their role: in fact the preoccupations of both these writers were limited to the similarities between the personalities of victims and their offenders and on the role of victims in precipitating their victimization. From the point of view of practical concern it was Margery Fry, a prominent British prison reformer, who in her book *Arms of the Law* (1951) revived the idea of offenders making direct reparation to the victim, and began the process of asserting the rights of victims to be heard and to be reckoned with.

However, it was the mid-1970s before researchers, justice policy-makers, and the broader community began to express concern about the predicament of crime victims, and victims themselves began to agitate about their own role, or rather its absence, in the criminal justice system.

In 1972, in a biting review of accountability practices in the American criminal justice system, Wolfgang (1972) reserved his severest criticism for the way in which victims were treated. He observed:

The whole criminal justice system—from police to parole—ignores the victim except as he contributes to the evidence against the offender . . . [and] fails to communicate information to the victim, who deserves at least the satisfaction of knowing that efforts have been made by the police to detect and apprehend the offender. . . . [T]his is a way of accounting to that segment of the public that has been hurt by the failure of the entire social system and of its subsystem called the police. (p. 18)

As Norval Morris stated (1974):

If the criminal process is the taking over by the state of the vengeful instincts of the injured persons—buttressed by the recognition that the harm to the victim is also harm to the state—then it would seem, at first blush, that the victim has a right to be informed of, and where appropriate involved in, the processes that have led to whatever is the state settlement of the harm that has been done to him. (p. 56)

Concern by the US Department of Justice about the growing reluctance of victims to become involved with the criminal justice system led to the commissioning of a study by Knutden *et al.* (1976) which concluded that this was caused in large measure by the inconvenience and expense experienced by most victims. These findings led researchers and policy-makers to speculate about what might become of the system itself if victims comprehensively withdrew their co-operation.

Gottfredson (1989), writing thirteen years later when the role and status of victims were finally receiving the attention both of academics and policy-makers, found that victims in the United States continued to suffer as a consequence of their circumscribed role in the justice system. The result, he observed, was a number of negative consequences for victims that he summarized as:

inconvenience, inattention, anxiety-provoking arrangements, the delayed return of property (evidence), a failure to validate the victim's status as the person harmed and a lack of information about what is happening in the prosecution of the case. (p. 210)

Other routine procedural insensitivities experienced by victims include difficult questioning by police and lawyers, poor protection against intimidation, unnecessary trips to court, long waits, mishandling of property, and a variety of other inconveniences (Lurigio & Resnick 1990).

As McBarnett (1988) observed:

The state is not just the arbiter in a trial between victims and offender; the state is the victim . . . If victims feel that nobody cares about their suffering, it is in part because institutionally nobody does. (p. 300)

It is difficult to disentangle the elements that resulted in the move over the past twenty-five years towards greater recognition of the importance of victims in the justice system. As Geis (1990) observed, their cause was so just and their condition so palpably unfair that now it appears extraordinary that their neglect could have continued for so long.

However, these elements were certainly connected with the social and demographic changes of the early 1970s which contributed to a greatly inflated crime rate—and victimization rate—around the world. This was brought home forcefully with the findings of new crime victimization surveys at this time, which revealed that only a small proportion of crimes were ever formally reported (Geis 1990). More victims meant more attention, especially when authorities were obliged to recognize the potential problem for civil society represented by large numbers of uncompensated, unsatisfied citizens, unhappy with the routinely insensitive reactions of the justice system to their circumstances.

A crucially important contributing factor in the growth of a crime victim constituency was the rise of the women's movement. Women's groups initially focused their interest on the plight of rape victims (Brownmiller 1975). Later they included on their agenda the experience of violence that was an ongoing part of many women's lives, especially domestic violence, and the position of victimized women in the criminal justice system. Geis (1990) suggested that the strong anti-offender stance taken by the more militant members of the women's movement had a profound impact on the shaping of the victim movement, which in some quarters, principally the United States, has been characterized by a vengeful and retributive attitude (see Chapter 2).

Indeed, the rise of victim advocacy at this time came with two aspects. On the one hand, it provided the means for much-enhanced support services to become available to victims of crime. This was the aspect of the victims' movement which tended to predominate in Europe and Australasia. On the other hand, it also became the vehicle for expressions of support for punitive and exclusionary policies (see, for example, Scheingold *et al.* 1994), and other 'get tough on crime' law-and-order politics which have characterized the crime discourse in the United States for the last two decades.

This renewed interest in the victims' plight, whether focused on support or on advocacy, resulted in research directed at both the extent and nature of the trauma of victimization and also on the 'secondary victimization' experienced at the hands of police, prosecutors, and court systems (see, for example, Elias 1986; Waller 1989). Norval Morris's comments (above) refer to two of the major concerns that victims were beginning to express about their lot, namely the state of ignorance that they suffered about the way the state was dealing with 'their' crime and their desire to be involved in the processing of their case. The remainder of this chapter addresses these and other shortcomings of the formal criminal justice system from the victim's perspective.

1.4   What Do Victims Want?

1.4.1   Victims want a less formal process where their views count

A central issue for victims was formulated by Nils Christie (1977), who argued that conflicts between victims and their offenders have been taken away from them—in fact, stolen—by the professionals of the criminal justice system, principally lawyers and welfare authorities. Christie accepted that there was an obligation on the part of the state to reduce conflict in the best interests of all its citizens and that taking conflicts out of victims' hands assisted in protecting victims from the consequences, material and emotional, of pursuing the prosecution of their offenders. But he believed that victims have been the real losers in this trend over the centuries: 'Not only has he suffered, lost materially or become hurt, physically or otherwise. And not only does the State take the compensation. But, above all, he has lost participation in his own case' (Christie 1977: 7).

A member of a victim advocacy group in the State of Washington, reflecting on her own experience as the victim of sexual assault, clearly felt that the state had stolen her conflict. She said:

I realised that it was a *criminal* [her emphasis] justice process and there was no room, according to the court's interpretation, any place for the victims to assert their rights. . . . . I felt [long pause] I'm trying to search for the right word. There's no connection between me and the crime. The crime happened to me but it was the state prosecuting this man. . . . I was just a piece of evidence. (Scheingold *et al.* 1994: 12)

Christie (1977) argued that there are many incentives for stealing conflicts, most of them relating to the 'professionalization' of the criminal justice system. He recognized that the system is not run for profit these days, at least not in the crass style of the Middle Ages, but that, more subtly, there are many interests at stake in preserving a state of affairs in which victims' views are comprehensively ignored.

The frustration victims feel about this lack of a voice in the justice system was expressed in a statement to the President's Task Force on Victims of Crime (1982): '[w]hy didn't anyone consult me? I was the one who was kidnapped, not the state of Virginia' (p. 9). Indeed, a judge of the Indiana criminal court in 1976 suggested that victims of violent crime should be encouraged to take civil remedies on the grounds that there was little deterrence to criminals in the legal system and that the threat of legal action might have some desired effect (*Indianapolis Star*, quoted by Carrington 1977).

Victims' imperative to put their side of the story, when they have been effectively silenced by a system that relegates them to witnesses subject to strict evidentiary rules, is strikingly illustrated by one such civil suit where a woman sued two men found guilty of her rape and was awarded $365,000. She said, 'The purpose of this trial wasn't to collect. The purpose of this trial was that it's high time somebody got off their tail and did something about "rape". . . . So what if these guys are sitting in jail, big deal. What about my doctor bills? . . . What about the mental anguish?' (quoted by Carrington 1977). The importance to this victim of the chance to express her outrage was all the more apparent because she knew before she began her action that the civil jury would hear details of her sex life and her job as a topless dancer.

The paradoxical relationship between victims and the criminal justice system was remarked on by Shapland (1986):

> The criminal justice system depends heavily upon victims for the reporting and detection of offences and for the provision of evidence in court. Yet, it does not appear to value the victim. The concern with attitudes, information, consultation shown by victims . . . is an expression of the need to be valued, to be wanted, to be considered an important participant. The system is not geared to the perspective of the victim. (p. 215)

Shapland reached this conclusion based on a review of several victim studies. Kelly (1982) found that the victims in her rape study expressed dissatisfaction with numerous aspects of the justice system, but principally the lack of consultation over proceedings in the case. They felt that the judicial system cared little about their wellbeing. In studies of burglary by Maguire (1982) and Howley (1982) victims expressed similar concerns about the importance attached to their views.

Plainly, the formality of the justice system, where victims have no opportunity for input beyond their role as prosecution witnesses—and not even that in those cases where the defendant pleads guilty—is a source of frustration and anger for many victims. Conversely, research shows that generally satisfaction with justice is increased when victims have the opportunity to express their views and when they feel that their wishes are not being ignored (Forst & Hernon 1985; Heinz & Kerstetter 1979).

1.4.2   Victims want more information about both the processing and outcome of their cases

In a review of several studies of victim attitudes in both the United States and Britain Shapland (1986) concluded that 'the rule was:

the more contact [with criminal justice authorities], the greater the level of satisfaction' (p. 214).

The paradox of the victim's role that Shapland refers to above—being both needed and unvalued—is partly explained by the variability with which victims are attended to at different points in the processing of their case. Shapland *et al.* (1985) found in their study of over 200 victims of violent crime in two English cities that there were initially high levels of satisfaction expressed by victims about their treatment by police—at the point of processing where victims are of highest value as a source of information for the prosecution of the case. By the middle of the investigation this was starting to decline and continued to do so, due largely to lack of information about progress with their cases, for which police were blamed, and a consequent feeling that the police did not care about them. Victims wanted to know all sorts of details about their cases and felt aggrieved if they were not told and could not easily find out.

The same pattern was found by Maguire (1982) in his study of English burglary victims, which he interpreted to mean that police response that displayed an appropriate level of engagement with the victim's situation was more important to the victim than was solving the crime. Similar findings were reached by Waller and Okihiro (1978) in their study of burglary victims. All these studies reveal that victims want to be kept informed throughout the various stages of their cases.

Shapland *et al.* (1985) further observed that the victim was regarded as 'supernumerary' when the offender pleaded guilty, and there was no requirement for officialdom to preserve a good relationship with someone who was not even required as a prosecution witness. Victims still very much wanted to know the outcome of their court cases, but there was no procedure for letting them know even that the case had been heard. They noted that:

in practice several victims in the study had no idea of the outcome and many more had only a partial knowledge of the sentence passed . . . 84 per cent felt they should have been informed of the sentence by the police. (p. 79)

Significantly, Shapland *et al.* also found that victims who were present at court for the outcome of their cases were more satisfied than those who were not. They attribute this finding to:

the greater information that participation brings, to the feeling of being involved in the case, to a greater knowledge of all the factors surrounding the case that the sentencer takes into account or to a better understanding of court procedure. (p. 80)

1.4.3 Victims want to participate in their cases

A major complaint of victims has been the fact that they are not encouraged to feel part of the criminal justice proceedings in their cases (see, for example, Smith 1983; Sebba 1996; Shapland 2000). In his small study of burglary victims, Umbreit (1989) found that nearly all victims wanted to be involved in the criminal justice system, whether actively or passively. A large German survey found that most victims (and non-victims) believed that the role of the victim should go beyond that of simple witness both at the investigation and disposition stages of their case (Kilchling 1991).

Studies conducted through the early 1980s (e.g. Forst & Hernon 1985; Hagan 1982; Shapland *et al.* 1985) repeatedly confirmed that victims not only felt frustrated and alienated from the justice system but, importantly, that this dissatisfaction focused on the process rather than the outcome of their cases. Erez and Tontodonato (1990) suggested that victim participation in the process assists both in 'restoration' of victims and in reducing the sense of alienation which results from believing they have no control and no status.

One of the strategies developed in the past decade for the purpose of increasing victim participation has been victim impact statements (VIS) ('victim statements' in the United Kingdom), which are statements tendered to the sentencing judge setting out the victim's view on the nature of the harm—physical, financial, psychological, and social—they have experienced. So popular has been this that by 1988 legislation providing for VIS had been enacted in almost all American states, Canada, and Australia (Sebba 1996). Concerns that VIS would result in harsher sentences seemed to be unfounded (Erez & Tontodonato 1990; Erez *et al.* 1994; Erez 2000).

However, a question mark remains over the capacity for VIS to improve victim satisfaction. A study of 239 victims of robbery, assault, and burglary concluded that '[t]here was no indication that impact statements led to greater feelings of involvement, greater satisfaction with the justice process, or greater satisfaction with dispositions' (Davis & Smith 1994: 11). This may be due in part to victims not being adequately informed about the availability of VIS, or given assistance and support in their preparation, so that they become 'well-kept secrets that only a few victims know about, or make use of, to their advantage' (Erez 1991: 6).

Erez *et al.* (1994) also warned that raising victims' expectations about their capacity to influence sentences via VIS may backfire if they feel that in fact their input had no influence on the outcome, which most often seems to be the case (Erez & Roeger 1995; Fisher 1991). She concluded (2000) that '[d]espite the high hopes of victim rights advocates, and the misgivings of opponents of victim participation, the inclusion of victim input in proceedings during the 1990s has had little effect on the criminal justice system and on victims' satisfaction with it' (p. 178).

1.4.4   Victims want to be treated respectfully and fairly

The revival of interest in crime victims from the mid-1970s resulted from research and from the actions of victim advocacy movements, both of which documented their plight and their 'secondary victimization' by the criminal justice system. Although complaints were usually focused on the court process, the tenor of many victims' experiences with the police is evoked by Wolfgang (1972), who quoted one as saying: '[b]y the time the police left I thought I was the criminal. I was questioned with discourtesy and abruptness. I was treated like a slob' (p. 19).

Overall satisfaction with the criminal justice system seems to be strongly correlated with the victim's satisfaction with the sentence the offender received, but the main variable influencing satisfaction with the sentence is perception of fairness in sentencing (Erez 1994), that is, the *process*. It is important to recognize that this satisfaction is not affected by participation in achieving the *outcome* of the case. Erez concluded that '[t]he victim's response to the system as a whole . . . may be viewed as an indicator of the system's ability to resolve the victim's personal conflict with the offender and to make the victim feel that justice has been done' (p. 412).

The victimological studies of Erez and others above link with psychological research undertaken since the mid-1970s on perceptions of procedural justice. Although Thibaut and Walker (1975) found that control over both the decision-making process and control over outcome made people feel that they had been treated fairly, subsequent research (Tyler 1988) found (like Erez) that control over process is more important than control over the outcome when citizens assess the fairness of legal procedures. Tyler showed that they made complex assessments in their judgements of fairness, and concluded that these assessments were composed of several elements: the authorities' motivation, honesty, ethicality and bias, opportunities for representation, opportunities for error correction, and the quality of the decisions. He further observed that:

the major criteria used to assess process fairness are those aspects of procedure least linked to outcomes—ethicality, honesty and the effort to be fair—rather than consistency with other outcomes. (p. 128)

In later research, Tyler (1990) found that:

people do not focus directly on the favorability of the outcomes they receive from third parties. Instead, they focus directly on the degree to which they are able to exert influence over third-party decisions . . . where people feel they have control over decisions they believe that the procedure is fair; where they feel they lack control they believe it is unfair. (pp. 6–7)

Tyler & Lind (1992) explored this finding further and concluded that three factors determine the perception of fairness: standing (acknowledgement of the individual status in the group or community), trust (in the benevolent intentions of an authority), and neutrality (of the authority in delivering an unbiased decision).

For victims of crime it appears that standing is an especially important aspect in their sense of being treated fairly: it refers to one's sense of being a valued member of a group or community, and in fact is defined by the extent to which the individual is treated with dignity and respect. It would not be surprising if victims were especially sensitive and aware of signals about their standing, given the effect of their victimization on their sense of self-worth. In a review of European research, Joutsen (1994) concluded that '[u]ltimately, the major factor in victim satisfaction with the operation of the criminal justice system is probably not the formal role of the victim, but the extent to which the victim is accorded dignity and respect'. (p. 65)

Not only is control over process more important than control over outcome in perceptions of fairness, but it appears that victims do not usually seek a decisive role in the outcome of their cases.

They certainly wish to be consulted throughout the criminal justice process, but research by Shapland (1985) in England, Smale (quoted in Wemmers 1996) in the Netherlands, and Kilchling (quoted in Wemmers 1996) in Germany all found that victims did not seek a role in the actual adjudication of their cases. Rather, it is the opportunity to present their perspective on the case—what Tyler (1988) referred to as the 'representation' component—which they found to be the crucial aspect for victims in attaining a sense of satisfaction with the justice system.

Where victims have been given the right to speak, either to the prosecutor, as in the Netherlands, or in court, as in parts of North America and Australia, it is apparent that they are not nearly as demanding as criminal defence lawyers had feared. Van Dijk (1994) observed that:

[V]ictims exercising their right to speak up in court about their feelings and opinions do not typically demand harsh punishment. Most victims do not apparently use their new rights as a retributive tool. They want to be recognised as concerned parties and to be notified of judicial decisions. (pp. 20–1)

These findings are supported by research conducted by Doob and Roberts (1988), who found that the more people knew about the circumstances and complexity of an offender's life, the less punitive they were. Presenting one's own point of view in the courtroom may also provide an opportunity to learn more about the offender. This research evidence will be addressed again below in the context of the restorative justice opportunities for finding out about one's offender's life circumstances.

1.4.5 Victims want material restoration

The right to material or financial reparation from the offender seems to have existed 'historically and almost universally' (Wolfgang 1965: 241) prior to the state's resumption of this entitlement. Zehr (1985) suggested that 'an eye for an eye' justice actually focused on compensation and restitution, limiting the retributive response to a measure equal to the offence and converting it to restitution. He also suggested that such justice was a way of vindicating the victim—that 'both restitution and vengeance may have been intended less to punish than to vindicate the moral rightness of the victim. . . . They needed moral compensation' (p. 10).

Christie (1977) argued that this right was 'stolen' by the state, which converted it to fines without reference to the victim. Although civil action has been available, it is rarely used, being possible only in the minority of cases where a successful prosecution has been made and only feasible if the victim can afford the cost of litigation and the offender has some assets.

The argument for reparation from the state for harm to the victim is derived from aspects of legal theory. First is Locke's assertion that citizens have the right to protection because of the 'social contract' they make with society, whereby they invest some of their own will for the sake of the benefit of society as a whole; that is, in this case the state monopoly on the right to punish criminals. When society cannot provide that protection, then it is morally obliged to compensate victims for that incapacity. Furthermore, as the state has removed the concept of restitution from the usual imposition of punishment, as well as claiming monopoly of the legitimate use of physical force (Weber 1948), it can be argued that there is an obligation to provide an alternative form of redress for victims (Galaway & Rutman 1974).

Throughout the 1960s and 1970s there was agitation around the world for victim-reparation schemes that would compensate victims for physical injury. In 1963 New Zealand became the first country to make compensation awards without regard to culpability. Criminal injuries compensation schemes are now the norm rather than the exception in North America, Europe, and Australasia. However, such schemes are not usually associated in any way with the judicial processing of the offence which resulted in the injury (Barton 1996) and are generally poorly funded.

Jeremy Bentham, in a 1838 essay examining various responses to crime, observed the moral advantage of compensation even though it was rarely provided:

Punishment . . . is scattered with a lavish hand; while satisfaction [defined as a benefit in consideration of an injury], which altogether produces good, is given with grudging parsimony. (p. 32)

He favoured payment by the offender to the victim as 'satisfaction' rather than the payment of a fine to the state:

What is paid by the offender as a fine is a punishment, and nothing more; what he pays as a satisfaction is also a punishment, and a punishment more than ordinarily strong, besides this, it is a satisfaction for the party injured; that is to say, a good. (p. 42)

The concept of direct restitution from offender to victim is argued by Barnett (1977), who believed it has the potential to overthrow the dominant criminal justice paradigm of punishment. In fact, Barnett approached the core concepts of restorative justice (see below) when he described the idea of restitution as viewing crime

as an offense by one individual against the rights of another. The victim has suffered a loss. Justice consists of the culpable offender making good the loss he has caused. . . . Where once we saw an offense against society, we now see an offense against an individual victim. . . . [The] debt, therefore, is not to society, it is to the victim. (p. 251)

Indeed, victims indicate a strong preference to be compensated directly by the offender (Shapland 1984). The amounts victims suggest as appropriate restitution are often small for this very reason—to make it feasible for the offender to pay it. One victim was very plain about this: '[i]t should be 50 pounds from the court or 200 pounds from the CICB' [Criminal Injuries Compensation Board]' (Shapland *et al.* 1985: 123).

Shapland (1986) found that victims saw compensation as a proper objective of the court process and integral to the criminal justice system. But more than that, it was seen as a means of making a symbolic statement about the offence:

Compensation was seen not according to the societal view as charity doled out to innocent, deserving victims, but according to the very much older view of compensation as restitution—as the giving back or recompensing to the victim what he had lost, not only materially but symbolically and in terms of suffering. . . . Victims saw compensation orders as part of the sentence, not primarily a civil measure. (Shapland 1986: 227)

Erez and Tontodonato (1992) also found that receiving restitution is a significant predictor of satisfaction with the criminal justice system (although it is not clear from the results they report whether this refers to restitution from the court or from the offender).

Although victims' preference for restitution from the offender is recognized, courts are relatively reluctant to become involved in making such orders. For example, in the United States federal courts in 1991 only 16 per cent of total criminal sentences included restitution orders (Tobolowsky 1993). It appears that criminal courts are generally unwilling to become involved with financial

assessments of harm because of the practical difficulties of determining both what amount is appropriate, what any given offender
may be in a position to pay (Sebba 1996), and determining who all
the victims are. Linked to this is the problem of enforcement of the
orders: Hudson and Galaway (1980), for example, reported that in
two studies they examined, one in Minnesota and one in England,
a quarter of restitution orders were not complied with at all, and
the larger the sum involved the less likely compliance became.
Sebba (1996) listed other studies with even more dismal results
(p. 175).

1.4.6   Victims want emotional restoration and an apology

Beyond the calculable material loss the victim of crime may experience, there are emotional and psychological dimensions to the
loss which have routinely been ignored by the justice system, and
which require redress if the experience of victimization is ever to be
satisfactorily resolved. Indeed, there is evidence to suggest that
victims see emotional reconciliation to be far more important than
material or financial reparation. Umbreit *et al.* (1994) found that
in their in-depth interviews with a sub-sample (n = 42) of their
subjects who had experienced mediation, a quarter spontaneously
mentioned the importance of the process for resolving their feelings
of distress resulting from the crime: this was a higher proportion
than mentioned material restitution as a primary benefit of the
process. Wright (1991) observed that victims 'often seek symbolic
reparation, an opportunity to try to persuade the offender not to
offend again, and, where the parties are related, a resolution of the
underlying dispute' (p. 113). Retzinger and Scheff (1996) elabo-
rated on the concept of symbolic reparation which they regard as
essential if true reconciliation is to be achieved. This subject is
addressed more thoroughly below in the context of victims' need
for apology.

    Crimes differ in the extent to which they are stressful, and the
most intrusive are usually the most stressful (Gottfredson 1989).
These kinds of offences 'upset a victim's balance in ways most
central to the self as well as the victim's sense of autonomy, order,
control or predictability in ordinary activities central to the victim's
identity' (Gottfredson 1989: 221–2). Victims, especially of unan-
ticipated incidents in familiar or benign settings, may have to re-

interpret the safety of these environments, which results in an increased sense of vulnerability and mistrust, anger, shame, or self-blame.

Different reactions to similar experiences result not only from how intrusive the crime is felt to be, but also from varying capacities of victims to recover from the event (Gottfredson 1989). The experience itself may involve a sense of loss of control and loss of belief in an orderly world, while the recovery has been described as a reordering or a 'sense-making' process (Gehm 1990). These findings illustrate the shortcomings from the victim's perspective of traditional criminal justice, which treats all similar offences in similar ways, regardless of the differential impact of the offence on different victims.

The emotional impact of victimization has been explained by Murphy and Hampton (1988) in the following terms:

> One reason we so deeply resent moral injuries done to us is not simply that they hurt us in some tangible or sensible way; it is because such injuries are also *messages*—symbolic communications. ... Intentional wrongdoing *insults* us and attempts (sometimes successfully) to *degrade* us—and thus it involves a kind of injury that is not merely tangible and sensible. It is moral injury, and we care about such injuries. ... Most of us tend to care about what others ... think about us. ... Our self-respect is *social* in at least this sense, and it is simply part of the human condition that we are weak and vulnerable in these ways. And thus when we are treated with contempt by others it attacks us in profound and deeply threatening ways. (p. 25)

All these research findings indicate the universality of the trauma of victimization and the high levels of dissatisfaction regarding the usual treatment victims receive at the hands of the criminal justice system. But beyond this, there is evidence of the need of victims for reintegration into their community before they can fully put the offence behind them. This is an issue only indirectly referred to in much of the victim literature, but directly by Braithwaite and Pettit (1990). The experience of victimization often results in a sense of being devalued and violated which, in Braithwaite and Pettit's terms, requires the restoration of the victims' sense of dominion. This can be achieved most effectively when the community:

> acts symbolically and tangibly to assure the victim that she is not devalued as a person, that her dominion is worthy of respect. Symbolically, this is done by condemning the crime and the criminal—reprobation. Tangibly it is done by restitution or compensation for the victim. (p. 91)

Braithwaite and Pettit specified a number of requirements of the criminal justice system if it is to be successful in restoring the victim:

providing aid and comfort in the period of initial distress; establishing contact for the victim with those who may be able to help her overcome any lingering problems; ensuring that compensation is available where appropriate; and, if this is something distinct, extracting where possible an act of recognition by the offender that he has wronged the victim. (p. 209)

In general, the victimology literature makes little mention of victims' desire for apologies from their offenders. This is surprising for anyone who has observed the interactions between victims and their offenders when they are unmediated by formal criminal justice processing. In this context the offer and acceptance of a sincere apology seem the most natural thing imaginable, and the *sine qua non* of a successful resolution of the offence and restoration of the participants.

The absence of discussion of apology in victimology is a consequence of operating purely within the dominant retributive paradigm—what is the point in asking victims whether they want an apology when no opportunity exists for a direct exchange between the principals? Wagatsuma and Rosett (1986) suggested that the relative absence of apology in American law—and, one may add, Western justice systems generally—may be related to the tendency for the legal system to reduce all harms to a monetary metric, even those where no economic loss is entailed. Indeed, this tendency can be found in victim–offender mediation programmes as well, with their emphasis on material restitution as the primary outcome. This contrasts with the Japanese situation where the offering of apologies is frequently used as an alternative to criminal charging (Wagatsuma & Rosett 1986); for example, following a 1982 Japan Airlines crash, the company president met with victims or their families to offer apologies and compensation, as a result of which no lawsuit was filed (Haley 1986).

Apology and forgiveness are so familiar and so much a part of everyday life in our society, for offences trivial and serious, that we need to look closely at the interaction to appreciate what Tavuchis (1991) referred to as 'the almost miraculous qualities of a satisfying apology' (p. 6). It is also worth considering whether what victims really want even more than an apology is the opportunity to forgive, and so to be relieved of the burden of anger and bitter-

ness resulting from a sense that their emotional hurt is unacknowledged. Arendt (1958) made the point that forgiveness releases the
victim from punishment and revenge, and works to terminate the
possibility of escalating dispute.

The seminal work on the sociology of apology is Goffman's
(1971) discussion in the context of 'remedial interchanges', while
the role of apology in everyday 'conversational routines' is the
subject of much linguistics literature (for example, Coulmas 1981;
Fraser 1981; Edmondson 1981). But these discussions have their
limitations when considering the emotional power of a sincere
apology to the victim of a criminal offence. Interestingly, this literature does reveal one important insight: that an apology is fundamentally a 'speech act' which in English must contain the word
'apologize' or 'sorry' (Owen 1983). Thus an apology must be artic-
ulated verbally before it can be acknowledged, in contrast to
forgiveness, which can be expressed by gesture as well as words,[1]
or simply implied in the demeanour of the victim toward the
offender.

Tavuchis suggested that an apology must minimally entail
'acknowledgment of the legitimacy of the violated rule, admission
of fault and responsibility for its violation, and the expression of
genuine regret and remorse for the harm done' (p. 3). However, the
magic of apology in restoring 'the antecedent moral order' (p. 5) is
that, while it cannot undo the past, somehow this is precisely what
is achieved. To illustrate this point Tavuchis quoted Disraeli's
epigram that 'apologies only account for that which they do not
alter' (p. 5).

Tavuchis further asserted that 'the singular achievement of
apologetic discourse paradoxically resides in its capacity to effectively eradicate the consequences of the offense by evoking the
unpredictable faculty of forgiveness' (p. vii); indeed, that the goal
of apology from the transgressor's point of view is the granting of
forgiveness. Thus the offender and the offended join in a ritual of
reconciliation, with the apology as a gift which must be accepted
through an expression of forgiveness, each party needing a
response from the other before social harmony can be restored.

---

[1] Indeed, it is often better communicated by an uncomplicated gesture than by
the rather arch expression 'I forgive you', which can be perceived as an expression
putting the speaker in a position of power.

Although Tavuchis was confident of the ability of apology to heal and restore relations in a one-to-one context, he was less sure of its capacity in other situations, whether it be from one person to many, from the many to one, from many to many, or in the presence of a mediating third party. In his discussion of rituals of apology and forgiveness observed in restorative justice processes in Wagga, New South Wales, Moore (1993) acknowledged that Tavuchis' concerns in these other social configurations were plausible, but reported that they had not been realized. He suggested that to explain why this should be so we should look beyond the sociology of apology to the moral psychology of forgiveness and to understand the role that anger and indignation play in the process. He further reported that the account by Murphy and Hampton (1988) of the internal and external motivations which work towards forgiveness is matched by empirical observation of the dynamics of restorative justice.

Murphy and Hampton (1988) suggested that forgiveness is acceptable only when it is consistent with self-respect and respect for others, as well as being consistent with rules of morality. They further argued that this can be the case only when we distinguish between the immoral act and the immoral actor, forgiving the one without tacitly approving of the other and allowing us to square forgiveness with self-respect. Zehr (1985) suggested that in achieving restoration '[a]bove all, perhaps, victims need an experience of forgiveness' and, although it is possible for victims to forgive in the absence of those who perpetrated the offence (Estrada-Hollenbeck 1996), sincere apologies are likely greatly to assist the process of 'letting go' of the crime experience.

Retzinger and Scheff (1996) placed the phenomenon of apology and forgiveness within a theoretical framework that they refer to as 'symbolic reparation', where these two steps are the 'core sequence' (p. 316). Based on their observations of nine Australian restorative justice conferences, they believed that:

[w]ithout the core sequence [apology and forgiveness], the path towards settlement is strewn with impediments, whatever settlement is reached does not decrease the tension level in the room, and leaves the participants with a feeling of arbitrariness and dissatisfaction. Thus, it is crucially important to give symbolic reparation at least parity with material settlement. ... Symbolic reparation is the vital element that differentiates conferences from all other forms of crime control. (p. 317)

Retzinger and Scheff went on to say that symbolic reparation depends upon management of the emotion of shame experienced by all participants in different ways, and that it 'will occur to the extent that shame and related emotions are evoked and acknowledged by the participants' (p. 318). But though sincere apologies may be accompanied by a feeling of shame, the shame results from the original offence that makes the apology necessary, and an understanding of the consequences of the offence, not resulting from the apology itself (Miller 1993). Scheff (1996) also argued that it is imperative for the burden of shame to be removed from the victim—the key element in the victim's future wellbeing. This is accomplished by ensuring that all of the shame connected with the offence is accepted by the offender through the core sequence of apology and forgiveness.

1.5 Summary

The common experience of victims in the Western criminal justice system is marked by routine lack of attention to the question of restitution, or, in broader terms, the repair of harm suffered. It is also marked by the persistent neglect of non-material dimensions of victimization: psychological and emotional consequences such as mistrust, unresolved anger, and fear. In addition, many victims experience frustration and alienation from the criminal justice system because of routine lack of communication, a perceived lack of procedural fairness, as well as dissatisfaction with the outcome of their case, owing to their exclusion from the decision-making process—or, indeed, any input at all beyond their role as witness for the prosecution. Finally, victims need their sense of dignity, worth, and respect to be restored before the harm caused can be properly repaired.

The agitations of the victim movement from the mid-1970s onward led to the development of a range of services for victims aimed at alleviating the negative consequences of both the crime and the criminal justice process, and in some cases increasing their involvement in the processing of their cases through victim impact statements at the sentencing stage. Other measures included a mass of legislative reform, particularly in the United States, the establishment of public funds to compensate victims, and the development of welfare plans to provide victim assistance through the criminal justice process and beyond. In 1985 the United Nations General Assembly adopted the Declaration of Basic Principles of Justice for Victims of Crime and Abuse of Power which recognized the victim's right to restitution (Sebba 1996).

The next chapter takes a closer look at the victim movement and the controversial subject of victims' rights. It pays special attention to the way that these issues have played out in Canberra, the site for a randomized controlled trial comparing the effectiveness of court with the restorative justice alternative known as conferencing, and opens up the debate on the possible advantages to victims of a restorative approach.

2

Victims of Crime and the Victim Movement

2.1 Introduction

In spring 1987 Mrs Cameron's[1] 14-year-old son was beaten to death at a Canberra school fete. His 17-year-old assailant was charged with murder but pleaded guilty to manslaughter. He was convicted, sentenced to six years' imprisonment, and served twenty-one months. Mrs Cameron described the treatment that she and her husband received from the justice system as 'just horrific—we had no support whatsoever . . . we felt so alienated'. She said that they felt so distressed by the way they were dealt with that they scarcely had time to think about their son's death.

In early 1988 the young daughter of another Canberra citizen was murdered. Soon afterwards, Mrs Cameron wrote to the father asking if she could help. In late 1988 the victim movement came to Canberra when the Victims of Crime Assistance League (VOCAL) was formed by these two people and twenty-four others who had suffered criminal victimization of some kind and who lived in the same community. Their objectives were primarily to provide support and assistance to victims of all crime in their community. Later they became important players in the struggle for recognition of the rights of victims to be treated as legitimate participants in the criminal justice process.

In the first part of this chapter I discuss the different forms of the victim movement in different places, its impact on the administration of justice, and its effectiveness in advancing the victim's cause. I then take the Canberra movement as a 'case study' to explore the resonances between a non-punitive model of victim advocacy and

---

[1] My sincere thanks go to Mrs Rita Cameron and others in the Canberra victim movement who generously gave their time to talk to me about their experiences.

the restorative approach, which will be discussed comprehensively in the next chapter. In the restorative approach, the emphasis on professional and adversarial conflict between the only two parties which count in our existing system—the offender and the State—is replaced by a focus on repairing the harm experienced by the victim and by community participation and reconciliation between victims, offenders, and the community.

2.2   The Victim Movement

The 'victim movement' is a social movement which takes many forms worldwide, ranging from a support-focused openness to restorative alternatives through to an extreme rights-focused retributiveness. Varied as its forms have been, the characteristic they have in common, not only across this movement but in common with the other great social movements of this century, is a shared sense of injustice. Frank and Fuentes (1990) suggested that this concern with injustice refers largely to 'us', so the movement serves both as a vehicle for working against the oppression 'we' experience, and as a means of reaffirming the identity of those working in the movement—and legitimating their concerns. They also argued that 'what most characterises social movements is that they must do their own thing in their own way' (p. 141) and, classically, outside existing institutions.

Movements do, however, often profit from support from existing institutions, but by doing so may risk being co-opted. This is a special risk for the victim movement because of its attractiveness to the 'law and order' lobby. Elias (1990) went so far as to say that the victim movement in the United States today can no longer be classified as a social movement at all, so completely has it been corrupted by right-wing political forces. Co-option can take other forms as well. For example, Victim Support in England and Wales, a non-government organization lobbying for victims and providing assistance services as well, has increasingly been seen as an adjunct to the formal justice system because of its success in securing a place at the centre of government policy, casting other victims' groups such as rape crisis centres to the margins (Crawford 2000).

It is relatively easy to put waves of public indignation at the service of punitive policies (Scheingold et al. 1994). Cynical politicians responding to community outrage over particular horrific events can easily channel such feeling into cries for retributive policies. Reeves and Mulley (2000) described how victim issues, as a popular political cause, have been used to support various criminal justice agendas: '[c]ampaigners for tougher sentences have used statements made by individual victims of crime as if they represent the views of "all" crime victims. In fact, victims' views on sentencing appear to be as varied as that of any other cross-section of the general public' (p. 142). On a hugely magnified scale we have seen this phenomenon at work in Rwanda and Cambodia, whose peoples were co-opted into genocide. Balint (2002) found that what actually happened in these and other episodes was that those with political power, or those with aspirations, fomented dormant racial divisions to assist their ambitions. Just as the racist vengeance of ethnic division can be captured and magnified by power-hungry leaders (Kuper 1981; Prunier 1995), the vengeance of crime victims has sometimes been captured by politicians with their own retributive agendas.

To understand the nature of the victim movement as it exists today, it is important to realize that twenty-five years ago there was no movement at all. As Chapter 1 discussed, for centuries victims were the forgotten third parties in a justice system which conceived of criminal behaviour as a matter between the offender and the state, with no formal role for the individuals who suffer the crime. As Geis (1990) remarked: '[t]heir condition for centuries aroused little comment or interest. Suddenly, they were "discovered", and afterwards it was unclear how their obvious neglect could have so long gone without attention and remedy' (p. 255).

Concern for victims was starting to emerge as an issue in the 1970s in Britain (Maguire & Corbett 1987) and continental Europe (van Dijk 1988), but it was really in the United States that the 'movement' had its genesis. Among the most important factors which contributed to its emergence as a social force was the exceptional rise in crime rates experienced through the 1960s by the United States and other Western democracies, turning 'law and order' into a major political issue. Suddenly there were more victims around; and many more than anyone, especially the politicians, had realized until the advent of victim surveys (Skogan 1978, 1984). These surveys gave an insight into the low regard for the justice system felt by crime victims, many of whom turned out to be reluctant to report even quite serious crime and extremely unwilling to act as prosecution witnesses (Biderman *et al.* 1967).

The American civil rights movement became a model for the early victim movement, inspired by its progressive, humanitarian ideals (Viano 1987). However, its success in improving the treatment of defendants in the criminal justice system was perceived in some quarters in the United States as further disadvantaging the interests of victims. Even at this early stage, those on the political right were portraying these developments as moves in a zero-sum equation where any protection of offender rights assumed a diminution in the rights of the victim (Elias 1986) (see Chapter 7 for a discussion of these views).

As mentioned in Chapter 1, another factor which contributed in a particular way to the victim cause was the attention given by the emerging women's movement to the treatment that women received as victims, especially with rape and domestic violence. Although these activists were at first perceived as radical and irrelevant to the mainstream victim movement, they became enormously effective in drawing attention to the plight of these victims and in setting up specialist services for them.

By the end of the 1970s, many diverse forces had converged to draw attention to the neglected role and importance of the victim in the justice system. The social movement that resulted encompassed a spectrum of activists from radical feminists to hardline law-and-order conservatives, an uncomfortable coalition whose varying priorities and philosophies were reflected in the disparate nature of the movement in different places and at different times.

2.3   Two Kinds of Victim Movement

These disparities resulted broadly in two kinds of movement: one focused on victim rights and the other on victim support. Van Dijk (1988) described it as a tension between 'being nice and being vindictive' and called it the international hallmark of the movement. He observed that the objectives of the movement have developed in an *ad hoc* way without any systematic attention to victims' needs. He commented: '[c]learly the movement's demands and achievements do not flow from a well-defined victimological theory, or in fact from any social theory at all', but rather they spring from 'ideologically inspired agendas for affirmative action' (p. 115), giving rise to markedly different philosophies and objectives in different places.

Although the American movement and the European movement contain strands of both advocacy and assistance, the former is characterized principally by a rights approach and the latter by support activities. Shapland (1988) suggested the difference is a result of the reliance by the movement on legislative change in the United States, and that when the response to victims involves the criminal justice system, it will inevitably have the flavour of the prevailing criminal justice tradition (see also Viano 1990). But the difference is still hard to account for, given the virtual unanimity in the research findings on victims' reactions to their victimization and subsequent experience of the justice system (see, for example, Waller 1989). Throughout the Anglo-American adversarial system and the inquisitorial system of Continental Europe as well, victims are consistently reported to be angry and bewildered, expecting to be able to turn to the police, to prosecutors, and the courts for assistance and advice, and invariably finding that they are regarded by each of these agencies as outside their area of responsibility (see, for example, Shapland *et al.* 1985; Elias 1986).

2.3.1   United States model: rights-focused

Geis (1990) argued that the fundamental basis of the power of the victim movement in the United States flows from the public and political perception that these are 'good' people who have suffered at the hands of 'bad' people. This view may render the cause politically irresistible, but it also works to support a narrow punitive focus. From the beginning there was a fierce retributive edge to the rhetoric supporting the interests of American victims. Carrington (1975), for example, a member of President Reagan's 1982 Task Force on Victims of Crime and other victim lobby groups, argued for a reversal of the Miranda exclusionary rule and increased use of the death penalty. He saw policy and policy-makers as occupying two distinct camps:

In recent years the lines have been drawn generally into two schools of thought regarding the treatment of those accused, or convicted of criminal acts. The first of these is the hard-line or victim-oriented viewpoint; the second is the permissive or criminal-oriented approach. (Carrington 1975: 124)

These views were echoed by many individuals and organizations in the United States newly interested in victims' issues (Viano 1983; Fattah 1986; Davis *et al.* 1984). This 'law-and-order' faction was extremely influential in setting the agenda for the American victim movement and the high priority it assigned to issues of victims *rights*—rights to be informed, rights to participate in the disposition of their cases, and, significantly, rights to influence sentencing decisions (Maguire & Shapland 1990). The dominance of this approach was probably due to the much greater volume and seriousness of crime in the United States than elsewhere, to differences in legal and political traditions, and to a much greater degree of dissatisfaction felt by American victims with the defects of their court system. Whatever the reason, victims' organizations in the USA tend to be punitively oriented, and there have even been claims that the real goal of some legislative amendments has been to advantage the prosecution rather than to establish victims' rights to participation (see Mosteller 1998).

Pressure on American politicians to be seen to act on victims' behalf, to 'tip the balance' in favour of victims, on the assumption that offenders had too many rights, certainly resulted in a huge volume of legislation conferring rights or benefits on victims in the decade after the President's Task Force on Victims of Crime in 1982 (Elias 1990). Inevitably, this emphasis on achieving rights through such wholesale amendment to criminal justice processes has added to the strong retributive tone to these rights.

The retributive ideology in the victims' camp resonates with the 'just deserts' jurisprudence which has been so influential in sentencing systems in the United States and beyond, where the aim is to punish a crime according to a notional scale of harm which the offence has caused to society (Von Hirsch 1976). Pressure from victims' rights advocates has resulted, for example, in the introduction of fixed sentences and the abolition of parole boards in some parts of the United States (US Department of Justice 1986).

An example of legislation introduced as a direct result of the political activism of a victim advocacy group was the Washington State Community Protection Act (1989) directed against sexually violent offenders. Three elements of this legislation were especially controversial: penalties were increased and their reach extended; sexual offenders were required to register with the police on release from prison and the communities in which they reside were to be notified of their presence; offenders classified as 'sexually violent predators' who have served their term might be subject to civil action which could result in further incarceration.

The people in Washington State working for the introduction of these measures had suffered terribly through the death or mutilation of their children, and they were not much interested in arguments about deterrence. In any case, there is a reluctance by citizens everywhere to engage in debate with people who have suffered so much, which in itself can be a serious impediment in moderating victims' demands. Scheingold *et al.* (1994) saw victims generally as problematic contributors to the crime debate because they tend to be incident-driven in their activities. They observed that the precipitating condition for victim advocacy is usually an especially horrifying or aberrant crime which stirs a moral panic in the community and the atmosphere generated by these events, as well as the attitudes of the victims concerned, is likely to be overwhelmingly punitive. Reiss (1981) expressed concern about policy being formed on the basis of misconceptions derived from the aberrant, while just deserts theorists are anxious about victim influence resulting in disproportionate sentences in particular cases (Ashworth & von Hirsch 1993; Ashworth 2000).

However, as we shall see, it is not axiomatic that all victims want punishment, or more of it, no matter how much they have been hurt. In fact, Scheingold *et al.* noted that the victim advocacy groups they observed in Washington State were actually not unremittingly punitive and short-term in their concerns and were interested in policies directed to crime prevention and the treatment of offenders as well. But local politicians chose to respond only to the punitive part of their agenda. Scheingold *et al.* concluded that retributive attitudes expressed by victims who have experienced especially horrifying crimes leave their communities vulnerable to manipulation by forces specifically concerned to introduce more punitive policies, even if retribution is only half of what victims say they want.

There has been pessimism expressed about the consequences of an appropriation of the American victim movement by the far right. Elias (1990), for example, saw a strident rights-based approach perpetuating a concept of victimization limited to 'street' crimes, with no room for 'suite' crimes, while the kinds of victims identified as the beneficiaries of the approach were likewise narrowed to those who 'deserved' them. In his view, the movement itself was conservative and manipulated, never likely substantially to improve the lot of victims because it was incapable of recognizing the relationships between criminal victimization and abuses of power. Elias concluded that victims in the United States:

> have gotten far less than they were promised. Rights have often been unenforced or unenforceable, participation sporadic or ill-advised, services as have been introduced precarious and underfunded, victim needs unsatisfied if not further jeopardised and victimization increased, if not in court, then certainly in the streets. (1990: 242)

2.3.2   European model: support-focused

By contrast, the emphasis in Europe has been far less on victim rights and much more towards victim support (Maguire & Shapland 1990; Mawby 1988). Organizations in these countries developed in the tradition of community-based voluntary associations whose objectives were primarily to alleviate suffering, and only secondarily to lobby for better treatment and more legal rights. Maguire and Shapland (1990) commented that outside the United States, 'relying on victims rights to speed change is considered impractical, unlikely and even scandalous' (p. 221). European victim support groups have deliberately avoided political activity or open campaigning, and in particular have consistently refused to comment publicly on sentencing policy. Their aim had been to be seen as politically neutral, thus maximizing its pool of volunteers and ensuring cross-party support (Zedner 1994), though in the United Kingdom they have been remarkably successful in mobilizing government towards helping victims (Rock 1990).

Activities involving support and assistance to victims tend to share similar characteristics across nations, probably because they have developed outside the ambit of criminal justice agencies or government generally and have their roots in their communities. Shapland (1988) argued that the similarity of victim assistance services across Europe is a result of their separateness from their respective criminal justice systems.

Underlying many of the activities of European victim organizations, as well as the American movement, is the assumption that victims are the virtuous 'us' and the offenders the culpable 'other'. But victims' organizations are well aware that victimization surveys routinely find that young men are the most victimized segment of the community (Van Dijk *et al.* 1990). In fact victims and offenders are often demographically indistinguishable from one another (Hindelang 1976; Fattah 1993). Not all victims are 'good', or in Christie's (1986) word, 'ideal', whom he characterized as respectable, weak, and unblameworthy, and this reality is recognized in Scandinavia where crime victims are not treated in any special way but are supported under the general provisions of the welfare state. Such an approach may not address the special difficulties many victims face in recovering from the loss of social trust and sense of violation resulting from their victimization, but it is unlikely that any rights-focus could help here either. What seems to be needed for all victims, the virtuous and the culpable, is what Van Dijk (1988) called 'an expression of care and solidarity by the community whose integrity is at stake' (p. 126).

2.4   How Useful, How Effective?

2.4.1   Rights groups

The effectiveness of rights-focused advocacy groups which have dominated the American picture is far from clear. There is no doubt about their success in raising the profile of crime victims, but much remains undone in giving victims the voice they believe should be heard in the justice system. The prior issue may be whether they have tested the limits of the capacity of the traditional justice system to fulfil their objectives. The 'noise level' they have generated, especially in the United States, has probably contributed in a positive way to drawing attention to the condition of crime victims and bringing about some necessary reform, but by doing so has made the movement vulnerable to appropriation by retributive conservative forces.

2.4.2   Support groups

In terms of effectiveness for the welfare of victims, support groups, which have sprung up in great numbers around the world, are very popular, and there is evidence of high levels of client satisfaction (Maguire 1991). However, the question whether they are either appropriate or effective in the services they provide has been the subject of a good deal of research with contradictory and inconclusive findings.

In terms of appropriateness, research has found that there may be a mismatch between the services offered and the needs of the victims. Several American studies (Brown & Yantzi 1990; Friedman *et al.* 1982; Skogan *et al.* 1990; Davis *et al.* 1999) found that property crime victims most often wanted practical help with repairs, security, insurance claims, and financial assistance, services not often provided by victims' organizations in the United States. They tended more often to be offered professional counselling, usually some considerable time after the incident. Skogan *et al.* (1990) suggested that the emotional support provided by family and friends is extremely important, but these connections were less likely to provide the practical help victims needed.

In Britain, Maguire and Corbett (1987) also found that victims needed both emotional and practical support, and that often they regarded the emotional impact of the crime as its worst aspect. Maguire (1991) argued that British support organizations may be more successful than their American counterparts, because they stress in their training that emotional support is enhanced through practical help and that the time of greatest need for help of all kinds is within two days of the crime.

In looking at the effectiveness of victim support groups, the evidence is mixed. When victims are asked whether victim assistance works, they tend to be very enthusiastic. For example, in Maguire and Corbett's (1987) study, 87 per cent of victims interviewed made positive comments. Similar results were also reported by Chesney and Schneider (1981), Norquay and Weiler (1981), and Skogan *et al.* (1990). But despite the positive views expressed by victims, no study has been able to demonstrate that these services are effective in actually assisting recovery from the effects of victimization (Maguire 1991).

In sum, the success of victim assistance groups is difficult to assess. But perhaps civil society is strengthened in any case when the motivation for such activity is primarily to demonstrate that 'someone cares' (Gay *et al.* 1987; Holtom & Raynor 1988) and to help restore victims' faith in others. As Van Dijk (1986) argues, it may be that 'a community that supports its crime victims does not offer charity, but makes an investment in its own survival' (p. 126).

2.5   A Third Way for Victims? Canberra as a Case Study

Canberra is not an important location in world victim politics, but it has been the setting for debates as vigorous as anywhere in the world on issues such as the treatment of rape victims, the establishment of women's refuges, the pros and cons of victim impact statements, and the like. The Canberra victim movement provides an interesting case study in which many of the competing forces in the wider movement have been played out, but which seems to have escaped the narrow choices, in philosophy and objectives, accepted by the movement, broadly speaking, in the United States on the one hand and Europe on the other. In fact, it may exemplify Roach's (1997) hopes for a 'progressive approach' which sees victims' rights as extending far beyond the frame of punishment and retribution.

While the Australian victim movement generally grew out of the same forces for change as it did in other countries, it mostly did so rather later than in Europe and North America. The exception was South Australia, where the Victims of Crime Service was established in 1979 through the efforts of a senior police officer, who was personally very concerned with victim issues and who worked with the families of the victims of a series of murders of young girls in the Adelaide area. Similar organizations were not established in other parts of Australia until a decade later.

In Canberra today, a booklet entitled *Victims of Crime: An Information Booklet for the ACT and Region* lists over fifty community and government organizations, excluding criminal justice agencies, which can provide information, advice, and support to victims of crime. Ten years ago most of these organizations did not exist, and of those that did, none was focused on victim support. The present network of support agencies is largely a result of the activities of two victim-focused groups, the Domestic Violence Crisis Service (DVCS) and the Victims of Crime Assistance League (VOCAL).

The DVCS is the organization most closely involved with victims of family violence and, like similar organizations across the world, is a strongly ideologically driven product of the women's movement. Over the past twenty years it has set up women's refuges and offered support of all kinds to women experiencing violence in the home. It lobbied for funds from a government which viewed its activities with some distaste. Sometimes uncompromising in attitudes and behaviour, these women succeeded in getting the funding they needed from government because of the palpable need for their services. The present head of DVCS was closely involved with this push for funding in the early 1980s through the use of direct action such as street demonstrations. She commented: '[t]he attitude was "you're funded because we've had to fund you but you're a damned mob of ratbags". That's very much how we were viewed from most quarters—the criminal justice system, bureaucrats and politicians' (personal communication, October 1998). But times have changed and so have the views of those who drive the organization. The punitive attitudes of the past have largely been replaced by a broader view of the problem. Some measures of this are the recent appointment of the first male worker for the DVCS, the extension of services to gay and lesbian relationships and the formation of MensLine, a telephone service for men concerned about their own violence or who are experiencing domestic violence themselves.

While DVCS limits its activities to the assistance of victims of domestic violence, VOCAL sees itself with a much broader area of responsibility and is widely seen as the premier victim support and lobby group in Canberra. Like a number of other grass-roots victims groups, it was formed as a result of local tragedies. It has about 120 members, almost all of them victims of crime themselves, and it provides services, mostly information and sometimes counselling, to around 800 clients each year. It supports on a long-term basis victims of nearly 100 offences, most of them violent crimes, through both personal contact by members and a government-funded full-time counsellor. It organizes telephone rosters of members for victims to call twenty-four hours a day and assigns two members to each new member wanting intensive help.

VOCAL states that its mission is primarily 'to help and support individual persons and their families, who, through a criminal act against them, are victims of crime, to overcome their anguish and suffering and assist them towards a state of understanding and acceptance of their adversity in order to resume a more stable mental and physical condition'. Other stated aims are to support victims during court action, to promote public awareness of victim issues, and to work co-operatively with the community, business, and government on victim issues.

From the outset the membership has consisted almost entirely of people who were victims themselves. The membership's view was that it was only those who had experienced crime who could really understand what it was like to be a victim. The original twenty-six victims of crime who came together in November 1988 to form the organization all have stories to tell of their experiences of the justice system. Mrs Cameron, whose son's death was described at the beginning of this chapter, told me:

We met every week because we were all new victims and really struggling and having terrible trouble with the system. Everybody had their story. Nobody was told very much at all and when we went to court it was just horrific—no support whatsoever, not knowing who was who. We couldn't understand all the lawyers laughing amongst themselves. That really hurt us. We felt like screaming out 'Don't you realise you're dealing with something serious here?'

Mrs Cameron described to me what it was like to confront her son's killer in the small area outside the courtroom, where everyone was required to wait together, and of finding herself face to face with his mother. She said that people told her she ought not to be there to run these risks and to hear the distressing evidence that was presented. She described how difficult it was to listen to character witnesses giving statements on behalf of the defendant while she had to remain silent. She said that she remembers sitting in the courtroom and wanting to shout '[c]an't I say anything about my son?'. Mrs Cameron said that any feelings she and her husband might have had towards the defendant were completely overshadowed by their anger towards what she called 'the system'. When they enquired at the office of the Director of Public Prosecutions about why the charge had been downgraded to manslaughter 'we were quickly told to leave. That really shocked us. It was dreadful. The way we were treated—we felt so alone.'

Mrs Cameron said that they were given no information at all about when court hearings would take place, and could find out only through their son's friends who had been subpoenaed to appear. She thought perhaps the police dealing with her case wanted to protect them from the experience of attending court but she said they did not understand that 'the not knowing is worse than the knowing. When you go to court at least you know what happened.'

Finally, Mrs Cameron reflected on the emotional pain caused by the defendant not showing any remorse for his crime: '[h]e never said that he was sorry. If he had it would have been so much easier on us—if he could have said he didn't mean to do it.'

Mrs Cameron's recollections mirror those of the victims whose needs and desires have been documented in the research literature (see, for example, Shapland *et al.* 1985; Mawby & Gill 1987; Waller 1989). They can be summarized as follows (see Chapter 1):

- victims want a less formal process where their views count;
- victims want more information about both the processing and outcome of their cases;
- victims want to participate in their cases;
- victims want to be treated respectfully and fairly;
- victims want material and emotional restoration, especially an apology.

At first glance, one would imagine that because membership of VOCAL consists overwhelmingly of those with first-hand experience of victimization, the organization would be vulnerable to the extreme punitiveness described by Scheingold *et al.* (1994) in the Washington State movement. But though individual members may have angry and vengeful feelings, overall the organization does not have a retributive character. None of the founders of VOCAL who met with judges, negotiated with the bureaucracy, or appeared before committees of enquiry had ever taken part in public life before. But they recall they decided very early that the organization needed to have a moderate, responsible style, because neither the community nor the government would be sympathetic to a radical, rights-focused approach. They agreed that reason, calm, and equanimity were the qualities needed in discussions to be held with politicians, police, the judiciary, and public servants to explain their case for reform.

Although there has been a great emphasis on victim support in its activities, VOCAL sees its objectives as both the advancement of rights and the enhancement of assistance services, and perceives no clash of interests between these roles. Both are informed by a restorative, non-punitive, approach which puts less emphasis on adversarial conflict and more on community participation and reconciliation. The organization has explicitly stated that it will never comment on sentencing decisions and it has no interest in curtailing offender rights. On the question of any clash of interests between their advocacy and support roles members respond that they must go together. Mrs Cameron said: '[i]t's the victims' problems that we go out to fight for changes to. That's what we did in the early days and that's where we're coming from now. It's because of the things that happen to victims that we go out and lobby for change.'

Perhaps because victims had already met with some success in other parts of the world in drawing attention to their neglect and revictimization by the criminal justice system, Australian victims groups generally, and Canberra VOCAL in particular, have been moderately successful in lobbying for improvements in the way victims are treated. Mrs Cameron said: '[i]t was almost as if the world was waiting for victims to stand up.' Compare this comment with the painful feelings of victim advocates in Washington State, where Scheingold (1994) believed that victims placed the blame for their situation on 'a callous and unresponsive state. They believed that much of the suffering was gratuitous, the result of the state placing its own bureaucratic concerns ahead of public safety' (p. 14).

VOCAL sees its proudest achievement as the passing of the Victims of Crime Act 1994 (and the Acts Revision (Victims of Crime) Act 1994). These followed from a Report of the Community Law Reform Committee of the ACT, published in 1993, which made recommendations concerning general needs of victims which should be met by the criminal justice system, and specifically addressing the issues of victim impact statements, victim–offender reconciliation, and criminal injuries compensation.

The first part of the Victims of Crime Act sets down 'governing principles' concerning the treatment of victims, based on a Charter of Victims' Rights devised by VOCAL members. These are as close as Canberra victims get to 'rights': they were deliberately described as 'principles' to ensure that no action could be brought for breaches of 'rights' in the event of non-compliance. Most of them concern obligations to inform victims about the progress of their cases and the way in which they are being dealt with by the various criminal justice agencies.

The remainder of the Act is largely concerned with the function and powers of a new statutory position, the Victims of Crime Co-ordinator. The occupant of this position sees it as a quasi-Ombudsman role whose function is to report to the

Attorney-General of the ACT on complaints and compliance with the Act. The majority of enquiries she receives are in fact complaints, usually about lack of information. She readily acknowledges that the Act is very seldom complied with regarding obligations to keep victims informed, and frankly doubts that it ever will be, because the justice system does not provide the opportunities for victims to be treated this way.

The Acts Revision (Victims of Crime) Act 1994 deals with three issues: notification of victims about bail decisions concerning their offenders, notification of victims concerning release on parole decisions about their offenders, and provision for use of victim impact statements. VOCAL members lobbied hard for all of these. The first two seem to work uncontroversially, but there is a good deal of dissatisfaction concerning the third. The dissatisfaction concerns the negative attitude of the judiciary towards them, as a result of which they are rarely used. It seems a prime example of the limitations of the legislative approach to giving victims what they say they want.

It is evident that even without a punitive rights focus, where the objective may be as much to curtail offender rights as advance victims' rights, there are limitations to what victims can achieve through conventional law reform. Victims in Canberra, for instance, are pleased with their success in lobbying for legislation which undertakes to ensure that they are given more information, which provides them with the Victims of Crime Co-ordinator to whom they can take their complaints, and which allows them to submit victim impact statements at the sentencing stage. There has also been funding supplied to the Office of the Director of Public Prosecutions to provide witness support.

But in many ways the legislative route has provided only marginal gains. Certainly victims in Canberra are treated more seriously than they were ten years ago, and are not as vulnerable to the sort of casual humiliations that they suffered then. But in terms of their larger objectives, namely being informed and consulted about the progress of their cases, participating actively in the disposition of their cases and obtaining material and emotional reparation and apologies from the offender, very little has been achieved. A growing number of people around the world believe that victims can achieve justice only by a radical reordering of the criminal justice process, whereby victims and offenders reclaim their stolen conflicts (Christie 1977).

The theory and practice of restorative justice will be comprehensively reviewed in the next chapter. At this point I observe only that there may be persuasive theoretical reasons for arguing that a restorative approach has the potential to deliver to victims those things they have identified as being of prime importance. Roach (1997) suggested that:

> less formal proceedings seeking restorative justice could empower crime victims, as well as offenders, their families and communities, to the detriment of the professionals such as police, prosecutors and defence counsel [and] include victims in decision-making without relying on increased punishment. . . . Less punitive approaches can give those who have been victimised in the past more power and justice than crime control measures which, increasingly undertaken in the name of victims, often affirm the powers of criminal justice professionals and frequently collide with due process claims. (pp. 4, 13)

In contrast to the punitive victims' rights approach, where the only action available is appeal to politicians, the judiciary, and the bureaucracy, who retain all the real power, the restorative approach may allow victims to play a central role in the disposition of their cases. In theory, through their participation in the process could they get most or all of the information they ever wanted, contribute towards the resolution of their cases, and obtain the reparation they seek? Does restorative justice have the potential to give a more meaningful role in responding to crime not only to victims, but also to offenders and their supporters and the community as a whole?

2.6   Summary

Canberra may be a rather good example of how victims can begin effectively claiming back from the state the role they believe they are entitled to in the justice system. Historically, victims have been deprived of their conflicts (Christie 1977)—and no doubt were sometimes glad to be rid of them. But now many want them back. Perhaps, as victims in Canberra seem to feel, they are there for the asking if conditions are right on both sides. On the victim side mature, responsible leadership is needed. On the side of the state there must be a recognition of the necessity for change: a responsive state that is willing to treat its citizens as adults with legitimate grievances. But at the same time VOCAL members recognize both the achievements of the organization and the limitations that the existing justice system places on its capacity to make a difference.

The victim movement worldwide has been enormously influential over the past twenty-five years in bringing to the attention of politicians, legislators, and the communities of which they are a part the needs and wishes of victims of crime. Whether it has reached the limits of the capacity of the traditional formal justice system to give victims what they want is an important question. Shapland (2000) argued that in reality there has been little substantive change over this period, with victims still perceived as separate from the criminal justice system, 'a rather annoying group which stand apart from justice, but to whom we now need to consider creating some kind of response and making some concessions. . . . There is little idea that victims are fundamentally woven into justice—that justice incorporates both victims and offenders' (p. 148). She identified the difficulties that victims still contend with as being characterized by the need for justice agencies 'to reach out and respond to victims' (p. 148), a task in which they have self-evidently failed. To succeed requires much greater appreciation of the legitimacy of the participation by victims in the disposition of the crimes they have experienced. This view is shared by Erez (2000) who commented that '[c]ourt inertia seems to result from the legal professionals' strong resistance against accepting victims as a legitimate party in the proceedings and practitioners' reluctance to recognize any value in victim input' (p. 178). The restorative approach may provide opportunities for this recognition in a way that may simply not be feasible for traditional justice, and the next chapter will explore the theory and practice of this alternative way of 'doing justice'.

3

The Theory and Practice of Restorative Justice

3.1 Introduction

In Chapter 1 I suggested that a 'restorative' approach has traditionally been the dominant paradigm of criminal justice. By this I
was referring to a response to crime that involved offenders making
amends to their victims, and that was achieved through various
mechanisms involving restitution. The purpose of this response was
to restore order and peace as quickly as possible and to avoid the
consequences of revenge (Weitekamp 1997). These mechanisms fell
away with the rise of the modern state, and were replaced by a
retributive model of state-centred justice with outcomes focused on
punishment of the offender, rather than reconciliation between the
disputing parties and restoration of the victim's wellbeing (Zehr
1985).

Dissatisfaction with the limited effectiveness of retribution in
deterring crime gave rise in the post-war period of the twentieth
century to the rehabilitation model, a 'welfare' model of justice.
This, in its turn, was found to have serious limitations (Martinson
1974) and was followed by a return to harsh punitive policies in
much of the industrialized world. Braithwaite (1999) suggests that
over the past fifty years, juvenile justice especially has been characterized by a see-sawing between the retributive and rehabilitative
models, neither of them satisfactory. Restorative justice is seen as a
third model, a new lens (Zehr 1990) through which to perceive
crime, taking into account its moral, social, economic, and political contexts.

3.2 What is Restorative Justice?

Restorative justice takes many forms, but usually refers to the

restoration of victims, offenders, and community (Bazemore &
Umbreit 1994; Brown & Polk 1996) (though Braithwaite and
Parker (1997) observed that this is an acceptable goal only if the
prior condition to which they were restored was a morally decent
one). It emphasizes the repair of harm resulting from the crime,
including harm to relationships (Daly & Immarigeon 1998).

Another essential strand of restorative justice is the attention
given to the context in which crime occurs: that, in Leslie Wilkins'
famous words (1991), 'the problem of crime cannot be simplified
to the problem of the criminal'. Bazemore (1997) observed that
restorative justice encourages a shift towards less formal responses
to crime that emphasize the role of citizens, community groups,
and other institutions of civil society. Bazemore and Umbreit
(1995) believe that in fact a core value in restorative justice is to
balance offender needs, victim needs, and the needs of the community as well (see also Bazemore & Washington 1995). Furthermore,
Bazemore (1997) has argued that the justice needs of communities
cannot be met merely by punishment or merely by treatment of
offenders: rather, an integrated approach is required for achieving
these multiple needs of sanctioning, offender accountability and
reintegration, safety and victim restoration, and that restorative
justice recognizes these needs.

Van Ness (1993) considered that the foundations of restorative
justice theory are the following propositions:

1. Crime is primarily conflict between individuals resulting in injuries to
victims, communities and the offenders themselves; only secondarily is it
lawbreaking.
2. The overarching aim of the criminal justice process should be to reconcile parties while repairing the injuries caused by the crime.
3. The criminal justice process should facilitate active participation by
victims, offenders and their communities. It should not be dominated by
the government to the exclusion of others. (p. 259)

Marshall, a British advocate for restorative justice, has defined
it as 'a process whereby all the parties with a stake in a particular
offence come together to resolve collectively how to deal with the
aftermath of the offence and its implications for the future'
(McCold 1997). Braithwaite (1999) argued that, while this defini-
tion is helpful in establishing a core meaning, it requires further
clarification. He suggested that those 'with a stake' in the offence
be defined as the victim(s), the offender(s), and the affected

community, which includes the families of the principals. As for what needs to be restored, Braithwaite (1996) specified the following as important for victims:

- restoring property loss;
- restoring injury;
- restoring a sense of security;
- restoring dignity;
- restoring a sense of empowerment;
- restoring deliberative democracy;
- restoring harmony based on a feeling that justice has been done;
- restoring social support.

Although the concept of 'restorative justice' has a lineage encompassing many indigenous as well as pre-industrial Western justice traditions, the term became widely used only in the 1990s (Zehr 1990; Colson and Van Ness 1990; Van Ness 1990; Wright 1991). It referred to the many programmes implemented since the mid-1970s which were characterized by mediated meetings between victims and offenders focused on reparation and reconciliation.

Prominent among these programmes are the victim–offender reconciliation programmes (VORPs) which originated in Kitchener, Ontario, in 1974 (Peachey 1989). These are community-initiated programmes which seek to mediate between victims and offenders, usually after sentencing. They are often Christian-based, having been established on principles of the Mennonite Church. Umbreit (1998) reported that by the mid-1990s there were over 300 such programmes in North America and over 500 in Europe. However, VORPs have been criticized for failing to take sufficiently into account the social and moral implications that more serious offences have for the whole community (Cavadino & Dignan 1997).

Victim–Offender Mediation (VOM) is similar to the VORP model, in that both focus on providing a process of conflict resolution, under the auspices of a mediator who is seen as fair by both parties, but with more emphasis on reparation and less on reconciliation. Umbreit *et al.* (1994) described the aims of VOM as being to:

hold offenders personally accountable for their behavior; emphasize the human impact of crime; provide opportunities for offenders to take responsibility for their actions by facing their victim and making amends; promote active victim and community involvement in the justice process; and enhance the quality of justice experienced by both victims and offenders. (p. 5)

Parties other than the victim and offender are rarely present (Marshall & Merry 1990), the programme is usually restricted to juvenile offenders, and involves collaboration between police, probation, and welfare agencies. Often the mediator meets separately with the offender and then the victim and sometimes the principals do not meet face-to-face at all: Marshall and Merry reported that in the English schemes a direct meeting was offered in about 85 per cent of referred cases but actually occurred in 34 per cent of cases.

Although there is a good deal of diversity in restorative justice programmes, essential to all of them is the principle of direct participation by victims and offenders. There has also been acknowledgement by many proponents, especially more recently, of the role of the broader community and repair of harm to that community. How this community is to be involved in the process, and indeed what the concept of community really means in this context, has not been so well conceptualized. However, over the past decade or so there have been important developments here, building on principles and practices in indigenous communities in Canada and New Zealand.

In Canada, circle sentencing emerged during the 1980s as a First Nations method of responding to offenders and is now used in a number of northern communities. It involves offenders, victims, the families of each, and other community members in a discussion of the circumstances that underlie the causes of a crime. It is built on principles of mediation, indigenous peacemaking processes, and consensus decision-making (Stuart 1996). However, these programmes have been criticized for their dependence on mainstream court processes and personnel in their operation (LaPrairie 1995).

In New Zealand, following a reassessment of the Treaty of Waitangi and its implications for white–Maori relations, legislation was introduced in 1989 establishing major changes in the way in which juvenile justice and family welfare was addressed (Daly &

Immarigeon 1998). These legislative changes applied to all youth, though they were primarily a response to the overrepresentation of Maori youth in the justice system and complaints by the Maori community that they were effectively shut out of decision-making in welfare matters affecting their children. The central feature of the Children, Young Persons and Their Families Act 1989 was the establishment of the Family Group Conference (FGC) as the primary mechanism for addressing almost all youth crime, including very serious offending.

The FGC, which involves a meeting of not only young offenders and (preferably but not always) their victims, but also their wider families, is based on traditional Maori ways of resolving disputes and dealing with criminal behaviour. FGCs are facilitated by specially trained Youth Justice Co-ordinators and administered by the Department of Social Welfare. They are now entrenched in mainstream criminal justice processing for all youth who 'decline to deny' their offence, and the programme has been extended in a limited way to some adults as well. The main difference between FGCs and VORPs and VOMs is the deliberate involvement in the former of the local community in discussion of the offence and acknowledgement of a wider community of victims as well (Maxwell & Morris 1993).

The idea of conferences was introduced to Australia in 1991 as part of police operations in the city of Wagga, New South Wales. Here the New Zealand model was adapted so that the police acted as conference organizers and facilitators, thus altering its character to a strict justice model. The programme was abandoned in 1995. However, police-run conferencing on the Wagga model was established in the Australian Capital Territory (ACT) in 1993 (see later in this chapter for a description of the Canberra conferencing programme).

Conferencing for juvenile offenders is now available in all Australian States and Territories, though the programmes vary in reach and size (Strang 2001). It continues to be run by police in the ACT, while in New South Wales, South Australia, Western Australia, the Northern Territory, and Queensland it is the responsibility of justice authorities. In Tasmania it is run by the Department of Health and Human Services, and in Victoria a small programme is operated by a church body. Variations exist in the offences and offenders eligible for conferencing, the existence of a legislative basis, and the agency in which the programme is located. In South Australia and New South Wales, it has become an established part of mainstream juvenile justice processing. Similar programmes have been introduced in several locations in the United States, Canada, and England.

All of these kinds of restorative justice in action share the aspiration of improving the treatment that victims experience in the official response to their victimization. Galaway and Hudson (1996), in reviewing the findings of the contributors to their edited volume, stated that victim outcomes reported include:

- providing an opportunity for participation in the justice process;
- receiving answers to their questions and a better understanding of why they were chosen to be victimized;
- restoring the emotional and material losses to victims;
- reducing their fears;
- giving them a sense of having been treated fairly (p. 9).

But there are problems too. The reparation and VOM programmes of the 1980s have been the subject of frequent criticism for their focus on offenders and their needs, sometimes at the expense of the victim's welfare, or, at best, their incidental benefit (see, for example, Wright 1991). Walklate (1989) concluded a review of English reparation and mediation schemes by stating that these

have been demonstrated to have little general value for the structural position of the victim. Whilst it is true that individual victims may have felt some benefit, the motivation for the generation of such schemes has largely come from the general problem with the rising prison population. There has been no demonstrable desire to promote these schemes in terms of their benefits to victims. The benefits for offenders seem clearer but the benefits to the state seem clearer still. (p. 129)

These criticisms have been addressed to varying extents by different conferencing models, but this subject will be addressed in detail below.

Although restorative justice is often referred to as a new paradigm of justice, it is not a complete model, because as yet it does not address major issues such as disputes over culpability, consequences of failure to reach an agreement, equity and proportionality in outcomes, or failure by the offender to comply with outcomes. These remain lively topics, with some proponents, such as Marshall (1990), recommending that these programmes should be independent of mainstream criminal justice because their objectives and practices are so different. Others see their future embedded in the mainstream, with New Zealand's legislation-based Family Group Conferencing as the exemplar. Still others look for ways in which forms of restorative justice might work with current criminal justice practices so that they can be informed and influenced by restorative principles (Walgrave & Aertsen 1996).

3.3   What May Restorative Justice Offer Victims?

In a review of her own and other research findings on victims' experience and attitudes, Shapland (1986) concluded:

[T]he similarity of victim attitudes over offences and in different systems is extraordinary. . . . If we adopt the more victim-centred system suggested by the findings of these studies . . . we may, in doing so, alter victims' attitudes and expectations so that a different model emerges, one perhaps closer to a mediated consensus form of dispute regulation.

Survey findings have revealed that victims are not nearly as punitive as has been assumed (Zedner 1994). Many victims said they would welcome the opportunity for reparation or even direct reconciliation rather than punishment. Zedner concluded her comprehensive review of the victim literature by reporting that:

Such evidence, together with growing disillusionment . . . with the existing paradigm of punishment has prompted discussion of models of reparative justice reoriented towards the aims of mediation and restitution. (p. 1234)

Similar findings emerged from a large German study of victim attitudes (Beurskens & Boers 1985). Only 13 per cent of almost 1,500 victims surveyed specified punishment as their primary need, while 33 per cent said restitution, 26 per cent said community service, and 17 per cent said apology.

These authors are suggesting that it may be time to consider another way of 'doing justice', another paradigm for addressing the wrongs of offenders and the rights of victims. Restorative justice is seen in some quarters as such a paradigm.

The practice of restorative justice includes programmes based purely on restitution, those based on mediation and reconciliation, and, more recently, the conferencing model. These three models may be said to represent different developmental stages in the restorative justice paradigm. From the early 1970s, those looking at ways of reforming criminal justice processing to fit better the needs of victims concentrated on the potential of restitution from offender directly to victim and compensation generally (for example, Hudson & Galaway 1975; Barnett 1977). During the 1980s, reconciliation became a major focus (Dignan 1992; Marshall 1985; Umbreit 1985; Zehr 1985; Van Ness 1990; Marshall & Merry 1990).

Since the establishment in New Zealand in 1989 of the Family Group Conferencing model for dealing with young offenders, a lot of attention has been focused on the potential of this kind of programme for overcoming problems with earlier restorative models and for 'mainstreaming' the principles of restorative justice (Maxwell & Morris 1993; Maxwell & Morris 1996; Morris *et al.* 1996; Braithwaite & Mugford 1994; Braithwaite & Daly 1994; Moore & O'Connell 1994; Alder & Wundersitz 1994) and for providing victims with the justice they seek. Braithwaite's *Crime, Shame and Reintegration* (1989) provides one of the most explicit theoretical frameworks for exploration of the model.

I will now review the principal shortcomings of the existing retributive system of justice from the victim's viewpoint discussed above, and explore whether restorative justice principles and practices may be superior in addressing these shortcomings and achieving the restorations victims seek.

3.3.1   A less formal process where their views count?

In the British Crime Survey of 1984, about half of respondents said that they would have accepted the chance of meeting their offender in order to negotiate direct restitution, and a further 20 per cent would have liked to reach such an agreement without meeting the offender directly (Maguire & Corbett 1987). For those who wanted to meet their offenders, the most common reasons given were to see what they were like, to find out why they committed the offence, to tell the offenders what they thought of them, to arrange for restitution, and to show the offenders the effect of the crime. Wright (1991) suggested that these findings indicate that 'many victims want not retribution, but a sufficient recognition of what has happened to them' (p. 128).

A study of fifty burglary victims who had been referred to a Minnesota VORP showed that their participation in the criminal justice process was the major determinant of their perception of fairness (Umbreit 1989). Three quarters of them wanted to be able to talk directly about the effects of the offence to the judge or other officials and a similar number wanted to express their concerns to their offenders so that they understood how the crime had affected them as people (p. 55).

In a comprehensive review of British victim–offender mediation programmes Marshall and Merry (1990) found that 82 per cent of victims felt that meeting their offenders was a valuable experience. Forty per cent of victims who had received reparation thought that compensation was a sufficient sentence, and only 10 per cent wanted the offender to be sent to prison.

In a study of over 500 victims of burglaries and muggings, a little over half of whom participated in mediation Umbreit *et al.* (1994) found that almost 80 per cent were satisfied with the conduct of their cases (compared with 57 per cent of those who had not participated). Being able to take an active role in their cases and the resulting sense of emotional closure were major reasons for their satisfaction. They particularly appreciated the chance to voice their opinions about the offence and the offender, which they felt had a humanizing effect on the meeting (p. 94). It also had the effect of reducing victims' fear because of the opportunity to see their offenders with all their frailties (p. 97). A plethora of small-scale studies concerning the success of various victim–offender mediation programmes, such as those reviewed by Sebba (1996), also suggest that most victims, when asked their views on the desirability of meeting their offenders, or when given the opportunity to do so, indicate that they are in favour of it.

In summarizing the available literature on victims' experience of restorative justice, Kennedy and Sacco (1998) suggested that central to this approach is the opportunity for victims to find closure through direct involvement in the justice process. They also appreciate being able to explain directly to their offenders the impact of their behaviour and to take an active part in the resolution of the offences. They concluded that there are positive signs that this model delivers a less formal process of the kind that victims seek.

3.3.2   More information about both the processing and the outcome of the case?

The structure of restorative justice programmes empowers victims to take an active role in the disposition of their cases, if they wish to do so. Victims are never *required* to take this role, but when it is made possible for them, there is plainly much greater opportunity to know about the state of play in their cases than the court alternative allows. Umbreit's 1989 study found that some victims simply wanted to be kept informed about what was happening in their cases, and derived their satisfaction from achieving that goal.

It is interesting to note that a source of dissatisfaction for some victims involved in New Zealand conferences concerned the same problems with being kept informed as is so commonly experienced by victims involved in the court system. Professionals sometimes failed to inform victims about what happened after the conference, and to make the necessary arrangements for the victim to receive the agreed reparation (Maxwell & Morris 1996).

3.3.3   Participation in the case?

In Umbreit *et al.*'s (1994) study of burglary and mugging victims who took part in restorative justice, respondents 'generally expressed satisfaction about participating in the process' (p. 94) and particularly emphasized the personal nature of the process, their opportunity to play an active role in the justice process, and their satisfaction with having a chance to make an impact on their offenders. These views were echoed in McCold and Wachtel's study (1998), which involved 215 property and violence cases, where one third were assigned to formal adjudication (the control group) and two thirds to a diversionary conference. Over 90 per cent of conferenced victims said that their opinions had been adequately considered, that meeting with the offender had been helpful, that the conference had allowed them to express their feelings about being victimized, and that conferencing allowed for fuller participation in the justice system.

Although the structure of restorative justice programmes theoretically provides much greater opportunity for victim participation, victims have not always been given the opportunity to take part and, in some cases, decline to do so in substantial numbers. For example, Dignan (1992) reported that in the Kettering Adult

Reparation Scheme in Britain not all victims wanted to meet their offenders: indeed, only about a third of cases were dealt with by a face-to-face meeting, and in the remaining cases, the bureau managing the Scheme acted as a 'go-between' in an attempt to negotiate an agreement between the parties (although it is not clear whether this was because of victim preference in all cases or whether it was a decision of the bureau).

Maxwell and Morris (1993) reported that in New Zealand just under half of victims attended their conference. The relatively low attendance rate was found to be related to inadequate attention to the victims' convenience in arranging the time and place for the conference; only 6 per cent of victims said that they did not want to meet their offenders (Maxwell & Morris 1996). Failure to keep victims informed about their cases was an important factor (together with lack of reparation and inadequate monitoring of outcomes) for the 38 per cent who felt dissatisfied about the conference. Likewise, Clairmont (1994) found a low level of victim participation in programmes designed for aboriginal offenders in Canada.

Similar problems have been found in the conferencing programme operating in South Australia. Wundersitz (1996) reported that during the first year of the programme's operation, in 1994–5, victims attended only 48 per cent of conferences. Conference co-ordinators acknowledged that when victims did not attend the effectiveness of the conference was significantly reduced. A number of strategies to increase victim attendance have been put in place and Wundersitz and Hetzel found by 1996 that victim attendance was estimated at 75–80 per cent.

In their 1993 evaluation of FGCs in New Zealand, Maxwell and Morris found that about 60 per cent of victims thought that attending the conference was 'helpful, positive and rewarding'; generally they felt involved and better as a result of taking part. The causes for victim dissatisfaction noted above in New Zealand and South Australia are a strong indication of how highly most victims regard the importance of participation.

3.3.4   Respectful and fair treatment?

Some evidence about the capacity of restorative justice to provide the fairness that victims seek has come from Umbreit et al. (1994). Their cross-site analysis of four programmes applying restorative justice techniques with victims and offenders indicated that the process 'was significantly more likely to result in a perception by victims that cases were handled fairly by the juvenile justice system ... 83 per cent of victims in the mediation group stated they experienced fairness in the processing of their case' (p. 83). This compared with 62 per cent for a control group whose cases were not referred to mediation in this quasi-experimental evaluation. Almost 90 per cent of victims who had experienced the mediation process felt that the negotiated restitution agreement was fair to them and a similar percentage felt that the mediators had been fair to them. In McCold and Wachtel's study (1998), 96 per cent of conferenced victims said they experienced fairness in the handling of their cases compared with 79 per cent of the control group.

3.3.5   Material restoration?

Although about 70 per cent of respondents in Umbreit *et al.*'s (1994) study indicated that receiving restitution from the offender was important, for many of them it was important only as a gesture of acceptance of responsibility for the harm on the offender's part. The compliance rate in restitution agreements was over 80 per cent in this study, compared with a matched group who received court-ordered restitution where the compliance rate was 58 per cent (p. 111). Overall, although victims sometimes complained about inadequate mechanisms for enforcing restitution agreements, it appears that most restorative programmes have a commendable record in terms of offenders complying with their agreements (see Braithwaite 1999: 23–4).

However, a serious problem exists in evaluating how well restorative justice restores, even on the apparently straightforward dimension of material restoration. Braithwaite (1999) observes that 'some victims will prefer mercy to insisting on getting their money back; indeed it may be that act of grace which gives them a spiritual restoration that is critical for them' (p. 20).

If we assume that material restoration matters, then it is important that some studies have found that victims are far more likely to obtain restitution through restorative justice than through the courts. For example, Coates and Gehm (1989) found that 87 per cent of the VORP agreements that they examined included an element of material restitution. Umbreit *et al.* (1994) showed that victims were more likely to receive material or financial reparation if the restitution plan were negotiated directly between victim and offender, rather than being imposed by a court.

However, early British victim–offender mediation programmes placed little emphasis on substantive reparation: Marshall and Merry (1990) reported that only 26 per cent of agreements in the schemes they examined involved substantive reparation. Nor was much attention given to the needs of victims generally, their focus being on the principle of diverting offenders from prosecution (Dignan 1992). For example, Blagg (1985) reported on a Northamptonshire programme which was offender-oriented to the point where its aims contained no mention of victims at all, and only about 60 per cent of offenders in the programme even met their victims. It appears that these early schemes contained little real reparative content (Marshall & Merry 1990). Sometimes there were mere offers to repair damage, dictated letters of apology, and token acts of material reparation (Davis *et al.* 1989). Marshall (1990) identified an ambivalence about the role of material compensation which he ascribed to the tension between the underlying philosophies of restorative justice and the prevailing criminal justice system. But later British schemes such as the Kettering Adult Reparation Scheme apparently took the needs and views of victims much more seriously: 61 per cent of all agreements entailed financial compensation with a very high level of compliance by offenders (Dignan 1992).

3.3.6 Emotional restoration and an apology?

A 1990 review of British victim–offender mediation programmes found that often what victims wanted most was not substantial reparation but rather symbolic reparation, primarily an apology (Marshall & Merry 1990). In these early programmes, apology was often all that victims came away with—57 per cent of all agreements in these schemes involved an apology only, while another 26 per cent combined an apology with some form of undertaking such as financial reparation. Dignan (1992) suggested that while material reparation was important 'many would argue that the psychological impact of receiving an explanation and an apology are of far greater value' (p. 460).

Clearly, the opportunity to come face-to-face with one's offender presented by restorative justice programmes of all kinds enhances the likelihood of an apology being offered. In restorative justice literature generally apology is regarded as a goal to be sought and a sign of victim satisfaction when it is achieved. But it is in the recent literature on conferencing that apology has come to be seen as central to the process of restoration. For example, it was the centrepiece of Stewart's detailed description of the process of New Zealand FGCs (1996), while Maxwell and Morris (1993) reported in their review that in 74 per cent of the cases in their sample apology to the victim was a conference outcome. McCold and Wachtel (1998) also found high levels of apology in their Bethlehem study: 96 per cent of conferenced victims said the offender apologized and 88 per cent said the offender seemed sorry about what he or she did. The significance of apology as an indication of remorse and a genuine desire for reconciliation was reinforced by Morris and Maxwell's later finding that the offenders who failed to apologize were three times more likely to re-offend than those who did so (1996: 107).

But beyond needing an apology, victims may also need to be able to forgive (Zehr 1985). Murphy and Hampton (1988) described forgiveness as essentially a 'private law paradigm' (compared with the 'criminal law paradigm' of mercy) because it can exist only where an emotional bond exists between offender and victim. Their view is shared by Moore (1993) who argued that conferences provide opportunities for the 'private' dimension of the offence to be explained and explored so that forgiveness becomes possible.

3.4   Shortcomings for Victims in Restorative Justice

The restorative literature indicates that although victims are generally approving of their experiences, they express lower levels of approval than do other participants in the process (Braithwaite 1999). Why is this so?

3.4.1   Some victims are more afraid as a result of restorative justice

It has been suggested that victims might fear retaliation if restorative justice were offered in serious criminal cases. However, Wright's (1991) view is that their situation would be no worse than in traditional criminal justice processing where, if the victim fears retaliation, the only way of avoiding it is not to pursue the case. By contrast, restorative justice may present the victim with an opportunity to negotiate an agreement that pre-empts retaliation and even to improve or restore the relationship. However, LaPrairie (1995) warned that, in discussions which are insufficiently structured or managed, victims may feel that what is revealed inside the meeting to participants whom the victim lives among may have the potential for resulting in their revictimization.

In a review of the New Zealand experience with restorative justice programmes, the Ministry of Justice (1995) observed that many victims may find meeting their offenders a threatening experience or may fear retaliation which may increase their anxiety. They suggested that for those wanting minimal involvement with the criminal justice system, whether because of their lack of emotional involvement (such as shop proprietors who routinely experience theft) or because of their emotional vulnerability (where victim and offender are well known to each other), the court process with its formality and impersonalness may be preferable.

3.4.2   Victims can experience power imbalance as a result of restorative justice

Restorative justice has been much criticized for its potential to replicate and perpetuate power imbalances already existing between victim and offender (Abel 1982; Stubbs 2002). Restorative interventions are said not to address issues of structural inequality and oppression which victims may experience, especially where they have a prior relationship with their offenders (Stubbs 1995, 2002). Marshall and Merry (1990) have also claimed that there has been little research on how to achieve equal treatment. LaPrairie (1995), in reviewing the operation of sentencing circles in Canada and conferences in Australasia, observed that '[p]ower and coercion may operate within informal structures to re-victimize the victim' (p. 88). But she suggested that conferencing may have the potential to address these criticisms, because it is less offender-focused, and hence victims feel more attention is being paid to their circumstances and needs. Victims may also be better served because of the capacity to involve more and less powerful supporters associated with each principal in the offence (see Braithwaite & Daly 1994; Pennell & Burford 2002).

3.4.3   Victims may be 'used' in restorative justice

Many mediation programmes of the 1970s and 1980s were unashamedly offender-focused (Wright 1991), whereas more recently restorative justice programmes have been much more victim-centred in their orientation (see, for example, Umbreit 1994; Ministry of Justice New Zealand 1995; Strang & Sherman 1997). However, the earlier view can be seen in the following quotation concerning a pilot programme using conferencing for young Aboriginal offenders in Winnepeg, Canada:

> All of the [offenders'] families thought that the victims should be invited. . . . Victims were all contacted and invited to attend the conference; they were briefed on the process and, if they were unable to participate, information for a victim impact statement was collected. (Longclaws *et al.* 1996: 197)

The Association of Victim Support Schemes, the umbrella organization for victim assistance groups in England and Wales, has warned (George 1999) that a key issue for success in restorative justice from the victim's point of view is that victims must be able to see the benefit of participation and must never be used simply as a tool for rehabilitating the offender, because of the danger of being revictimized. Umbreit *et al.* (1994) reported that some of their respondents said that they felt coerced into participation and revictimized because of a perception of bias towards the offender on the part of the mediator. Braithwaite and Parker (1997) also suggested that restorative intervention generally may fail victims by mediators or facilitators not taking the harm they have experienced seriously enough.

3.5   Summary

This review of the victimological and restorative justice literature has revealed three things:

- there has been considerable and justified complaint about the dominant criminal justice paradigm where the victim of crime is perceived to be only the state and where the focus is on retribution towards the offender;
- the restorative justice paradigm, after a faltering start based purely on restitution and mediation, shows promise of offering crime victims more justice than they currently receive

from an adversarial justice system;
- studies of restorative programmes reveal a number of weaknesses, as well as strengths, which need to be addressed.

3.6   The Canberra Reintegrative Shaming Experiments

The Reintegrative Shaming Experiments (RISE) in Canberra present an opportunity to answer questions about the comparative advantages and disadvantages for victims of a restorative justice alternative compared with the traditional court system. The Canberra programme is derived from the New Zealand adaptation of traditional Maori practice in dealing with offenders, but modified according to the model developed by the police in the New South Wales town of Wagga Wagga (Alder & Wundersitz 1994; McDonald *et al.* 1995; O'Connell & Moore 1992; Moore *et al.* 1995). The programme operates in the following way.

Offenders making full admissions to the police about responsibility for a crime may be diverted from being charged and going to court by voluntarily agreeing to attend a conference. This entails the police bringing together those most affected by the crime—the offenders and their supporters, the victims and their supporters, and anyone else with a stake in the offence. If there is no direct victim, such as in most drink-driving offences, then representatives of the community are invited to attend instead. Canberra conferences are led by a police officer who is a trained facilitator. This group of citizens discuss the harm that has been caused by the crime, how this has affected each of them, and what may be done to repair the harm. A consensus is then reached by all participants (in principle excluding the police facilitator, whose role is limited to that of a 'boundary umpire', but including the offender(s)) about what needs to be done to restore the victims, the community, and the offenders themselves. An outcome agreement for the offenders is decided upon which may include direct restitution and apology to the victims, work for the community, and any other undertakings which everyone present believes to be just and appropriate. The police monitor implementation of the agreement: if offenders fail to fulfil their obligations then the police may reconvene the conference or, on rare occasions, send the matter to court.

The theoretical underpinning for diversionary conferences is Braithwaite's (1989) theory of reintegrative shaming, whereby a sense of shame is engendered in the offenders and their supporters through providing the victims with a forum to explain directly all the harm they have experienced flowing from the offence. In a successful conference, the shame is sufficient to elicit a sincere apology by offenders, which, in turn, gives rise to the expression of forgiveness by victims and by offender supporters, and the reintegration of the offenders into their 'community of care'.

We saw in Chapter 2 that when members of the Canberra victim movement were asked what they wanted from the justice system, they echoed what the research shows to be the views of victims worldwide (see, for example, Shapland *et al.* 1985; Mawby & Gill 1987; Waller 1989; Chapter 1 (above)). They said they wanted:

- a less formal process where their views count;
- more information about both the processing and outcome of their cases;
- participation in their cases;
- respectful and fair treatment;
- material restoration;
- emotional restoration, including an apology.

Given that the restorative justice conferencing programme operating in Canberra sets out to deliver most of what victims themselves have identified, it should come as no surprise to find a very high level of support for the programme among members of the Canberra victim movement (Victims of Crime Assistance League, or VOCAL). The programme brings offenders and victims together to discuss the crime and its consequences, to require offenders to take responsibility for their actions, and to work out what is needed to repair the harm experienced by the victim. VOCAL sees the programme as resonating with its view of how criminal justice should be reformed to meet victims' needs: rather than being focused on the criminal sanction, they put more emphasis on crime prevention and making amends, with less control by the criminal justice professionals who dominate the formal system. Mrs Cameron of VOCAL said:

Often victims of serious crimes say 'I wish we could speak to the offender and ask why they did it, did they mean to, was there a reason?' I'd certainly go to a conference. The offender can learn too, what the effect of the crime has been. It gives the victim the opportunity to confront the offender and tell them, and that has a healing effect. It's especially important in dealing with the emotional harm, telling the offender the emotional consequences.

On more than one occasion, VOCAL has publicly supported the programme when it has been under fire in the media. For example, when the outcome of a poorly run conference was that the young offender should walk through the shopping mall where he has shoplifted wearing a t-shirt saying 'I Am a Thief', VOCAL thought the programme should be defended, not because it approved of this stigmatizing outcome but because it saw it as a mistaken outcome in a fledgling programme. In sum, VOCAL takes a strongly supportive view of restorative justice. The Chair, Steve Prothero, said:

It's how you get the human face of the victim's experience. . . . Victims feel just a part of the furniture in court and dissatisfied with their inability to communicate to a judge or magistrate in simple language. [They think] 'Why isn't the judge listening to what I want to say?' . . . We are support-ive of conferencing because we want our victims to be able to show their injuries and damage in a human way to their perpetrators so they can recover their own lives and also perpetrators will see we aren't cardboard cutouts, it's not an American cop show, these are real people, just like their own family. (Personal communication, October 1998)

The most methodologically compelling means of determining whether in fact conferences can deliver what victims want in a way superior to normal court processing is through a randomized controlled trial comparing these two methods of doing justice. The next chapter will examine the research design and methodology employed by RISE.

4

The Reintegrative Shaming Experiments: Research Design and Methodology

4.1 Introduction

In Donald Campbell's seminal article, 'Reforms as Experiments' (1969), an explicit connection is proposed between experimental methods and social reform:

The United States and other modern nations should be ready for an experimental approach to social reform, an approach in which we try out new programs designed to cure specific social problems, in which we learn whether or not these programs are effective, and in which we retain, imitate, modify or discard them on the basis of apparent effectiveness. (p. 409)

Experimental methods have long been accepted in the physical sciences where manipulation of variables can be readily controlled and their effects on other variables observed. What Campbell was suggesting was a commitment in the social sciences to experimental methods which would allow factual questions about reforms in social policy to be answered using the same scientific principles and procedures. Not surprisingly, useful experiments have been found to be much more difficult to implement in the social sciences, mainly because of difficulties in retaining adequate control over the implementation of the research design in the 'real world' as compared to the laboratory setting, or even field settings available in biochemistry, agriculture, and the like. Nevertheless, over the past two decades or so, much has been learned about when experimental procedures are appropriate in social science, how to implement them in the field, and how results can be applied by policy-makers (Berk *et al.* 1985).

It is useful to consider at the outset some features of the theory of experimentation. Campbell and Stanley (1963) urge us to remember that experimental results never 'confirm' or 'prove' a theory: rather the theory may escape being 'disconfirmed'. The 'null hypothesis', which is employed as a convenience in theory-testing can never be 'accepted' by the data obtained; it can only be 'rejected' or 'fail to be rejected'. Popper (1959) emphasized the impossibility of obtaining deductive proof for inductive laws. However, the benefits of experimentation are summed up by Campbell and Stanley as follows:

Varying degrees of 'confirmation' are conferred upon a theory through the number of plausible rival hypotheses available to account for the data. The fewer such rival hypotheses remaining, the greater the degree of 'confirmation'. . . . This fewness is the epistemological counterpart of the positive affirmation of theory which elegant experiments seem to offer. (p. 36)

There are numerous experimental and quasi-experimental research designs which have been used satisfactorily to secure data for theory testing. However, the 'gold standard' of evaluation in medicine (Pocock 1983) and in many other fields is the randomized controlled trial. This model entails the random assignment of subjects to treatment and control groups with known probability, thus minimizing the risk that prior to treatment the two groups were, on average, different in ways that could affect the outcomes of treatment. The special quality of the randomization procedure is that it substantially fosters between-group equivalence, not only on known variables, but also on variables which are unknown and perhaps not even imagined (Gartin 1995). It then follows that any post-treatment difference between the groups can be attributed to the treatment rather than to the characteristics of the individuals making up each group (within the statistical limits). Randomized trials are so powerful in their capacity to test for cause and effect that the US Food and Drug Administration, for example, requires that all new drugs be tested using this methodology before they are deemed safe for public use (Pocock 1983).

Over the more than thirty years since Campbell's plea for the adoption of scientifically rigorous testing, the experimental approach in the development of social policy has had a chequered career, with initial reluctance by public officials to embrace—or fund—experiments in this realm. Berk et al. (1985) suggested that some of the reasons for this revolve around the admission of ignorance that is entailed in approving them, the time they take to complete, unrealistic expectations about the ease with which they can be undertaken, the equivocation in some of the results, their ethics, and their expense. All of these objections have been encountered in the experiments which are the subject of this book.

However, since the early 1980s there has been growing recognition of the superior qualities of randomized trials in developing social policy generally (Berk *et al.* 1985) and a move towards their increased use in the evaluation of criminal justice programmes (Farrington 1983; Weisburd *et al.* 1993). Some of these have had a dramatic impact on policy: for example the findings of Sherman and Berk's (1984) experiment on police responses to domestic violence affected law enforcement policy across the United States and in other countries as well.

Randomized trials have been endorsed by the US Federal Judicial Center's (1981) Advisory Committee to the Chief Justice of the United States and by the Australian National Health and Medical Research Council guidelines on human subjects experimentation under the following ethical conditions:

- there is substantial uncertainty about the superiority of current practice over an alternative practice;
- the experiment has adequate sample size, statistical power, and research management to ensure the achievement of strong conclusions about the relative effects of the two practices.

A third criterion for ethical experimentation in criminal sanctions has been proposed by Professor Norval Morris (1966): the principle of less severity, that is, that the proposed experimental treatment ought not to be more severe than the control.

In 1994 the Australian Federal Police (AFP) in Canberra undertook to collaborate with the Australian National University in a randomized controlled trial based on these ethical criteria. The aim of the research was to determine the effectiveness of the AFP restorative justice conferencing programme, compared with traditional court processing of offenders. Data collection began in July 1995.

The key criteria for comparing court processing to conferencing were these:

- prevalence and frequency of repeat offending;
- victim satisfaction with the process;
- perceptions by victims and offenders of procedural justice and protection of rights;
- equity in sentencing in conferences versus courts;
- offender changes in drinking or drug-use behaviour;
- increased police effectiveness through less time spent in court-related activity;
- estimated cost savings.

Policy implications of the results of the study would emerge from a consideration of all these criteria together, rather than results from any one alone.

4.2   Overall RISE Research Design

RISE was not one but four separate experiments. Each of the experiments was structured in the most rigorous scientific method possible—the randomized controlled trial. Separate randomized controlled trials, with separate random number sequences, were conducted for separate offence types and offender groups, so as to identify possible differential effectiveness of conferences and court. This design has the benefit of distinguishing different effects of conferencing under different circumstances. At the same time, the greater homogeneity within each of the four experiments had the additional benefit of increasing statistical power (Weisburd et al. 1993), defined as the probability of accepting a true conclusion as correct and not due to chance (i.e. 1 minus the probability of a Type II error). The four experiments were:

1. Drink-driving with blood alcohol content above 0.08 by offenders of all ages;
2. Shoplifting from stores employing security personnel by offenders aged under 18 years;
3. Property crime involving personal victims by offenders aged under 18 years;
4. Violent crime by offenders aged under 30 years.

All analyses and discussion will relate only to experiments 3 and 4 above. From this point, experiment 3 will be referred to as the *property experiment* and experiment 4 will be referred to as the *violence experiment*.

4.2.1   Suitability of Canberra for the experiments and generalizability of its findings

Every city has its own profile of offenders and offending patterns. In Canberra this profile tends towards less serious violent offending, especially among juveniles, than is sometimes found in large North American cities, for example. However, no matter where these experiments were conducted, the aim would have been to focus on a narrow group of homogeneous offenders whose offences were neither very serious nor very trivial. If, by contrast, the aim had been to conduct the experiments based on very serious offenders, then a city with far higher rates of serious offending than Canberra's would have been preferable, but this was never the intention. Every city has its share of the middle-level offences that are the subject of RISE, and to that extent the findings of RISE in Canberra may be generalized to other locations. To the extent that Canberra's courts are already less stigmatizing and less prone to employing incarceration than those in other cities, any difference detected between court and conference will represent a minimum likely to be more starkly revealed in other less caring jurisdictions. I will discuss questions of internal and external validity later, and at this point note only that internal validity is a necessary condition of external validity but not vice versa (Cook & Campbell 1979).

4.2.2   Sample size

Sample size was calculated on the basis of the number of cases required in order to detect a difference in recidivism rates between experimental (conference) and control (court) groups. Preliminary analysis of Australian Federal Police (AFP) criminal records suggested recidivism rates around 50 per cent over one year as measured key arrests for both juvenile property and juvenile violent offenders. There were 175 cases in the property experiment (with 251 offenders) and 100 cases in the violence experiment (with 121 offenders).

4.2.3   Unit of analysis

In this study the unit of analysis was incidents, not individuals, and where there were co-offenders they were treated together for all analytical purposes. Each new incident accepted into RISE was treated as a separate case. Thus, repeat offenders appeared in more than one experimental case and were treated as if they were different people: similarly there were repeat victims, though all of these were victims of shoplifting and are not included in these analyses.

4.2.4 Offence eligibility

Because the aim of the research was to compare cases which were assigned to court with equally serious cases that were assigned to conference, a case could be accepted into the experiments only if it would normally be dealt with by court. But the research protocol also required that eligible cases must not be so serious that, in the estimation of the apprehending police officer, they could be dealt with *only* in court, as there was a 50 per cent probability that they would be assigned to a conference. So the aim of the research team was to include in the experiments 'middle-range' offences, neither so trivial that they would normally be dealt with by a simple caution or warning, nor so serious that police would be reluctant not to have them dealt with in the court system.

The process of deciding what offence categories would be *ineligible* for conferencing entailed some negotiation at the outset. Both the then Chief Police Officer for the Australian Capital Territory (ACT) and the then ACT Attorney General were broadminded in their approaches and wanted to declare ineligible as few offences as possible. It was agreed with the police to declare *ineligible* only serious indictable offences, sexual offences, and domestic violence offences.

Offences eligible for the property experiment were:

- burglary;
- theft;
- shoplifting (where the shop manager or sales assistant, rather than security personnel, had apprehended the offender);
- receiving/possession stolen goods;
- criminal damage (vandalism);
- fraud (excluding offences involving a driver's licence);
- car theft;
- vehicle break-in;
- attempts at any of the above.

Offences eligible for the violence experiment were:

- armed robbery (later withdrawn);
- assault occasioning actual bodily harm;
- common assault;
- act endangering life;
- fighting;
- possession of an offensive weapon;
- arson;
- attempts at any of the above.

4.2.5   Offender eligibility

In all the experiments, offenders had to meet the following criteria in order to be eligible for RISE:

- they (and all co-offenders) had made full admissions about committing the offence;
- they (and all co-offenders) had no outstanding warrants or bonds which would require them to attend court;
- they (and all co-offenders) lived in the Canberra region;
- the apprehending officer's sergeant approved the case being sent to RISE;
- the apprehending officer agreed to accept the RISE recommendation (based on random assignment) for the case regardless of whether it was court or conference.

For entry to the property experiment, besides meeting these eligibility criteria, at least one co-offender had to be under 18 years of age. For entry to the violence experiment, in addition to meeting these eligibility criteria, at least one co-offender had to be under 30 years of age.

4.2.6   Pipeline tracking

To determine the extent to which cases referred into the experiments were representative of the total population of offences apprehended during the course of the study, a record was kept of all cases of these kinds that came to police attention—the 'pipeline' of cases. Some of these cases were RISE-eligible and some RISE-ineligible. Of the RISE-eligible cases, some were sent to RISE and others were not. Of those that were not, the reason was usually that, in the judgement of the apprehending police officer, the nature or circumstances of the offence required that it *must* be dealt with in court or *must* be dealt with by caution or *must* be dealt with by conference (officers were free to send cases to a conference outside RISE).

Analysis of the property incidents involving juvenile offenders in the period from May 1997 to December 1997 shows that cases coming into RISE accounted for 12 per cent of the total *eligible* population in the 'pipeline'. Analysis of the violence incidents involving offenders aged under 30 in the same period shows that cases coming into RISE accounted for 11 per cent of the total *eligible* population in the 'pipeline'. For both offence categories, the main reason for ineligibility was difficulty in determining whether all the offenders admitted responsibility for the offence at the time of apprehension.

4.2.7   Police discretion

This principle is of paramount importance in Canberra policing, where police officers have very great latitude in deciding how their cases are to be dealt with. It is very rare for sergeants to overrule the decisions of any of their constables, nor do these constables have to account in any formal way for the decisions they reach. In squaring the principle of discretion with the implacable requirements of randomization, it was agreed with the police at the outset that officers' discretion would be exercised in their decisions whether or not to refer any ostensibly eligible case to RISE. If they believed that it *must* be dealt with in a particular way, they were not compelled to forego their discretion and refer it into the study.

There was no alternative for the research team but to agree to this regime, which had both good and bad consequences. The good consequence was the low level of misassignment to the alternative treatment. (It was constantly emphasized to police that it was fatal to a randomized trial to misassign cases to the alternative treatment and that we would much prefer not to have the case at all than have it misassigned.) The bad consequence was that, despite very close contact and co-operation between the researchers and police at every level throughout the course of the study, RISE missed many ostensibly eligible cases.

4.2.8   Random assignment

Prior to commencement of data collection, treatments were randomly assigned by a computer program using a sequence of quasi-random numbers. Separate listings were made for each of the experiments. Envelopes were prepared containing slips of paper bearing the assignment for each case, carefully double-folded so that they could not be read without opening the envelopes. They were then sealed and numbered according to the case number and experiment to which each applied.

4.2.9   Assigning the cases

When police officers apprehended offenders whom they believed to be eligible for one of the RISE experiments and whom they were equally prepared to process by court or by conference, they then rang one of two mobile phones staffed by RISE researchers on a rostered basis twenty-four hours a day. The staff member taking the call then ran through the relevant eligibility questions (listed above) before taking down the following details about the case and the offender:

- date and time the call was received;
- initials of the person taking the call;
- case number;
- offender(s)' name;
- offender(s)' date of birth;
- offender(s)' sex;
- offender(s)' attitude (good, bad, indifferent);
- police informant's name and badge number;
- informant's sergeant's name and badge number;
- police incident database unique identifying job number;
- police station referring the case (there are four in Canberra);
- nature of the offence;
- offender(s)' address and telephone number.

When all this information had been supplied and entered in the log book, the staff member then opened the envelope corresponding to the offender's now-assigned case number and told the police whether the assignment was court or conference. The assignment was also entered into the log book. At this stage nothing at all was known by RISE staff about the characteristics of the victim (if any) of the offence. In fact, nothing at all was known of the victims until the observation of the conference, in the case of conference-assigned cases, or until details were obtained for interview purposes from the police databases in the case of court-assigned cases.

Following assignment by RISE, police then (almost always) processed the case accordingly. In a few cases, police decided to process the case differently from as assigned (some court cases were cautioned, some conference cases were sent to court or cautioned). There were a number of reasons why misassignment might happen:

- the offender re-offended while the case was being processed and a conference assignment was altered to court;
- the offender withdrew his/her full admissions to the offence;
- the offender persistently failed to turn up for the conference, or did so in an intoxicated state;
- information obtained after random assignment revealed that the offence fell into one of the ineligible categories of offence;
- the conference failed to reach an outcome agreement acceptable to all parties and the facilitator referred the matter to court;
- because of an administrative error on the part of the police, the case was sent to court when it had been assigned to conference;
- the police failed to reveal that there were co-offenders that were not being included in the case and who were being sent to court outside RISE.

The last of these reasons resulted in four cases assigned to a conference going to court instead; each of the other reasons led to either one or two cases being misassigned. All of these circumstances were misassignments in relation to the randomized research design which, for the purpose of this study, is defined as encompassing:

- crossover to the comparison treatment (court to conference or conference to court);
- treatment with another regimen besides the assigned or the comparison treatment (in this study the regimen was invariably a caution);
- no treatment at all.

But not all misassignments to the comparison treatment were true crossovers: assaulting a police officer after assignment, for example, or withdrawing full admissions were not foreseeable at the time the case was deemed eligible. Changing assignment from conference to court in such cases did not entail a true crossover because they did not violate random assignment to a policy stream. But where the decision to change the assigned treatment resulted from inadequate checking of facts about the eligibility of the offence or the offender, these were true treatment failures and designated as crossovers.

Every effort was made prior to the commencement of data collection to alert all police officers to the dire consequences to the integrity of the experiments of treatment failures (and no experiment in criminology without such failures has ever been reported). It was pleasing, and indicative of a good understanding of the nature of the experiments as well as a good working relationship between officers and the research team, that there was only one misassignment in the property or violence experiments resulting simply from the officer preferring the alternative treatment.

4.2.10   The ethics of random assignment

Prior to the finalization of the research design a good deal of careful consideration was given to the ethical aspects of a randomized controlled trial in criminal justice. The research team was mindful of Norval Morris's ethical criterion mentioned above (that the experimental treatment is not designed to be more severe than the control treatment). Although a judgement regarding the relative severity of each treatment was bound to be subjective without substantial experience with conferencing in Canberra, the research team assumed that the lack of any criminal record in the outcome of a conference made it less severe in conventional terms.

When the research design had been finalized it was put to the Committee on Ethics in Human Experimentation of the Australian National University (ANU). It was agreed that it was not necessary to obtain the informed consent of offenders to their taking part in the experiments, given that all of them would have gone to court without the conferencing programme. However, no offender assigned to a conference was compelled to take part and all could opt for normal court processing of their case at any time up to and including the end of a conference (in fact, none of the conference-assigned property or violence offenders opted for court).

A primary concern of the research team, the Ethics Committee, and the police was preserving the privacy and confidentiality of the offenders coming into the experiments and all information held about them. This was also the concern of the Australian

Government's Privacy Commission which was consulted prior to the commencement of data collection about the basis on which the research could be conducted and on which private information obtained from the police could be held for analysis by the researchers. These and other issues were spelled out in a twenty-seven-page Memorandum of Understanding drawn up between the ANU and the AFP. Among the issues addressed was that of the confidentiality of the data collected in terms of police access to them: the Memorandum stated that under no circumstances would the researchers reveal to police any information disclosed by any identified participant in the experiments.

The Ethics Committee decided that the informed consent of participants in the experiments would be required on four occasions:

1. When a case was diverted by random assignment from normal court processing to a conference, the investigating police officer was obliged to explain to offenders that they had the right to have their matters heard in court rather than a conference, if that was their preference. The officer obtained in writing their agreement to diversion from the normal option of court to the experimental condition of conference.

2. At the beginning of every conference the police officer facilitating the conference reminded offenders of their right to stop the conference at any time and ask for the matter to be dealt with in court.

3. At the beginning of every conference and prior to any case being heard in the Children's Court, it was necessary to obtain the agreement of the offenders and, where relevant, the victims, to the case being observed by the researcher. This was not required for cases in adult court, which was an open court and where the practicalities made it impossible to identify offenders prior to their case being heard.

4. Prior to interviewing any offender, victim, or supporter of either party it was necessary for the respondent to read and sign an Informed Consent form. This form set out the reasons for the interview and gave assurances regarding the confidentiality of the information which the respondent was asked to reveal.

4.3 Methods of Measurement

There were three principal sources of data in RISE:

- observation by trained research staff of court and conference treatments to which cases had been randomly assigned;
- self-completion questionnaires completed by the police officer facilitating each conference and the apprehending police officer in each case;
- interviews with victims, offenders, and their supporters.

Victims in the property and violence experiments were contacted as soon as practicable after the disposition of their cases to arrange an interview. A response rate of 88 per cent was achieved for property victims and at least 87 per cent for violence victims (see 4.4.2). There was no difference between response rates for court and conference cases. A second wave of interviewing was conducted two years after the case came into RISE, but those data are not yet available.

4.4 Analysing Victim Effects: Research Designs and Response Rates

Two basic research designs are used in this book's analysis of the effects of restorative justice on victims. Neither of these designs technically constitutes a randomized controlled trial, although one is a close approximation. That design is a quasi-experimental comparison of victims whose offenders were randomly assigned to court or conference. The design is only *quasi*-experimental with respect to victim effects because the victims themselves were not the unit of random assignment. The other design is limited to victims who actually participated in a restorative justice conference. This design compares victims' statements about how they felt before the conference to their statements about how they felt after the conference, with both statements taken in the same interview, usually taken within six weeks after the conference occurred.

Two kinds of subsidiary research designs are also employed in these analyses. One is simply a breakdown of the findings from the two separate RISE trials for violence and from property crimes. These breakdowns are presented both for the quasi-experimental comparison of victims in court and conference cases, and for the before-and-after comparisons among only those victims who experienced a restorative justice conference.

The second subsidiary research design is used only in the quasi-experimental comparison of victims whose offenders were randomly assigned to court or conference. The subsidiary research design compares victims on the basis of what *actually happened*, as distinct from what the random assignment called for. Virtually all randomized controlled trials experience some fraction of cases in which actual treatment diverges from the assigned treatment (Weinstein & Levin, 1989). The extent to which this occurred in RISE varied across the four experiments (Strang *et al.*, 1999). What is relevant to this analysis is not the overall variance between assigned and delivered treatment, but the variance between assigned and delivered treatment among the cases in our victim interview sample. This raises two important questions: the nature of the sampling frame from which the victim interview sample was drawn, and the extent of the variance between assigned and delivered offender treatments among the victims who were actually interviewed.

4.4.1 Sampling frames and response rates

The sampling frame for the victim effects analysis is all victims associated with the RISE cases randomly assigned to court or restorative justice conference. This sampling frame differs from the research design for RISE in three important respects. First, RISE was based on cases, but not all cases had victims. Secondly, it was not the victims who were randomly assigned to court or restorative justice, but the offenders. Thus the random assignment sequence does not proceed to create comparability across victims in the same ways it did for offenders. Thirdly, the criminal justice records that accompany prosecution must identify each offender arrested, but not each victim affected. Thus the sampling frame target of 'all victims' associated with RISE cases could not be fully compiled from police records.

There were two reasons why not all RISE cases had victims. First, in many criminal offences, the victim is the public at large, rather than any specific individual. Examples of this in RISE included the discharge of a firearm in a public place, or the possession of a concealed weapon. Secondly, in other criminal offences, the victim is technically an institution rather than an individual, such as a school, the Post Office, or a bus company. In those cases where an individual employee of the institution could be identified who was personally affected by the crime—such as a school principal whose school was the target of arson—we defined that person as a 'victim' for research purposes. In many crimes against institutions, however, no affected victim could be identified from police records.

Even if a case had individual victims, it was often not possible to identify any or all of the victims affected by the crime. In some cases, no named individual victim was included in the police record (due to poor record-keeping), even when the description of the incident made it clear that one person had been victimized. Some individual victims who were named lacked accurate or complete enough contact information so that we could make contact with the named individual. When cases had more than one victim, not all victims were named in the police record—such as vandalism to every letterbox or parked car on a street. The identification of the complete universe of 'victims' in each case was often highly arbitrary, as in the case of a residential burglary, since police reports rarely list all occupants of a home that has been burgled. Only one victim was therefore identified to be interviewed for each residential burglary. Similar rules guided the identification of victims of other property crime, such as car break-ins and car thefts.

For all of these reasons, the identification of the sampling frame as a universe of victims who *could* have been interviewed is highly problematic. Estimation of the number of victims who could have been added to a denominator of potentially affected victims is subject to the biases of the respondents, as well as the response rates among the victims who were named in the police reports. A victim-based randomized design might have avoided these problems, by introducing random assignment of cases after the sub-sample of cases with victims was identified. Such a design would have to assign all the victims of one offender to one treatment or another, but it could then estimate the mean effect of each treatment in each case by averaging responses across all identified victims in the case—as well as the average response rate (percentage of victims responding) per case.

Given the focus of the RISE research design on repeat offending effects, the current study cannot estimate the probability of each victim affected by these crimes having completed an interview.

Rather than characterizing the data as a probability sample of all affected victims, it is more accurate to describe the interview data as a convenience sample of victims associated with random assignment of restorative justice. That is, they are the victims who (1) were associated with the cases that were identified on the basis of offender and offence characteristics, and who (2) had their cases assigned to either court or conference.

4.4.2 Case-based and Victim-based response rates

One way of assessing the possible extent of bias in this convenience sample is to estimate response rates on the most relevant denominator and numerator. The appropriate denominator for the response rate is limited to those cases for which at least one victim has been identified. The most appropriate numerator is the number of such cases for which one or more victims have been interviewed. This procedure accepts the convenience basis of the sample, but then estimates the probability that each case has at least one victim viewpoint about how it was dealt with. Whether this viewpoint is representative of all possible victims of each offence cannot be determined. But it is at least one viewpoint about each case. Using this method, Table 4.1 shows that the case-based response rate was 87 per cent for the violence experiment, and 90 per cent for the personal property crime experiment, for an overall response rate of the merged experimental samples of 89 per cent.

TABLE 4.1   Case-based Response Rate

	Interviews of 1+ Victims	Total Cases with 1+ Contactable Victims	Response Rate (%)
All Victims			
Court	98	110	89
Conference	98	111	88
Total	196	221	89
Property Victims			
Court	66	72	92
Conference	58	66	88
Total	124	138	90
Violence Victims			
Court	32	38	84
Conference	40	45	89
Total	72	83	87

Another way to estimate response rate is to list all of the victims whom I actually attempted to contact. This list is based on the availability of victim names, as well as some diligence in unearthing names of all known victims in such unusual offences as an Internet fraud. While this list has no clear relation to an underlying universe of victims, it is in fact the list from which the interviews were requested. The response rate to that list is an indication of the extent to which each individual victim who granted an interview may have been different from all victims from whom interviews were sought. Using this method, Table 4.2 shows that the response rate was 91 per cent for the violence experiment, and 88 per cent for the personal property crime experiment, for an overall response rate of the merged experimental samples of 90 per cent.

4.4.3　Assigned versus actual treatment

The high response rates of the interview sample offer great confidence in our interpretation of the data as a quasi-experimental test of the effects of restorative justice on victims. The major threat to that conclusion is the difference between treatments randomly assigned and actually delivered in each case. This section assesses the joint effects of the high response rates and the medium rates of treatment misassignments on the internal validity of the comparison of victims on the basis of assigned (rather than actual) treatments.

The high response rates mean that the victims did not select themselves into or out of the sample based on their views about

TABLE 4.2　Victim-based Response Rate

	Interviews of Victims	Total Victims Approached	Response Rate (%)
All Victims			
Court	116	123	94
Conference	116	137	85
Total	232	260	89
Property Victims			
Court	80	84	95
Conference	71	87	82
Total	151	171	88
Violence Victims			
Court	36	39	92
Conference	45	50	90
Total	81	89	91

restorative justice. While there is a slight tendency for victims to respond more often if their cases went to court than if they were assigned to conference (89 per cent versus 88 per cent, respectively, for case-based response rates, and 94 per cent versus 85 per cent for victim-based), this difference is not large enough to explain away the much larger differences in most comparisons of victim attitudes towards court and conference. Thus we can be confident that the sample is a relatively unbiased estimate of the views of people whose offenders happened to go to court or conference.

The most important thing about those people is that they were *not* selected for restorative justice on the basis of any of their personal characteristics or attitudes. The assignment of these victims to restorative justice was completely exogenous to the victims themselves, and was not determined by any factors that could also affect their interview responses about the way their cases were handled. While this design does not control selection bias as effectively as a randomized experiment based upon pre-identified victims, there is a strong causal inference that any difference in attitudes between 'court' and 'conference' victims was caused by the way the case was dealt with. The fact that the victims themselves are a convenience sample within the randomized design is little different, in principle, from the fact that the cases were a convenience sample of what the police decided to refer to RISE, or even from the fact that RISE was conducted in Canberra as a matter of convenience, rather than in Sydney, London, or Stockholm.

The more substantial threat to any inference of causation in comparisons of 'court' and 'conference' victims is that so many of the 'conference' victims never actually attended a restorative justice conference. As Table 4.3 shows, almost one out of four victims whose offenders were randomly assigned to a conference never actually attended a conference. This victim-based non-attendance rate was higher for victims of property crime (28 per cent) than for victims of violent crime (16 per cent). The rate has three components:

- cases in which no conference was ever organized by police;
- cases in which a conference occurred, but no victim was notified to attend;
- cases in which a conference occurred and at least one victim was present, but not all victims were notified or were present.

TABLE 4.3   Actual Treatment by Assigned Treatment—Victim Sample

Actual Treatment	Assigned to Court		Assigned to Conference	
	N	%	N	%
All Victims				
Conference	0	0	89	77
Court	108	93	15	13
Caution	8	7	4	3
Untreated	0	0	8	7
Total	116	100	116	100
Property Victims				
Conference	0	0	51	72
Court	72	90	12	17
Caution	8	10	3	4
Untreated	0	0	5	7
Total	80	100	71	100
Violence Victims				
Conference	0	0	38	84
Court	36	100	3	7
Caution	0	0	1	2
Untreated	0	0	3	7
Total Victims	36	100	45	100

The misassignment rates for court cases, in contrast, are much lower. Table 4.3 shows that 93 per cent of all court cases were actually prosecuted in court, with the other 7 per cent cautioned.

The effect of the difference in treatment misassignment rates between court and conference cases in this respect is to bias the results against restorative justice. This effect may pose an internal validity threat to the analysis where the differences between court and conference cases are small. But since most of the results show substantial benefits of restorative justice, the effects of the actually delivered cases appear to overwhelm the effects of not getting a conference when the police promised victims they would be invited to attend one.

In order to examine the possibility that effects of actual treatment may be different from the effects of assigned treatment, all the analyses in the quasi-experimental comparisons of court and conference victims have been done both ways. That is, the analyses examine the effects of actually delivered treatments as well as the effects of treatments as randomly assigned. The comparison of the actually delivered treatments is reported wherever the effects of assigned treatments do not show statistically significant differences (p = .05) between court and conference cases, but the delivered treatments do.

Some analysts might question the decision to present most of the findings in this book on the basis of assigned, rather than actually delivered treatments.[1] The argument in favour of this approach is that it maximizes the reduction in bias produced by the random assignment of the cases. The differences between assigned and actual treatments are driven by characteristics of the offences and offenders that could, in turn, have effects on the views of victims. This is the most conservative possible procedure for avoiding any over-statement of the benefits of restorative justice. The argument against this approach, however, is that it increases the threat to internal validity by analysing the effects of conferences that never occurred. Thus whatever view the reader takes on this issue, it is important to keep in mind the fact that *23 per cent of the 'conference' victims did not actually attend a restorative justice conference.*

4.5   Designing the Victim Questionnaire

The objective of the victim questionnaire (see Appendix 4.1) was to represent systematically the key concepts identified and discussed in Chapters 1, 2, and 3 as the principal shortcomings of the court system from the victim's point of view. Chapter 1 summarized these as follows:

(a) *A less formal process where victims can participate and where their views count*:
     Questions designed to address this issue were asked only of victims who had attended the disposition of their cases, which effectively meant only conference victims. They were asked whether they believed in fact that the conference had taken account of what they had said in deciding what should be done and had taken account of the effects of the offence on them.

---

[1] There is another method that has been recommended for dealing with this issue that combines randomly assigned with actually delivered treatments into a single equation. But whether such a model is appropriate when the promise of treatment has been broken is not at all clear from the literature (see Angrist *et al.* 1996).

(b) *More information about both the processing and outcome of their cases:*
Questions about the amount and quality of the information they received about their cases were asked of all victims. Conference victims were also asked about the extent of their preparation by the police for their conferences, while court victims were asked what they had been told about both their offenders' charges and the outcomes of their cases.

(c) *Participating in their cases:*
Victims who had attended the disposition of their cases were asked about the importance of participating and having their views counted as a reason for deciding to attend compared with other possible motivations, whether they felt they had an opportunity to express their views, whether they felt intimidated.

(d) *Fair and respectful treatment:*
Questions were devised to address all the dimensions of fairness and respect that victims might be looking for in the disposition of their cases (but could be answered only by those who had attended the disposition). These included such facets of procedural justice as impartiality, ethicality, lack of bias, correctability, and control over the process (Tyler 1990).

(e) *Material restoration:*
All property victims were asked a series of questions about the extent of their material and financial loss. Similarly, violence victims were asked about the extent of physical injuries and associated financial costs. These questions were followed by another series designed to ascertain the extent of material restoration they had received following the disposition of their cases.

(f) *Emotional restoration, including an apology:*
All victims were asked about the emotional harm and restoration they had experienced. This included questions concerning whether they believed they were owed an apology from their offenders, whether in fact their offenders had apologized to them, the sincerity of the apology if one had been offered, and the circumstances in which it had been offered.

There was a major impediment in seeking these views from victims whose cases went to court: very few of them (n = 4) actually attended 'their' court cases for one of the following reasons:

- the Children's Court is a closed court, which means that no one other than the offender's immediate family and professional staff are permitted to attend the case. The only basis on which a victim can be present is if the young person pleads not guilty and the victim is required as a prosecution witness. As an eligibility criterion for entry to RISE was that full admissions had been made to the police, theoretically all cases assigned to court should have been guilty pleas, though in the event two cases were contested;
- the great majority of victims whose cases were dealt with in court were not informed about when the cases were to be heard and, at the time they were contacted for interview, were not aware that their matters had been dealt with. This was despite the governing principles of the Victims of Crime Act 1994 which state (Section 4(k)) that 'a victim should be given an explanation of the outcome of criminal proceedings and of any sentence and its implications'. Consequently, they did not attend their cases, even if it had been heard in the adult (open) court.

Although few victims could be interviewed about their experiences of court, the evidence of the literature review is persuasive enough for an assumption to be made regarding victims' usual views of court processing. Most victims think court fails to deliver satisfaction on the six identified issues. It will be against this putative standard that victim satisfaction with the conference alternative will be assessed when insufficient RISE data exist about the experiences of victims whose cases were dealt with in court.

4.6 Conducting the Victim Interviews

4.6.1 Who were the respondents for the victim interviews?

Sometimes a case involved the victims of several offences committed at different times, which were being dealt with simultaneously either by court or conference. In these cases each victim was approached for interview. Sometimes there were several victims of the same offence, e.g. members of a family whose house had been burgled: in these cases, RISE staff selected for interview the person who acted as the complainant to the police. As already mentioned, this rule may have served to underestimate the amount of emotional harm suffered as a result of the offence, as the complainant where a family had been the victim of an offence was usually the husband/father, who often disclosed at interview that his spouse/children had been much more affected emotionally by the offence than he had been.

In cases where both or all the participants had been fighting and there was no obvious victim or offender, it was decided that all parties should be treated as both offenders and victims, and interviewed as both.

In twelve cases where offenders were cautioned rather than dealt with in court or conference, all victims were given the version of the questionnaire modified for victims who had not attended the disposition of the offence. In a further eight cases where offenders were not dealt with after twelve months (usually because they could not be located even when a warrant was issued, or because the file was lost by the police), victims were given a version of the questionnaire where all questions relating to the offenders' treatment were removed.

4.6.2   Making contact

Normally at the time the case was dealt with in court or in conference, the research team had no information about the identity of the victim. When the disposition was completed, the narrative summary of the incident was obtained from the AFP incident database, as this normally contained details of the victim. A letter was then sent to each victim explaining that the ANU was conducting a survey of the Canberra justice system and that we would like to have their views on how their cases had been dealt with. This was followed up by a telephone call or home visit to make an appointment for the interview. All interviews were conducted face-to-face wherever possible: most of the eight interviews not conducted face-to-face were with victims residing outside Canberra. All victim interviews were conducted by the author.

4.6.3   Privacy issues

Victims were assured that RISE was being conducted in close

collaboration with the police, and that their contact details had been provided by the police. Assurances were also given about the confidentiality of the information they disclosed in the course of the interview. Before the interview the victim read and signed an informed consent form which set out the purpose of the research and the conditions under which the information was collected and stored.

4.7   Comparison between Victim Characteristics and Offender Characteristics

It is useful to compare the characteristics of interviewed victims and offenders[2] (Tables 4.4 and 4.5). In the property experiment there were marked differences between them on all the variables ($p < 0.01$). In the violence experiment the differences were less marked; victims were older ($p < 0.01$), better educated ($p < 0.01$), and more often foreign-born ($p < 0.01$).

TABLE 4.4   Property Experiment—Characteristics of Victims and Offenders

	Victims	Offenders
Average age at entry into experiment*	38 years	16 years
Average years of education*	13 years	9 years
% male*	59	85
% born outside Australia*	25	11
% Aboriginal or Torres Strait*	2	9
% unemployed*	1	15

*$p < 0.01$

TABLE 4.5   Violence Experiment—Characteristics of Victims and Offenders

	Victims	Offenders
Average age at entry into experiment*	25 years	19 years
Average years of education*	12 years	10 years
% male*	68	77
% born outside Australia*	21	6
% Aboriginal or Torres Strait*	6	12
% unemployed*	10	18

*$p < 0.01$

[2] There were a total of 251 offenders in the property experiment and 121 offenders in the violence experiment, of whom 69 per cent were interviewed.

4.8   Summary

This chapter provides the foundation for the analyses presented in the rest of the book. It shows how the two major research designs provide a reasonably sound, if not perfect, basis for testing the effects of restorative justice on victims. While the full benefits of the two randomized controlled trials in Canberra cannot be applied to the victims associated with the randomly assigned criminal cases, the quasi-experimental design employed in this book is a close approximation of a fully randomized trial. In both designs, the assignment of the treatment is independent of any characteristics of the victims that might affect the measured benefits or harms of restorative justice.

The main threat to internal validity of the test is not the slight variance from random assignment of *cases* to the assigned status of *victims*. Rather, it is the large variance between the assigned and actual treatment of cases randomly assigned to conference. While the overall RISE experiments had low rates of treatment crossover, the sample of individual 'conference' victims interviewed for this study had a much higher rate of not getting the conference they expected to get. *Fully 23 per cent of the victims whose cases had been assigned to a conference were never able to participate in a restorative justice meeting with their offenders.* As it happens, the effect of this threat is to understate the benefits of restorative justice for victims. Presenting the data on the basis of assigned rather than actual treatment offers the reader the most conservative test of the effects of restorative justice, so that the selection factors affecting whether conferences happened do not bias the interpretation of the independent effects of the conferences on victims.

The external validity of the analyses depends in part on how typical Canberra is of other places where restorative justice might be tried. The answer to that question may depend on which other place one chooses, and on numerous factors of similarities and differences between that place and Canberra (size, demographic characteristics, income levels, level of incarceration, etc.). Canberra is a place, for example, where criminals are less often sentenced to prison for offences that would lead to prison in other parts of Australia, as well as in both England and many parts of the United States. How much this may or may not affect victim views of restorative justice is not clear.

The external validity of these analyses also depends on how representative the cases police referred into RISE are of all similar cases in Canberra. The fact that police referred only about 12 per cent of all eligible offences restricts the external validity of the results to the same kinds of cases. That is, the study reflects the kinds of cases in which police did not have strong views either way about whether a case should be cautioned or should result in a prosecution in court. These judgements may vary from one police officer to the next, and between police officers on average in Canberra and elsewhere. All this book can do to assess external validity is to note the basis on which the cases were referred, and to ask the reader to keep in mind these limitations on both internal and external validity.

5

The Lived Experience of Victims

5.1 Introduction

The discussion in Chapter 1 concluded that the common experience of victims in the Western criminal justice system was marked by:

- routine lack of attention to the question of restitution or, in broader terms, the repair of the material harm suffered;
- persistent neglect of non-material dimensions of victimization, that is, psychological and emotional consequences such as mistrust, unresolved anger, and fear;
- routine lack of communication between criminal justice agencies and victims, leaving them ignorant of progress about both processing and outcome of their cases;
- absence of a legitimate, participating role in the disposition of their cases;
- exclusion from the decision-making process which leads to perceptions of a lack of procedural fairness and dissatisfaction with outcomes.

This chapter explores whether the lived experience of RISE victims coincided with what the literature suggests about the experience of justice that victims seek, both in the processing and outcome of their cases. The data consist of the responses of 232 victims of property crime or violent crime to the structured questionnaire described in Chapter 4 (see Appendix 1). These data are supplemented by qualitative comments from the victims made in the course of the interviews. These 232 victims, of 196 separate cases, represent a response rate of 89 per cent of all personal victims (see Chapter 4 for a discussion of response rates).

The cases involving these victims were assigned either to court in the normal way *or* to a restorative justice conference. Victims whose cases went to court were not required as witnesses for the prosecution because a guilty plea was an eligibility criterion for the experiments: they therefore almost never attended their cases. Those whose cases were assigned to a conference were intended to meet their offenders, together with their own and the offenders' supporters, in the presence of a trained facilitator: the purpose of the conference was to discuss what had happened in the incident, the way everyone had been affected, and how the harm done could be repaired. As the previous chapter (see 4.4) discussed, however, not all cases assigned to a conference actually received one.

For simplicity, throughout the chapter the terms 'court victim' and 'conference victim' will be used to refer to those whose cases were *assigned* to those dispositions, even though not all cases were treated as assigned. All victim responses were analysed both by *assigned* treatment and *actual* treatment. However, the chapter reports only on responses by assigned treatment (Peto 1976) unless there is a statistically significant difference in the actual treatment not apparent in the assigned treatment, in which case the actual treatment data are also included.

Wherever possible, comparisons are made between the court-assigned and conference-assigned victims. When the difference between them is statistically significant at an alpha level of at least 0.05, this is noted throughout in the text and beneath the figures (where the exact p value is given). The figures also indicate, wherever possible, the effect size.[1] However, there were a number of questions court victims could not respond to because they had not attended the disposition of their cases (see Chapter 4). For example, court victims could not be asked how they felt after their cases were dealt with, compared with beforehand, because to do so would merely have measured the effect of the passage of time. By this I mean that not only did they not attend court but they usually did not know the outcome of their cases, and most often did not even know the cases had been held, so it was impossible to put these before/after questions to them meaningfully. This problem was especially apparent with questions concerning perceptions of procedural justice: it was simply not meaningful to ask people how

---

[1] Cohen's d, the measure of effect size, is defined as the degree of departure from the null hypothesis of zero difference: 0.2 is usually seen as a small effect, 0.5 as a moderate effect, and 0.8 as a large effect.

procedurally just they felt their treatment had been when they had no experience of it. I note throughout whether the data concern *all victims* or *conference victims only*. As Chapter 4 notes, the latter sample is analysed in a before-after design, with any differences attributed to the experience of going through the restorative justice conference.

5.2   Material Harm and Restoration

All victims were asked whether they had experienced financial, housing, employment, or any other material harm as a result of the offence. Only around 20 per cent of both court and conference victims said that they had experienced financial *problems* (and most of these were property victims), though about two-thirds of *property victims* and about one third of *violence victims* had incurred financial *loss* (Tables 5.1 and 5.3)). A further 13 per cent had had employment problems, and almost all of these were violence victims: their problems usually arose from the injuries they had suffered which led to their taking time off work for recovery or because of embarrassment (many of the injuries were facial); in addition, others who were looking for work said they could not approach employers while injured. Another 11 per cent had experienced housing problems; most of these had been victimized by offenders living near them.

Table 5.1 sets out the kinds of *specific* material harm faced by *property victims*. None of these victims incurred any loss relating to medical or legal costs. The 'other' costs refer principally to loss of unrecovered goods or cash. There was no significant difference between the two groups on any of these measures.[2]

Table 5.2 shows that similar percentages of court and conference victims had goods stolen and recovered.

Table 5.3 sets out the material harm suffered by *violence victims*. Again, for violence victims as for property victims, there was a high degree of equivalence in the material harm suffered by

---

[2] The data set includes two outliers for financial harm, one for $120,000 (arson of a kindergarten) and one for $35,000. The person who suffered the loss of $35,000 was the victim in six separate cases. For the data analysis as a whole, this case has been replicated five times in order to preserve random assignment. When these cases are excluded, there is no significant difference between court-assigned and conference-assigned victims on any measure of financial harm.

TABLE 5.1 Property Experiment—Material Harm, Court vs Conference

	Court (n = 80)		Conference (n = 73)	
	(n)	%	(n)	%
Damage/repairs >$500	(26)	33	(35)	49
Loss of wages	(10)	13	(5)	7
Costs to improve security	(6)	7	(6)	9
Other costs	(24)	30	(34)	48
Total with any costs	(57)	73	(47)	67

TABLE 5.2 Property Experiment—Recovery of Stolen Goods, Court vs Conference

	Court (n = 82)		Conference (n = 77)	
	(n)	%	(n)	%
N/A	(20)	24	(20)	26
No	(11)	13	(9)	12
Partly	(14)	17	(15)	20
Completely	(37)	45	(33)	43

TABLE 5.3 Violence Experiment—Material Harm, Court vs Conference

	Court (n = 35)		Conference (n = 44)	
	(n)	%	(n)	%
% with injury requiring medical attention	(22)	63	(24)	55
% of those requiring medical attention needing hospital treatment	(12)	55	(15)	63
% of those requiring medical attention needing hospital admission	(1)	8	(5)	33
% with financial costs incurred	(12)	34	(19)	43

the court and conference groups as a result of the offence. The largest difference in the table concerns hospital admission: 33 per cent of conference victims compared with 8 per cent of court victims required hospital admission.

In summary, there was no significant difference between the court and conference groups in the extent of material harm they had experienced in either the property or violence experiments.

Although material restoration is a legitimate and significant part of a restorative process, it is interesting to note that victims themselves evidently do not always regard it as being of primary importance. When victims were asked why they decided to attend a conference, only 31 per cent said that wanting to ensure repayment for the harm experienced was a 'quite important' or 'very important' reason (see Figure 5.24). This tendency to regard material restitution as no more than secondary was well expressed by the victim in JPP115, whose babysitter had stolen from her family: in the conference she said: '[i]t's not just money, that's nothing, it's the way it's affected all of us. We aren't here because money's an issue at all. We aren't here for our pound of flesh. We're here for Ben [the offender].'

The victim in JPP069 had been assaulted while riding his bicycle by an angry motorist, and said that he felt he probably should have received some money from the offender but made a decision in the conference not to ask for it: this was not because he felt too powerless but because the emotions in the conference had been so raw that he felt it was inappropriate to ask for it, and also because he discovered that he and his assailant were in the same kind of employment and he felt a sense of solidarity with him.

Table 5.4 sets out the material restitution actually awarded to court and conference victims. The majority of both groups received nothing, and both groups were awarded restitution less often than they said they should have been. About the same percentage of each group received money, but significantly more conference victims than court victims received some other form of material restitution ($p < 0.05$), such as work for people affected by the offence. In addition, on many occasions the outcome involved community service work by the offenders to organizations nominated by the victims, such as the Salvation Army or the Brain Injury Foundation.

TABLE 5.4   Material Restitution Awarded, Court vs Conference

Form of Restitution	Court (n = 116)		Conference (n = 116)	
	(n)	%	(n)	%
Money	(14)	12	(16)	14
Work	(0)	0	(7)	6
Other	(0)	0	(6)	5
None	(102)	88	(87)	75

Case JPP082 provided an example of an attempt at financial restitution in a court case which went awry: the solicitor from the Office of the Director of Public Prosecutions, in discussion with the offender's solicitor, had agreed not to offer evidence in court (which always leads to dismissal of the case), provided the offender's solicitor undertook to ensure that the offender approached the victim and arranged to pay for the damage he had caused to his shop window. The offender did indeed ask the victim the cost of repairs arising from the incident: the victim did not know the cost at the time the offender contacted him, and he never heard from the offender again. He said that he felt that if it were court-ordered compensation then he ought to have received the payment from the court rather than directly from the offender; and if it were not court-ordered he felt he did not have the right to approach the offender for payment.

Given that conferences appear to be no more effective than court at delivering financial restitution to victims, it is useful to know whether there is any difference between the two groups in terms of how much they wanted it awarded. When victims were asked whether they believed they should have received any money from their offenders to compensate them for loss and harm, 47 per cent of court victims and 37 per cent of conference victims thought they should have done so ($p < 0.05$) (Table 5.5). On the question whether the offenders should do some work for them or their families, 15 per cent of court and 20 per cent of conference victims said they should do so.

Thus, although victims were not often awarded money either in court or conference, fewer conference victims than court victims wanted money as an outcome of their cases. It appears that the

TABLE 5.5   Financial Restitution Sought and Received, Court vs Conference

	Court (n = 112)		Conference (n = 103)	
	(n)	%	(n)	%
Wanted and awarded money	(13)	12	(16)	16
Wanted money but not awarded	(39)	35	(22)	21
Did not want money	(60)	54	(65)	63

conference experience affects victims' opinions of whether financial restitution constitutes an appropriate outcome.

It is difficult to discern a pattern in the making of orders for material restitution in court, though the financial circumstances of the offender are a consideration, just as they are in the conference. The victim in JPP016, who had experienced a burglary, said he was pleased the matter was dealt with in court because he received a cheque in the mail for $800, though there was no accompanying explanatory letter (several victims spoke of receiving cheques in the mail from the court with no covering note and being puzzled about them). He said he did not care about the money—he was not hard up and insurance had covered most of the loss—but appreciated the acknowledgement that he had experienced harm. He had no idea how the amount was arrived at: his estimated loss was much greater than $800 before his insurance claim, and much less after the claim.

The victim in JPP041 had a rather different experience of court-ordered financial restitution. Her offender was ordered to pay $1,000 to the court and the court was to pay her. After about eighteen months she rang the court to find out whether the offender had paid anything yet and when she might expect to receive her compensation. She was told: '[i]t's not your business and you can't be told anything about whether the offender had paid anything yet.' She was very taken aback by this response to her query and resigned herself to not receiving the money. But a few months later she received a cheque from the court for the full amount, though without any covering note.

In summary, many victims believed they ought to have received more material restitution than they did. About the same proportion of both groups received money, but conference-assigned victims were more likely to receive other forms of restitution. The experience of most court-assigned victims was as reported in the literature: routine lack of attention to the question of restitution or, in broader terms, the repair of the material harm suffered. It appears that conferencing provided more opportunity for material reparation, including money, work from the offender, or other tangible outcomes, even if this did not take place as often as victims said they would have liked; it also appears that conference victims did not attach as much importance to financial restitution as court victims did.

5.3 Emotional Harm and Restoration (Including Apology)

Overall, it is a little more difficult to interpret the data on emotional harm experienced as a result of the offence. Most of it could be expected to occur pre-treatment, and therefore to be randomly distributed in the same way as material harm, and this appears to be the case. On the other hand, especially in more serious cases, further emotional harm could be expected in the period between disposition and interview. However, because of confidence that random assignment has rendered the two groups equivalent (see Chapter 4), I propose that any difference in levels of emotional harm and restoration will be due to the treatment they received.

Tables 5.6 and 5.7 set out the emotional harm suffered by property and violence victims. A concept missing from this list is one that was spontaneously mentioned by a number of property victims—that of a sense of violation. This was the word that recurred when victims of these crimes, especially house break-ins, talked about their experience, and which seemed to encompass many of these harms. For example the victim in JPP016 said: '[i]t was very upsetting. My wife felt quite violated with her things all over the room. It happened the day before we went overseas: they moved the tickets and passports so they could see we would be

TABLE 5.6 Property Experiment—Emotional Harm, Court vs Conference

	Court (n = 80)		Conference (n = 70)	
	(n)	%	(n)	%
'Have you suffered from any of the following as a result of the offence?'				
Fear of being alone	(6)	8	(7)	10
Sleeplessness and/or nightmares	(7)	9	(7)	10
Headaches or other physical symptons	(3)	4	(4)	6
General increase in suspicion or distrust	(42)	53	(39)	56
Loss of confidence	(9)	11	(7)	10
Loss of self-esteem	(0)	0	(3)	4
'You felt you suffered a loss of . . . as a result of the offence' (% agree or strongly agree)				
Loss of self-respect	(6)	8	(12)	17
Loss of dignity	(24)	30	(28)	40
Loss of self-confidence	(15)	19	(14)	20

TABLE 5.7   Violence Experiment—Emotional Harm, Court vs Conference

	Court (n = 36)		Conference (n = 45)	
	(n)	%	(n)	%
'Have you suffered from any of the following as a result of the offence?' *(% yes)*				
Fear of being alone	(11)	31	(16)	36
Sleeplessness and/or nightmares	(12)	33	(10)	22
Headaches or other physical symptons	(14)	39	(19)	42
General increase in suspicion or distrust	(24)	67	(31)	69
Loss of confidence	(12)	33	(21)	47
Loss of self-esteem	(10)	28	(20)	44
'You felt you suffered a loss of . . . as a result of the offence' *(% agree or strongly agree)*				
Loss of self-respect	(17)	47	(21)	47
Loss of dignity	(20)	56	(28)	62
Loss of self-confidence	(14)	39	(25)	56

away. We worried the whole time that we would come back and find they had been there again.' One of the victims in JPP099 (a series of letterbox vandalisms) said she felt 'intruded on' and was surprised at the strength of her feelings, both of violation and anger. She said: 'I've got friends who have had their houses broken into and I wonder how they must feel when I feel so badly about something which just happened in my garden.'

In both court and conference groups, by far the most common emotional harm flowing from the offence for both *property* and *violence victims* was increased levels of suspicion and distrust (Tables 5.6 and 5.7). As would be expected, there were much higher levels of emotional harm experienced by violence victims than property victims, but there was no significant difference between the court and conference groups on any of these measures.

In summary, for both property and violence victims there was no significant difference between the court and conference groups in the extent of emotional harm they experienced. For both violence and property victims in both groups the most common emotional harm experienced was increased suspicion and distrust.

5.3.1 Safety and fear

An important measure of emotional restoration for victims after their cases were dealt with was a sense of safety, or, conversely, a

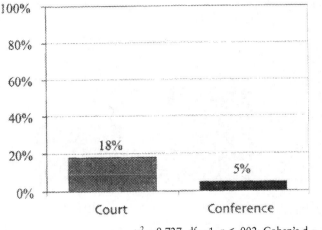

$\chi^2 = 9.727$, df = 1, p ≤ .002; Cohen's d = .777

FIGURE 5.1. Anticipate the Offender will Repeat the Offence on Me—all victims

fear of revictimization. *All victims* were asked: 'do you anticipate that the offender(s) will repeat the offence on you?': significantly more court victims than conference victims expected to be revictimized (18 per cent vs 5 per cent: Figure 5.1) (p < 0.005).

Among *property victims*, three times as many of the court as conference victims believed the offender would repeat the offence *on them* (21 per cent vs 7 per cent, p < 0.05). Among *violence victims*, more than five times as many court as conference victims believed the offender would repeat the offence *on them* (11 per cent compared with 2 per cent, p = 0.01).

All victims were asked: 'do you anticipate that the offender(s) will repeat this offence on another victim?' Significantly more of the court victims than conference victims believed their offenders would repeat the offence on *another victim* (55 per cent vs 35 per cent: Figure 5.2) (p < 0.005).

A significantly higher percentage of court than conference *property victims* believed they would repeat it on *another victim* (54 per cent compared with 31 per cent) (p < 0.05). Similarly, significantly more of the court than conference *violence victims* believed they would repeat the offence on *another victim* (58 per cent compared with 40 per cent) (p < 0.01).

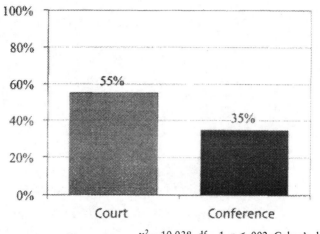

$\chi^2 = 10.038$, df = 1, p ≤ .002; Cohen's d = .468

FIGURE 5.2. Anticipate the Offender will Repeat the Offence on Another—All Victims

The opportunity to make a personal assessment of the offender seems to be important here. JPP071, a case involving an assault on a taxi driver by a passenger, demonstrated the capacity of the conference setting to calm fears of revictimization. At the end of the conference both parties remarked that the other was completely unlike the person they had imagined them to be: both of them also spontaneously said that they had each been fearfully looking out for the other since the incident, expecting further trouble if they met. The offender said: '[n]ow I can see things from [the victim's] point of view. I thought you were totally different. I thought you wanted to fight me. I've been keeping an eye out for you in case you wanted to run me down.'

The victim in JVC055, a young mother who was the victim of a random drive-by shooting, said: '[o]nce I saw him that was it—he was just a young boy. I felt sorry for him, towards the end [of the conference] to tell you the truth.' In JVC047 a case involving a drunken street assault, the victim's father said: 'I wanted to see what kind of fellow he was ... I can see where he's coming from now.'

Conference victims only were asked whether: 'you were afraid of the offender(s) before (after) the conference' (no corresponding

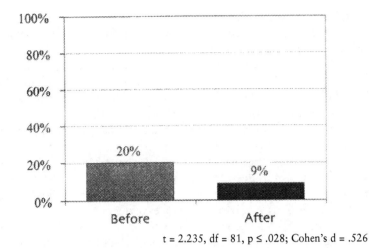

t = 2.235, df = 81, p ≤ .028; Cohen's d = .526

FIGURE 5.3. Fear of Offender Before and After Treatment—conference victims

court data). The percentage of conference victims who said they felt afraid before the conference was not large, but fell significantly further after the conference (20 per cent vs 9 per cent: Figure 5.3) (p < 0.05).

As might be expected, there were striking differences here between property and violence victims. Four per cent of *property victims* agreed they were afraid of their offenders before the conference and this was unchanged afterwards. By contrast, significantly more *violence victims* said they were afraid before the conference but not afterwards (38 per cent vs 14 per cent, p < 0.001). Fear of their offenders was not a major issue for the property victims, it appears, but it plainly was important in the violence cases, and the data indicate that for these victims meeting their offenders tended to be a reassuring experience rather than one engendering more fear.

It was not possible to obtain the same kind of before/after measures for *court victims*. However, the lack of opportunity for court victims to see their offenders means there is no chance for this kind of reassurance. For example, the victim in JPP052, whose car was stolen from her driveway with her housekeys in it, was very afraid after the offence. She had a sick baby and an absent husband at the time of the incident, and said that while she was not upset about losing the car, she was consumed with fear about the possibility of the offenders coming into the house. Even after she had all the locks changed she said she could not stop worrying. The victim in JPP050 was an elderly woman who had had a number of garden ornaments smashed. She was quite terrified about this apparently trivial incident and her life had been greatly affected—frightened to stay in her house alone and frightened to leave it.

Even those not much affected by the experience of victimization themselves may readily acknowledge that those they care about have been deeply affected: in JPP087 a Cabinet Minister's chief of staff was uncomfortable even with the idea of being a victim ('Well, I don't think I'm exactly that, am I?'), but spoke with feeling about the nightmares his 7-year-old son had experienced since their house was burgled. (This accords with Morgan and Zedner's (1992) study of child victims, which found that a significant minority of children whose households had been burgled were deeply affected.)

5.3.2   Sense of security

Conference victims only were asked: 'since the conference have you felt your sense of security had been restored?' (no corresponding court data). While about one third (35 per cent) said they had never lost it, 46 per cent said it had been completely or partly restored (Figure 5.4).

Again there were notable differences between property and violence victims: significantly more *violence victims* said that they had lost their sense of security, but that since the conference it had been restored, either partly or completely (p < 0.05).

There are no before/after measures for *court victims*, but the difficulty of restoring security in a court case was illustrated by the victim in JPP052. This case appeared at first sight to be a very trivial one, involving the theft of a child's pet rabbit, but the interview revealed that this offence was the latest in a long line of incidents between neighbours with abusive relationships between the adults carried on by their children. After the court case the young victim said: 'she [the offender] keeps telling me she'll steal the rabbit again and bash me up as well, and her parents say it too.'

5.3.3   Helpfulness of the conference

Conference victims only were asked: 'how helpful did you find attending the conference?' (no corresponding court data): only a small minority called it unhelpful (Figure 5.5).

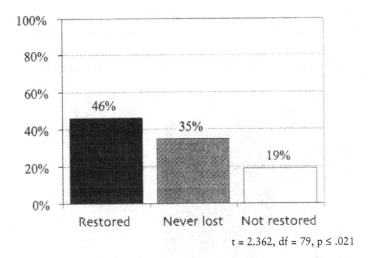

t = 2.362, df = 79, p ≤ .021

FIGURE 5.4. Effect of Treatment on Sense of Security—conference victims

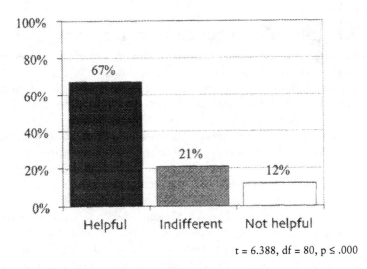

t = 6.388, df = 80, p ≤ .000

FIGURE 5.5. Helpfulness of Attending Treatment—conference victims

They were also asked: 'do you think the conference helped to solve any problems?' The results here were similar: the great majority (88 per cent) said that it had helped quite a lot while only 12 per cent said that it had failed to do so at all (Figure 5.6).

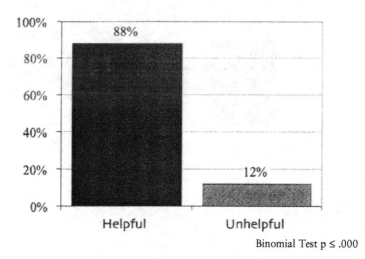

Binomial Test p ≤ .000

FIGURE 5.6. Helpfulness of Treatment in Solving Problems—conference victims

5.3.4 Anger and sympathy towards offender

Conference victims only were asked: 'before (after) the conference how angry (sympathetic) did you feel towards the offender(s)?' (no corresponding court data). Significantly more had felt angry beforehand with their offenders, compared with afterwards (63 per cent vs 29 per cent, Figure 5.7) (p < 0.001).

Significantly more conference victims had felt sympathetic towards their offenders after the conference, compared with beforehand (48 per cent vs 19 per cent, Figure 5.8) (p < 0.001).

The victim in JVC071 said at the end of the conference dealing with the assault he had suffered: 'I have to sympathize with you. Everything you've said I've experienced as well since it happened— feeling guilty, wondering how this is going to affect my career.' Similarly, before the conference 60 per cent said they felt sympathetic towards their offenders' families and supporters, compared with 72 per cent afterwards.

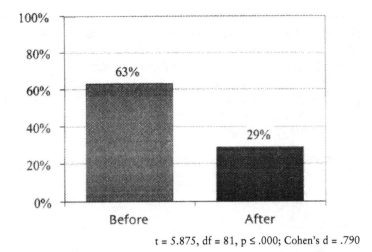

t = 5.875, df = 81, p ≤ .000; Cohen's d = .790

FIGURE 5.7. Anger Towards Offender Before and After Treatment—conference victims

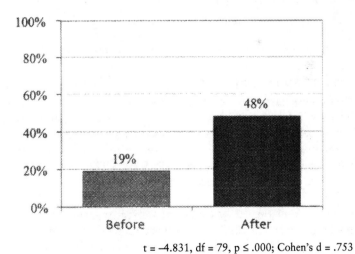

t = –4.831, df = 79, p ≤ .000; Cohen's d = .753

FIGURE 5.8. Sympathy Towards Offender Before and After Treatment—conference victims

Table 5.8 shows these responses for *property and violence victims* separately. It is interesting to note that while feelings of anger before and after the conference were at similar levels for the property and violence victims, there was significantly more sympathy felt for both the offenders and their families by the property victims, both before and after the conference, than was felt by the violence victims (p < 0.05): indeed, sympathy felt by violence victims for their offenders' families actually declined after the conference.

TABLE 5.8   Feelings of Anger and Sympathy, Before and After Conference, Property and Violence Victims

	Property*		Violence**	
	(n)	%	(n)	%
(quite/very) angry with offender before conference	(26)	58	(26)	67
(quite/very) angry with offender after conference	(10)	24	(14)	36
(a little/very) sympathetic for offender before	(10)	22	(5)	14
(a little/very) sympathetic for offender after	(26)	58	(13)	34
(a little/very) sympathetic for offender's family	(27)	63	(20)	57
(a little/very) sympathetic for offender's family	(37)	86	(18)	53

* n of property respondents to these questions varied from 43 to 45.
** n of violence respondents to these questions varied from 34 to 37.

5.3.5   Dignity, self-respect, self-confidence

Conference victims only were asked: 'was your sense of dignity (self-respect, self-confidence) increased or reduced after the conference?' While two-thirds of all respondents said that they felt no different about any of these, most of the remainder felt there had been a beneficial effect (Figures 5.9, 5.10, 5.11).

5.3.6   Trust

Conference victims only were asked about trust and the loss of it resulting from the offence, a subject that recurred repeatedly in conference discussions (no corresponding court data). It was particularly salient for young offenders' parents, who frequently commented that the biggest harm they had experienced was the loss of trust, the feeling of being 'let down', and how much they

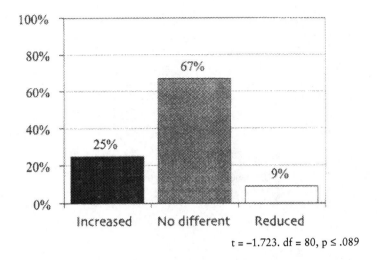

t = −1.723. df = 80, p ≤ .089

FIGURE 5.9. Effect of Treatment on Dignity—conference victims

regretted the loss of their former confidence in their children. The young offenders themselves recognized this cost as well: in JVC041, a youth involved in a street fight said 'I feel bad about my parents, of course I do. I guess they don't have much trust in me

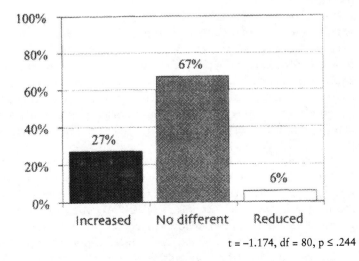

t = −1.174, df = 80, p ≤ .244

FIGURE 5.10. Effect of Treatment on Self-respect—conference victims

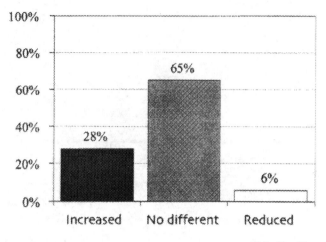

t = −.913, df = 80, p ≤ .364

FIGURE 5.11. Effect of Treatment on Self-confidence—conference victims

. . . my mum was upset because I didn't tell her what happened . .
. because I felt too ashamed.' It also arose frequently for victims
who felt that the way they normally interacted with others had
been affected.

When conference victims were asked: 'before the conference,
what would you say the offence had done to your trust in others?',
over half of them (56 per cent) said that they felt less trusting than
they had done before the offence. However, the conference experience had a beneficial effect on some of them. When conference
victims were asked: 'after the conference, how did you feel regarding your trust in others?', 20 per cent reported that they felt more
trusting, but a further 26 per cent said they remained less trusting
(Figure 5.12).

Although there are no quantitative data regarding court victims'
experience of the loss of trust, it was mentioned spontaneously by
several of them at interview. Typical of the views expressed were
those of a 14-year-old schoolgirl (JVC004) who had been the
victim of an assault by two fellow students on her way home from
school. One of the offenders had previously been a friend, and the
victim was shocked by the assault as well as physically hurt. She
said that since the attack she had suffered from nightmares and

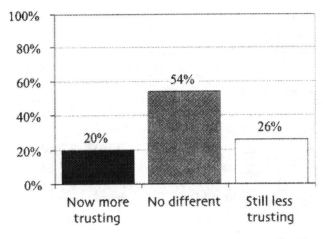

t = −.913, df = 80, p ≤ .364

FIGURE 5.12. Effect of Treatment on Trust in Others—conference victims

headaches but that 'the worst part is I don't know who to trust anymore'.

5.3.7 Anxiety

Conference victims only were asked: 'before (after) the conference, how anxious did you feel about the offence happening again?' (no corresponding court data). The percentage feeling anxious declined significantly after the conference (40 per cent vs 31 per cent: Figure 5.13) (p < 0.05).

Violence victims were moderately reassured—42 per cent of them reported still being anxious after the conference compared with 58 per cent beforehand (p < 0.01). The victim of the drive-by shooting incident (JVC055) said in her conference that her initial thoughts after the incident were 'Do they know me? Do they know my son? Did they mean to do it?' Then she looked directly at the offender and said: 'Why did you do it? Did you pick me?' The offender looked very embarrassed and said that he and his friends were 'just mucking about', that his friend was holding the barrel and he was firing the trigger at random, and that he definitely had not meant to hit her. She visibly relaxed at that moment, a turning point for the conference.

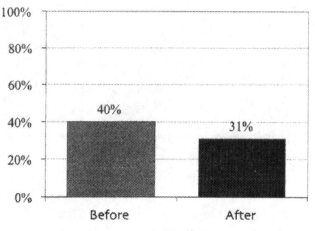

t = 2.402, df = 79, p ≤ .019; Cohen's d = .211

FIGURE 5.13. Effect of Treatment on Anxiety—conference victims

The anxiety that *court victims* experience may not be so readily resolved. The victims in JPP110, whose motorcycles were stolen from their garage, said that their offenders continued to harass them by turning up in their garden late at night, trying to steal their family car, and attempting to break into the house, as payback for 'dobbing them in'. The family knew that the offenders were 'just kids' but the mother said: 'I'd like to see a judge put up with what we put up with. Knowing that sometime every week they'll be around . . . it's awful having to be watchful all the time and worry about all the noises . . . and our kids too, they've been really frightened.' The father in this court case added: 'We don't want to know who they are and where they live because I might get so angry I'd go down to their place and punch their lights out.'

5.3.8 Embarrassment and shame

Conference victims only were asked whether: 'the conference has helped you in dealing with any feelings of embarrassment (shame) you might have about the offence' (no corresponding court data). More than half of them (59 per cent) said that they had not felt any embarrassment, but most of the remainder found the conference helpful rather than unhelpful in dealing with it (28 per cent vs 14 per cent: Figure 5.14).

Although more than half of them (58 per cent) said that they

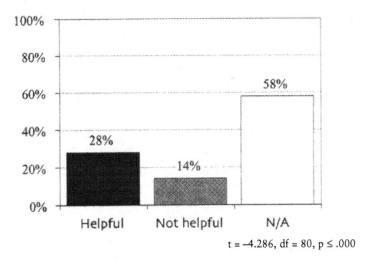

t = –4.286, df = 80, p ≤ .000

FIGURE 5.14. Effect of Treatment on Overcoming Feelings of Embarrassment—conference victims

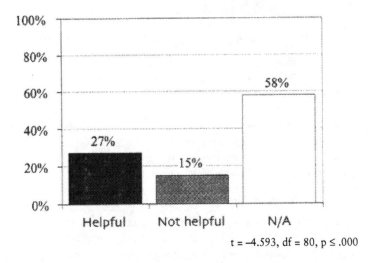

t = –4.593, df = 80, p ≤ .000

FIGURE 5.15. Effect of Treatment on Overcoming Feelings of Shame—conference victims

had not felt any shame, most of the remainder found the conference helpful rather than unhelpful in dealing with it (27 per cent vs 15 per cent: Figure 5.15).

5.3.9   Feeling emotionally settled

Conference victims only were asked: 'did the conference make you feel more or less settled emotionally about the offence?' While half said it had no effect, most of the remainder said that they felt more settled rather than less settled after the conference (41 per cent vs 6 per cent: Figure 5.16).

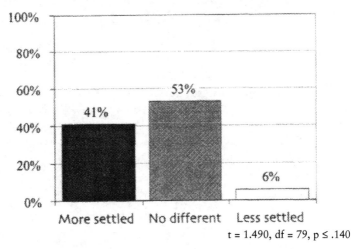

t = 1.490, df = 79, p ≤ .140

FIGURE 5.16. Effect of Treatment on Feeling Emotionally Settled—conference victims

Again, as might be anticipated, there were big differences between the property and violence victims. Significantly more *violence victims* said they felt some shame (p < 0.05) and embarrassment (p < 0.05) about the offence (Table 5.9).

5.3.10   Forgiveness

Conference victims only were asked: 'since the conference, in thinking about the offender(s), you have felt very unforgiving, unforgiving, neither forgiving nor unforgiving, forgiving, very forgiving' (no corresponding court data available). Almost half the victims (45 per cent) said that since the conference they had felt neither forgiving

TABLE 5.9   Effect of Conference on Shame, Embarrassment, Feeling Emotionally Settled, Property and Violence Victims

	Property (n = 45)		Violence (n = 37)	
	(n)	%	(n)	%
Felt some shame about the offence	(13)	28	(21)	57
Of those who felt some shame				
Conference alleviated shame	(8)	62	(14)	67
Felt some embarrassment about the offence	(15)	33	(19)	51
Of those who felt some embarrassment				
Conference alleviated embarrassment	(12)	80	(11)	58
More settled emotionally after the conference	(18)	39	(16)	43
Less settled emotionally after the conference	(1)	2	(4)	11

nor unforgiving, but most of the remainder said that they did in fact feel forgiving (39 per cent vs 16 per cent: Figure 5.17).

A sense of forgiveness often accompanied the feeling that after the conference offenders had a proper understanding of the harm caused (52 per cent of all conference victims agreed that they did) and a belief that their offenders had learnt their lesson and deserved a second chance (48 per cent of all conference victims agreed that they had). A forgiving disposition may be indicated by the 36 per cent of all conference victims who said that wanting to

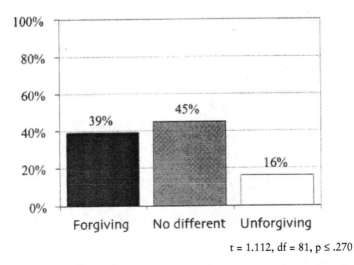

t = 1.112, df = 81, p ≤ .270

FIGURE 5.17. Effect of Treatment on Forgiveness—conference victims

help the offender was an important reason for their attending the conference at all (see Figure 5.24). For example, in JPP049, the victim of a small-store shoplift said: 'When everyone let their feelings out by talking I felt better. She [the offender] apparently learned by the conference which made me feel better about what happened. . . . Next day she came past the shop and saw me and waved hello. To me that meant she had learned from what happened. It was reassuring—she showed a bit of respect. . . . She would have gone to Quamby [a detention centre] if she'd gone to court. It was good to have an opportunity to give her maybe her last chance.' The victim in JPP009, a medical practitioner, was alarmed when the offender said in the conference that she had stolen the purse in order to buy cigarettes: all the victim wanted from the outcome was for the offender to undertake a 'quit smoking' course.

5.3.11   Closure

Conference victims only were asked whether 'the conference made you feel you could put the whole thing behind you' (no corresponding court data). Three times as many agreed as disagreed with this statement (60 per cent vs 20 per cent: Figure 5.18) (p < 0.001).

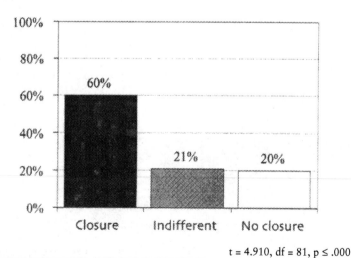

t = 4.910, df = 81, p ≤ .000

FIGURE 5.18. Effect of Treatment on Sense of Closure—conference victims

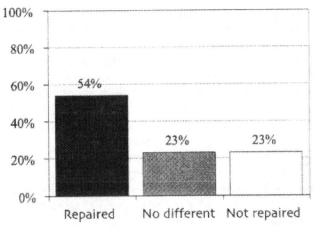

t = 3.729, df = 81, p ≤ .000

FIGURE 5.19. Effect of Treatment on Repair of Harm—conference victims

Conference victims only were asked whether 'you felt the conference allowed the harm done to you by the offender to be repaired' (no corresponding court data). More than half felt that the conference had allowed the harm done to them to be repaired, compared with less than a quarter who disagreed (54 per cent vs 23 per cent: Figure 5.19) (p < 0.001).

The victim in JPP115, whose house had been broken into by her children's babysitter, explained her complex and conflicting emotions this way: 'I went to the conference for Ben's sake [the offender]. I was terribly nervous and I didn't want to go. I was really surprised how much better I felt afterwards. I felt so much more settled—I could put it behind me. I felt I could forgive him for betraying my trust.'

5.3.12 Apology

Perhaps the most significant factor in emotional restoration relates to whether victims feel they can accept their offenders' apologies. While Brown (1994) is concerned that the restorative setting with its focus on reconciliation 'could harm victims who are not ready or willing to forgive their offenders' (p. 1263) and 'may inhibit victims' expression of anger and pressure them to forgive their offenders' (p. 1274), this did not appear to be an issue for these victims. For example, in the conference for the drive-by shooting incident already referred to (JVC055), both the victim and her husband noticeably relaxed as the conference progressed. They accepted the apology from the offender when it was offered, and also accepted the apologies offered by the offender's father, mother, and grandmother (as well as a hug from the grandmother). When voluntary work was discussed as an outcome for the offender, the husband said: 'This can be good for you too, if you get a good reference. Because I want to see you get a good job too . . . and I hope you'll do more hours if you enjoy it.' At the end, the facilitator, who knew how nervous and stressed the victim had been in the week or so prior to the conference, asked her: 'Do you feel better now?' to which she replied: 'Yes I do, I have to admit I do. . . . I wanted to put a face to him. I wanted to know what he looks like . . . it was hard coming to Canberra [on visits] not knowing.'

All victims were asked: 'do you believe you should have received [an apology] from the offender(s) to compensate you for loss and harm?' The great majority of both groups said they should have done (88 per cent of court victims and 91 per cent of conference victims: Figure 5.20).

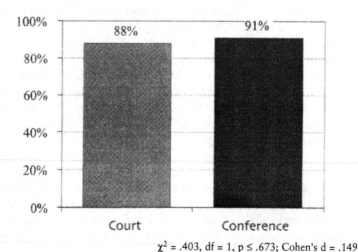

$\chi^2 = .403$, df = 1, p ≤ .673; Cohen's d = .149

FIGURE 5.20. Felt Should have Received an Apology—all victims

When *all victims* were asked: 'has the offender apologised to you?', almost three quarters of the *conference* victims said that they had done so (and 86 per cent of those who had actually attended a conference), compared with only 19 per cent of the *court* victims (Figure 5.21) (p < .001). Of those who had received an apology, none of the *court* victims said that it was part of the court outcome, while 91 per cent of the *conference* victims said that it was part of the conference outcome.

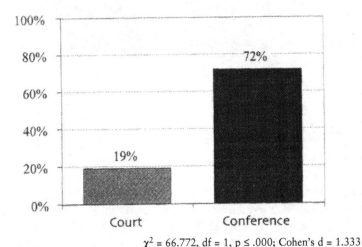

$\chi^2 = 66.772$, df = 1, p ≤ .000; Cohen's d = 1.333

FIGURE 5.21. Received an Apology—all victims

Interestingly, there was also a significant difference between the groups when they were asked how they rated the sincerity of the apology: over three quarters of the *conference* victims (77 per cent) believed it was 'sincere' or 'somewhat sincere', compared with only 41 per cent of the *court* victims (Figure 5.22) (p < 0.001).

Conference victims, it seems, not only received more apologies but also higher quality apologies (if sincerity is a measure of quality). This may be due to the circumstances in which they were offered: most of the apologies received by victims whose cases went to court seem to have been coerced, while apologies forthcoming at a conference usually emerged spontaneously as the discussion evolved. For example, the offender in JPP106, who had stolen the jacket of a fellow school student apologized tearfully for her

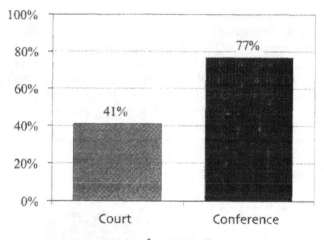

$\chi^2 = 10.755$, df = 1, p ≤ .001; Cohen's d = .872

FIGURE 5.22. Felt Apology was Sincere—all victims

actions: the victim's father said very solemnly that he accepted her apology provided she undertook never to do anything like that again. When they were all leaving the conference, he had said to her: 'Now, you remember your promise to me.' The victim's mother said that she felt the girl's face had lit up, as if she was glad to be given this limit on her actions and a sense that somebody cared. The shopkeeper victim in JPP105, who said he was not interested in conferencing and had in any case forgotten to attend, said that he had plenty of experience of the court system with shoptheft and was impressed with conferencing, to the extent that this was the first occasion on which the offender had come into the shop and apologized sincerely (as was agreed as part of the conference outcome). The victim told the offender's mother that it took 'real guts' to do that and he appreciated it.

Finally, those who had *not* received an apology were asked whether they thought that an apology would have helped them to forgive their offenders. Fifty-three per cent of the *court* victims and 50 per cent of the *conference* victims said that it 'probably' or 'definitely' would have helped them to do so.

It is worth noting that possibly many offenders who go before the court experience genuine remorse for their behaviour. The victim in JPP065, a music shop proprietor with a large clientele of young people, frequently experienced shoplifting attempts and always called the police, but his attitude toward these offenders often resulted in their thanks for the way they were treated: in fact the offender in this case, which was dealt with in court, had spontaneously written him a letter of apology, which the victim described as 'very nice'. In JPP044, the police incident report stated: '[the offender] stated that he did not know why he committed the burglaries and took the property, . . . *He wanted to apologise to the people for what had been done.*' When one of the victims in this case was interviewed she said: 'I got most of my stuff back—all except the roller blades. I really wanted the roller blades back as I'll never be able to afford another pair. But mostly I wanted an apology for all the mess.' She added that she would have been glad to settle the matter out of court if the offender had returned the goods. But neither the police nor the court conveyed to her that the offender wanted to apologize, nor was any compensation ordered for the loss of the blades. In JPP040, at the end of the court case concerning his theft of a motorcycle, the offender apologized for his behaviour and his parents and his class teacher, all of whom were present in court, responded in a forgiving way. But the victim was not there to hear the apology and had no idea that it had been offered.

In summary, *court-assigned* and *conference-assigned* victims were very different in the degree of emotional restoration they experienced (differences were usually even more marked between victims who *actually* experienced a conference and victims whose cases were *actually* dealt with in court). Victims who had attended a conference were asked about feelings of anger, fear, and anxiety about their offenders before the conference: these tended to fall markedly after the conference, while feelings of sympathy and secur-ity rose. The conference usually had a beneficial effect on feelings of dignity, self-respect, and self-confidence and reduced levels of embarrassment and shame that some felt about the offence. Throughout, there was a minority of victims who felt worse after the conference: violence victims tended more often than property victims to feel either better or worse, with fewer indifferent to the experience.

Court victims, by contrast, could say little about emotional restoration because the court provided no opportunity for restoration to take place. They expressed higher levels of fear of revictimization: in the violence cases, five times as many court-assigned as conference-assigned victims believed their offender would repeat the offence on them. Differences in levels of confidence in the likelihood of their offenders desisting from victimizing others were marked as well: almost twice as many court-assigned as conference-assigned victims believed their offenders would repeat the offence on someone else.

In addition, the vast majority of both court-assigned and conference-assigned victims believed they should have received an apology. Nearly four times as many of the conference-assigned as court-assigned had actually received an apology. Conference-assigned victims also rated more highly the sincerity of the apologies they received.

These findings confirm that court processing neglects the non-material dimensions of victimization, that is, psychological and emotional consequences such as mistrust, unresolved anger, and fear. Conferences, by contrast, provided an opportunity for the resolution of these harms and were moderately successful in providing the restoration that victims sought, especially in providing a forum for apology and forgiveness to be transacted.

5.4   Communication of Information about Processing and Outcome

When victims are not required as witnesses, courts tell victims nothing about their cases. Victims must contact the police officer involved in the apprehension of their offenders if they want to know anything about their cases, a frustrating experience as 'their' police officers are usually out on patrol or not on shift. This is in spite of specific legislation on victims' rights to be informed, found in many jurisdictions. Canberra's legislation is typical: section 4 of the Australian Capital Territory Victims of Crime Act 1994 states:

In the administration of justice, the following principles shall, as far as practicable and appropriate, govern the treatment of victims: . . .
(b) a victim should be informed at reasonable intervals (generally not exceeding one month) of the progress of police investigations concerning the relevant offence . . .
(c) a victim should be informed of the charges laid against the accused . . .
(k) a victim should be given an explanation of the outcome of criminal proceedings and of any sentence and its implications.

The proviso 'as far as practicable' means that victims have little basis on which to compel police or the courts to keep them informed, so that the onus is always on the victims to find out for themselves. The practical difficulties of doing so are compounded when their offenders are juveniles when most children's and youth courts are closed to the public.

All victims were asked whether they had been informed 'in good time' about when their cases were to be dealt with, whether by court or by conference (Figure 5.23). In cases dealt with in court,

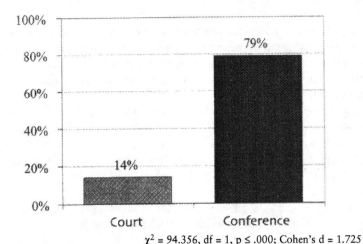

$\chi^2 = 94.356$, df = 1, p ≤ .000; Cohen's d = 1.725

FIGURE 5.23. Informed in Good Time About When the Case was to be Dealt With—all victims

this effectively meant whether victims had been informed at all: where they had been, this was usually though their own efforts. Evidently *violence victims* were more persistent in finding out about their court cases: 28 per cent of them had been informed about when their cases were to be dealt with, compared with 8 per cent of the *property victims.*

This lack of communication was the single greatest cause for dissatisfaction from victims whose cases were dealt with in court. Usually the first they knew that their cases had been dealt with at all was when they were contacted for interview. They often said that it was premature to talk to them because the cases had not been dealt with so they could not make intelligent comment on how they felt. When they were told that indeed they had been before the court the reaction was often one of disbelief and almost always of annoyance. Victim JPP023 was a typical example of this reaction. A victim of a bag snatch, she said she had been assured by the arresting police officer that she would be asked to give evidence against her offender. When told that the case had been dealt with, she said she felt let down and angry, especially as she had had no success in making contact with the officer since the incident despite repeated calls. She said: 'I'm supposed to be the victim and I'm treated like this.'

Victim JVC062/2 was also very dissatisfied with her experience. She had intervened in an argument at the motel where she worked as a receptionist. She was assaulted with a baseball bat and her wrist was broken after the offender demolished the door of the room where she had locked herself in. She was not sure whether she would be needed for the court case and made numerous calls both to the court and to the office of the Director of Public Prosecutions (DPP) about the progress of the case. She said: 'Basically I was made to feel like a complete nuisance by both of them.' It was only through persistence and contacts—her father was a police officer and she had a friend at the DPP's office—that she found out eventually when the case was to be dealt with and what the outcome was. She was invited to make a Victim Impact Statement but the police told her that the offender would see it. She declined to make one because she did not want the offender to know how upset she had been by the incident: she felt he had enjoyed the power during the incident and she did not want to give him the satisfaction of knowing how frightened she was.

Only a little over a quarter of *court* victims (27 per cent) said that they had been officially informed about what their offenders were charged with. Of those who had *not* been informed, two-thirds (68 per cent) said they felt they should have been, and many were astonished that this had not happened as a matter of course. A third of all the *violence victims* (32 per cent) were officially informed about what their offenders were charged with, and 24 per cent of all the *property victims*: of those who were *not* so informed, 79 per cent of the violence victims felt they should have been, and 64 per cent of the property victims.

Only 18 per cent of all *court* victims knew what the outcome had been from their offenders going to court: none of them had been officially informed but had found out for themselves. There was a difference between the offence groups: 39 per cent of the *violence victims* knew what the outcome had been, compared with only 9 per cent of the *property victims* (p < .05). Of those who did *not* know, three-quarters of both offence groups said they felt they should have been informed.

By contrast, conferences provide an opportunity for victims to be as closely involved as they wish to be with the disposition of their cases. Their desire to be involved was indicated by the fact that 88 per cent of the victims in this data set whose cases were ultimately dealt with by a conference (see Chapter 4) chose to attend their conferences (across all cases with an identified victim, including those where the victim was not interviewed, the attendance rate was about 80 per cent). Most of those who did not attend were victims of corner-store shoptheft who said they were not interested: in two cases they were visitors who left Canberra before their conferences were held. This high attendance rate was in large part due to the attention the facilitators gave to arranging the conferences at a time and date convenient to the victims and by the amount of time they put into talking to victims, reassuring them about their role and suggesting to them that it could be in their interests to take part. This is in contrast to the much lower victim attendance recorded in restorative justice programmes in Britain (Dignan 1992), New Zealand (Maxwell & Morris 1992), Canada (Clairmont 1994), and South Australia (Wundersitz 1996) (see Chapter 3 for a fuller discussion of these findings).

Victims assigned to a *conference* were asked about the amount of information they were given on what would happen at the conference and what would be expected of them. More than three-quarters (80 per cent) said they had been given 'some' or 'a lot' and only 3 per cent said they had been given no information at all. Somewhat fewer (64 per cent) said that they had been given information on possible outcomes from the conference; this lower figure was partly due to the concern of facilitators not unduly to influence or limit the range of outcome possibilities that participants could arrive at for themselves. They were also asked whether they had been informed in a timely fashion about when the conference was to be held: 79 per cent said they had been, while of the remainder, 3 per cent (two cases) complained about short notice, and one said he had not been informed at all. (The remaining 17 per cent who were not appropriately informed were victims of offenders ultimately dealt with in court or cautioned or not treated at all. Of those victims who actually attended a conference, 87 per cent said they had been informed in a timely way.)

In summary, conferences provided victims with the opportunity to be as closely engaged with the processing and outcome of their cases as they wished. They were consistently much better informed than victims whose cases were dealt with in court, and had an opportunity for direct input in the way the case was dealt with.

5.5 A Participating Role

The absence of any opportunity to participate in their cases was a revelation to many victims whose cases went to court. Nevertheless there were low expectations of the process: when *court victims* who had not attended their cases were asked if they thought they would have got any benefit from going to court only 35 per cent thought they would have done (31 per cent of property victims and 45 per cent of violence victims).

When *conference victims* were asked what were the most important reasons for their decision to attend their conference, their desire for a process in which they could participate and be taken seriously was strongly evident (Figure 5.24).

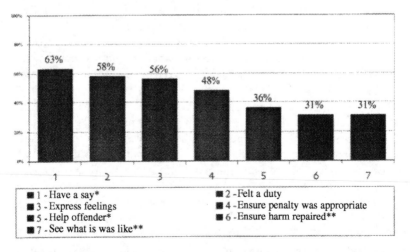

1 - Have a say*
3 - Express feelings
5 - Help offender*
7 - See what is was like**

2 - Felt a duty
4 - Ensure penalty was appropriate
6 - Ensure harm repaired**

Binomial test *p ≤ .05, ** p ≤ .001

FIGURE 5.24. Reasons for Attending Conference—conference victims

Both property and violence victims felt very similarly in their reasons for attending (Table 5.10): for both groups 'having a say' and 'expressing feelings directly to the offender' were major reasons for attending. The victim in JPP026, for example, was a young girl in her first job who was glad to be able to say directly to the boy who stole her purse: 'I'm not any better off than you are—why are you stealing from me?'

The victim in JPP112, whose car was broken into, said: 'Conferences are useful for confronting offenders and for victims to express their anger. The shaming effect can be quite profound. Some fundamental rethinking of the justice system is needed. There is no point in a victim attending court just as an observer—the offender needs to know who the victim is. Offenders need to be confronted with what they've done—the consequences of their stupid, thoughtless act. The shaming of unsocial behaviour has been lost and we need clever, innovative ways to bring it back.'

Many also felt a strong civic duty to take part: the victim in JPP008, for example, said 'I went to the conference because I have a strong sense of social responsibility—if the system can't handle juveniles, then friends, family and neighbourhood should do so.' The victim in JPP032 said that she 'felt a responsibility to attend—I can't complain about the justice system if I don't do my part'.

The victim in JPP081 explained how pleased she was at this opportunity to participate meaningfully: 'At the conference I was

TABLE 5.10   Quite/Very Important Reasons to Attend a Conference, Property and Violence Victims

	Property (n = 45)		Violence (n = 36)	
	(n)	%	(n)	%
Attended to have a say in how the problem was resolved	(28)	62	(23)	64
Attended because felt they had a duty to attend	(28)	62	(19)	53
Attended to express feelings and speak directly to offender	(29)	64	(16)	44
Attended to ensure that the penalty was appropriate	(23)	51	(16)	44
Attended to help the offender	(22)	49	(7)	19
Attended to ensure repayment	(11)	24	(14)	39
Attended because curious to see how conferencing works	(17)	38	(9)	25

amazed how much power I had. When the facilitator turned to me and said "Well, what do you think should happen now?" I was astonished . . . it was wonderful.' (The outcome in this case was that the offender spent twenty hours doing voluntary work at the RSPCA).

The importance of 'wanting to express feelings and speak directly to the offender' was well expressed by the victim of the drive-by incident in JVC055, who said: 'I had to see him. I had to look in his face and I needed to know why—why he shot me.' When the victim of a burglary in JPP081 was asked what she wanted out of the conference she expressed her wish to help the offender, and added with a smile 'and to make him feel as bad as possible to make sure he never does it again'. But then she said: 'I don't feel he should be punished but he should do something for others: it's a helping hand he needs more than a stick.' When the offender's mother thanked her for participating she responded: 'It's a pleasure if he gets something out of it', then added to the offender: 'Come and visit us sometime, but next time come through the front door.'

Although one of the victims in JPP099 (a series of letterbox vandalisms) did not have an opportunity to meet her offenders because the case was dealt with in court, at interview she spontaneously said that she felt the best way of dealing with them would have been 'to give them a chance to see face to face the people they've affected. . . . When I was a kid, the feeling of being embarrassed and ashamed was a lot more effective than a smack on the bum.' (She added that she had been surprised that when she had her property returned by the police, the names of the offenders were on a label still attached to it. She immediately looked up the names in the telephone book, found that they lived nearby, and that she knew the mothers of two of them. She said she felt guilty about doing this, but relieved that she had been able to find out that the offenders were 'just local kids', rather than anything more sinister.) Likewise, in another court-treated case, JVC030, which involved an assault on a 10-year-old child by an older girl on the school bus, the victim's mother expressed an intuitive wish for reconciliation as the most appropriate way of dealing with the incident: she had suggested to the police that she might invite the offender to her house 'so that we can talk it out and [the victim] can explain her point of view'. The police discouraged her from this course of action and she was very disappointed that she could not do something to reconcile these children.

Several commentators on restorative justice have expressed concern about the inhibiting character of the conferencing forum from the victim's point of view. For example, Brown (1994) suggested that such programmes serve to suppress victims' feelings of outrage and loss 'by assuming that these negative feelings can be expressed and resolved in the course of a few hours spent meeting with the offender' (p. 1250). She also comments that 'in these types of confrontations the victim often has difficulty expressing anger . . . victims must speak and act for themselves and the directness of their contact with offenders may actually inhibit them' (p. 1276). The mother of the victim in JVC051 felt this way. She said that she and the victim's supporters were not equipped to deal with the situation (a poorly constituted conference in which the offender, who had assaulted the victim, was accompanied only by the five friends who had been with him when the incident occurred and who endorsed his actions) and lacked the experience and background to feel confident and able to contribute properly. She said: 'Courts are better because the lawyer can speak for you.' Facing the offender and his supporters she felt intimidated and unable to express what she felt: 'In court the lawyer would have been able to say "you're lying", but if I'd said that in the conference they would have just thought I was a bitch.' (Of course, because the offender admitted the offence the court would not have provided the opportunity for such an interchange.)

However, the data indicate that such views were not often held and that conferences more often provided victims with the chance to have their opinions taken seriously. Ninety-three per cent of *conference victims* agreed that they had had an opportunity to explain the loss and harm that resulted from the offence and 88 per cent felt they had been able to express their views. A further 92 per cent said that all sides got a fair chance to bring out the facts at the conference and only 11 per cent said that they had been too intimidated to say what they really felt. There was no significant difference between the property and violence conference victims on any of these measures.

As far as the outcome was concerned, 85 per cent of victims said they believed that the conference took account of what they said in deciding what should be done. However, there was a difference here between property and violence victims: 93 per cent of *property victims* agreed with this compared with 76 per cent of *violence victims* (p < .05). Similarly, while 74 per cent of *all victims* agreed that the conference had taken adequate account of the effects of the offence on them in arriving at the outcome, differences appeared between the offence groups: 84 per cent of *property victims* agreed, compared with only 62 per cent of *violence victims* (p < .05). The victim in JPP116, a shop assistant, expressed her satisfaction about being able to participate and express her views. She said: 'I'm so glad the conference gave me a chance to explain that when people steal clothes I have to pay for it and I could lose my job too.' Likewise, the victim in JPP092 said: 'This is the fifth time my house had been broken into . . . I know nothing happens to these kids in court and they learn nothing. The conference gave me a chance to tell them what I wanted to say.' On a more conciliatory note, the victim in JPP125, which involved a burglary of his house by two young offenders, said: 'The conference was a great opportunity not only to show the offenders the consequences of what they did, but also for so many people to show that they cared.'

In summary, the great majority of conference victims believed that conferences provided them with the opportunity to participate in the processing of their cases and have their views taken into account. By contrast, court victims had no role unless they were present as witnesses (or, in two cases, as offenders also).

5.6   Fair and Respectful Treatment

Chapter 1 reviewed research by Tyler (1988) showing that control over process is more important than control over the outcome when citizens assess the fairness of legal procedures. He found that assessments in judgements of fairness were composed of several elements: the authorities' motivation, honesty, ethicality and bias, opportunities for representation, opportunities for error correction, and the quality of the decisions. Tyler further observed that:

the major criteria used to assess process fairness are those aspects of procedure least linked to outcomes—ethicality, honesty and the effort to be fair—rather than consistency with other outcomes. (p. 128)

In later research, Tyler (1990) found that:

people do not focus directly on the favorability of the outcomes they receive from third parties. Instead, they focus directly on the degree to which they are able to exert influence over third-party decisions . . . where people feel they have control over decisions they believe that the procedure is fair; where they feel they lack control they believe it is unfair. (pp. 6–7)

In summary, Tyler argues that perceptions of fairness and justice in procedures consist of the following elements:

- confidence in the impartiality of the process;
- confidence in the ethicality of the process;
- confidence in lack of bias in the process;
- a belief that any errors that occurred in the process could be corrected;
- a sense of control over the process.

Conference victims only were asked about the facets of procedural justice set out in Table 5.11. Their responses indicate a strong perception of fairness by these victims, and there was no significant difference between property and violence victims on any of these dimensions. The great majority of all conference victims (81 per cent) also agreed that they had been treated with respect during the conference, and, again, there was no significant difference between property and violence victims.

Some feminist writers have expressed concerns about disadvantage that women victims may suffer in restorative justice settings. Most of these relate to issues expected to arise in domestic violence cases and are focused on mediation; for example Stubbs (1995) observed that '[f]eminist critiques of mediation have drawn attention to the dangers of assuming that a woman who has been the target of violence is able to assert her own needs and promote her own interests in the presence of the person who has perpetrated that violence. . . . Requiring women to participate may be disempowering and punitive for them' (p. 281).

Domestic violence cases were ineligible for inclusion in RISE (see Chapter 4), so it is not possible to comment here on these critiques. However, Table 5.11 reveals that there was no difference between men and women, including victims of violent offences, on questions relating to perceptions of procedural justice. It appears that, at least in relation to non-domestic assaults, women do feel able to assert and express themselves in the presence of their male offenders.

There have also been concerns raised about equality of participation by men and women in restorative justice settings. Astor

TABLE 5.11   Perceived Procedural Justice: Percentage of Male and Female Conference Victims who Agree/Strongly Agree

	Male*		Female **	
	(n)	%	(n)	%
Impartiality:				
The police were fair during the conference	(40)	89	(35)	95
All sides got a fair chance to bring out facts	(41)	91	(34)	92
The conference was fair for me	(38)	86	(34)	92
The conference was fair for the offender	(42)	98	(37)	100
Ethicality:				
Felt the conference respected my rights	(37)	84	(34)	87
Lack of bias:				
Felt disadvantage in the conference by age, income, sex, race or some other reason (% disagree/strongly disagree)	(37)	82	(35)	95
Correctability:				
If conference got the facts wrong, felt able to get this corrected	(32)	71	(33)	89
If treated unjustly by conference or police, believe I could have got complaint heard	(36)	78	(31)	84
Control:				
I felt I had enough control over the way things were run in the conference	(31)	67	(26)	71
I undersood what was going on	(41)	89	(33)	89
I felt pushed into things I did not agree with (% disagree/strongly disagree)	(38)	88	(29)	85
I felt pushed aroundby people with more power (% disagree/strongly disagree)	(38)	88	(29)	85

  * n of male respondents to these questions varied from 43 to 45.
 ** n of female respondents to these questions varied from 34 to 37.

(1994) stated that '[w]hat mediators perceive to be an equal hearing is inevitably affected by their values. We know for instance that the way we judge equal participation is strongly affected by gender, that our reactions to the expression of emotions such as anger or assertiveness differs according to whether it is expressed by a man or a woman' (p. 153). The data in Table 5.11 indicate that, even if Astor is right, women victims themselves do not believe that they have been disadvantaged in terms of equal participation with their offenders: there was no significant difference between men and women victims on feeling 'disadvantaged at the conference by age, income, sex, race or some other reason'.

For victims whose cases were dealt with in *court*, little quantitative information was available about their experience of fairness and respect. They were effectively excluded from any part of the processing of their cases. Some victims were indifferent to this; others were dismayed and interpreted their exclusion as unfair and unjust.

In summary, victims who experienced a conference said they were treated fairly and with respect. Predictions that women would feel disempowered or intimidated appear to be unfounded.

5.7 Summary

On the indicators identified through the literature in Chapter 1 as the principal areas of shortcoming in formal justice, the victims who participated in conferences usually found the experience a better one than did victims whose cases were dealt with in court. Specifically:

* in terms of material restoration, neither court nor conference provided a great deal financially, but conference victims received other kinds of restitution such as work from the offenders, more often than court victims. Court victims felt that financial restitution was a more important consideration than conference victims did, but neither group received as much as they said they wanted. It may be the case that sometimes in the conference setting victims do not feel powerful enough to ask for what they really want and more attention needs to be paid to this by facilitators (see Chapter 6);
* in terms of emotional restoration, big differences emerged between conference victims and court victims regarding fear of revictimization: it is clear that the opportunity to see and talk to their offenders was immensely reassuring for the majority of conference victims. The before/after measures for conference victims on sympathy, anger, anxiety, trust, and fear were very positive (though no comparable data were available for court victims), and it appears that the conference is especially beneficial for violence victims in reducing fear of their offenders;
* whereas around 90 per cent of both court and conference victims believed they should have received an apology, almost four times as many of the conference victims as court victims had in fact received one;

- one of the biggest differences between court victims and conference victims concerned their unresolved anger towards their offenders. Overall, 20 per cent of court victims said they would harm their offenders if they had the chance, compared with only 7 per cent of the conference victims. This difference was especially stark for the violence victims: nearly half (45 per cent) of those whose cases went to court would harm their offenders, compared with only 9 per cent of those who went to a conference (see Chapter 6);
- conference victims were much more satisfied than court victims about the amount of information they were able to get about both the processing and outcome of their cases;
- conferences were usually very successful in delivering the opportunity for victims to participate and have their views taken into account (but tended to be more successful for property victims than violence victims);
- conference victims were very satisfied about the fair and respectful treatment they received (though property victims tended to be more satisfied than violence victims).

The next chapter looks specifically at what victims say about their satisfaction with court and conference.

6

Victim Satisfaction with the Restorative Justice Alternative

6.1 Introduction

Chapter 5 showed that victims whose cases were assigned to the restorative alternative of conferencing consistently expressed relatively high levels of approval about most aspects of their experience. On many of these aspects we do not have comparable data for victims whose cases were dealt with in court: so few of them actually attended their court cases that it was not possible to gather enough information to compare their experience meaningfully with that of the conference victims. This does not necessarily mean that court victims were unhappy with the way their cases were dealt with. Indeed, some victims, especially small-shop proprietors and managers who are repeatedly victimized, were pleased to have as little to do with their cases as the court provided.

This chapter looks at both comparative levels of satisfaction between court and conference victims, and absolute levels of satisfaction expressed by conference victims. (Where comparisons are made, as before statistically significant differences at an alpha level of at least 0.05 are noted throughout; the figures also indicate effect size wherever possible.) We find that these victims do not appear as happy with their experience as victims who have taken part in some other studies (see, for example, Umbreit 1994; Hayes et al. 1998; Goodes 1995; Trimboli 2000). In Chapter 4 we discussed why a randomized controlled trial comparing court with conference was desirable in order to discount systematic biases which may be at work in some of these restorative justice studies and which may have eliminated some of the victims likely to be dissatisfied with the process. Chapter 4 also explained why the decision was taken to analyse the data on the basis of assignment, rather than on the basis of actual treatment delivered. In brief, failing to analyse the data on the basis of assignment would result in a loss of initial equivalence between the groups and a consequent weakening of causal inference about differences emerging between them (Peto 1976). Moreover, it misleads with respect to the real policy choice, which is to *attempt* to organize a conference versus a court case.

One of the consequences of this decision was to include in the 'conference' data twenty-seven victims (23 per cent) whose cases were *assigned* to conference but who never experienced conference: that is, victims who were told that their cases would be dealt with this way and who were often disappointed when their expectations were not met. These victims turned out to be some of the most unhappy in the entire data set: of the twenty-nine conference-assigned victims who said they felt dissatisfied with the way their cases were dealt with, eleven of them were not in fact treated by conference: either their cases went to court or the offenders were cautioned or not dealt with at all.

Analysing the data on the basis of assigned rather than delivered treatment thus allows us to include the views of conference-assigned victims 'discarded' along the way, that is victims whose cases were ultimately dealt with in court (thirteen cases), by caution (three cases), or not treated at all (three cases). As discussed in Chapter 4, the reasons for failure to treat as assigned were various, but almost always related to the offender: either the offender withdrew his/her full admissions, or something was discovered subsequent to assignment that rendered the case ineligible for a conference (for example, an outstanding warrant or bond), or the offender could not be located, or s/he failed to attend the conference, or an outcome could not be agreed. The views of these victims are important too: the restorative process has failed them and they deserve to be counted. However, they are inevitably excluded from any study which reports only on the views of victims who have *experienced* a conference.

This chapter will first of all review all the data concerning satisfaction felt by victims in both the court and conference groups. Next, it examines data concerning dissatisfaction in each group. Finally, it looks at some good conference experiences, then, in greater detail, some bad conference experiences. For the latter, seven conference cases are reviewed: all of them were highly unsatisfactory for victims in different ways. As Tolstoy might have said, all good conferences are alike, but a bad conference is bad after its own fashion. There is much to be learnt from the variety of ways in which conferences can fail victims. However, it is vital to bear in mind that these seven cases are to some extent outliers in the data set: they are seven of only twenty-nine cases where conference-assigned victims were not satisfied, and of these a further eleven were not actually dealt with by a conference.

6.2   Satisfaction: Court vs Conference

All victims were asked whether: 'you are satisfied with the way your case was dealt with by the justice system.' There was a significant difference between the groups on this question: 46 per cent of the court-assigned victims vs 60 per cent of the conference-assigned victims were satisfied (p < 0.05) (Figure 6.1). Significantly more of those who actually *experienced* a conference were satisfied, compared with those whose cases were dealt with in court (70 per cent vs 42 per cent, p < 0.001): there was no difference between property and violence victims here.

As a further indicator of overall treatment satisfaction, all victims were asked whether they were pleased that their cases were dealt with in the way they were (whether by court or by conference), rather than by the alternative treatment. This was a more

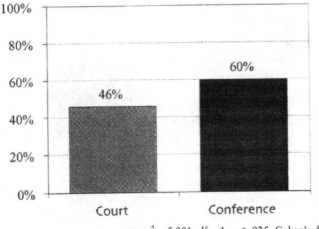

$\chi^2 = 5.001$, df = 1, p ≤ .025; Cohen's d = .327

FIGURE 6.1. Satisfied with the Way Case was Dealt With—all victims

difficult question for the court victims to answer than for the conference victims: most people have an idea about what it would be like to have their cases dealt with in court (even if it is a mistaken idea, given the surprise many court victims felt about their lack of role in the process), whereas only about half of the court victims had actually heard of conferencing. They were asked to form a comparative idea based on a brief description of conferencing given at the interview. Significantly more conference victims than court victims agreed that they were pleased their cases were treated the way they were, rather than by the alternative treatment (69 per cent vs 48 per cent, p < 0.005: Figure 6.2).

When *violence victims* were asked whether they were pleased their cases were dealt with the way they were (rather than the alternative) 66 per cent of conference victims were satisfied compared with 58 per cent of court victims. For the *property victims*, 70 per cent of the conference victims said they were pleased, compared with 43 per cent of the court victims (p = 0.005) (Table 6.1).

Conference victims only were asked whether: 'the government should use conferencing as an alternative to court more often.' Seventy per cent said that it should be used more often while 10 per cent disagreed: there was little difference between violence and property victims. Both satisfied and dissatisfied victims sometimes

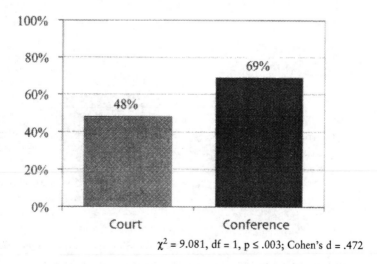

$\chi^2 = 9.081$, df = 1, p ≤ .003; Cohen's d = .472

FIGURE 6.2. Pleased with the Way Case was Dealt With—all victims

TABLE 6.1 Satisfaction with Treatment, Property and Violence Victims

	Court (n)	%	Conference (n)	%
'The government should use conferencing as an alternative to court more often' (conference victims only)				
Property victims (n = 43)	–	–	(30)	70
Violence victims (n = 34)	–	–	(23)	68
'If you were the victim of a young person's offending again, you would attend a conference again' (conference victims only)				
Property victims (n = 45)	–	–	(35)	78
Violence victims (n = 36)	–	–	(25)	69
'If you were the victim of a young person's offending again, you would NOT attend a conference again' (conference victims only)				
Property victims (n = 45)	–	–	(5)	11
Violence victims (n = 36)	–	–	(6)	17
Satisfied with outcome immediately post-conference (conference victims only)				
Property victims (n = 45)	–	–	(37)	82
Violence victims (n = 36)	–	–	(19)	53
(If yes) % still satisfied with outcome at interview				
Property victims (n = 37)	–	–	(31)	84
Violence victims (n = 19)	–	–	(19)	100
Satisfied with the way the case was dealt with (all victims)				
Property victims (n = 151)	(37)	46	(43)	61
Violence victims (n = 81)	(16)	44	(27)	60
Pleased that my case was dealt with in the way it was (rather than by the alternative treatment) (all victims)				
Property victims (n = 134)	(30)	43*	(46)	70*
Violence victims (n = 77)	(21)	58	(27)	66

* p = 0.005

agreed with this question. The conference victim in JPP002 was most
unhappy with his experience: he had not been given enough information about the process by the police, the whole onus of the
outcome had been placed on him, and the facilitator was an older
man whose body language said that he did not want to be there. In
spite of this he said: 'This is a good programme, worth a try, even
though I question its value for people with a criminal history.' He
also queried the value of a facilitator who apparently did not support
the programme. On the other hand, the victim in JPP049 was very
happy with her conference: she said it was well organized and went

smoothly and that 'it felt like a serious event'. She also commented that she believed conferences were more suitable than court for recidivist offenders so that more attention could be paid to their family circumstances and the reasons for committing the offence.

A moderately high degree of satisfaction was indicated by the percentage of all conference victims—74 per cent—who said that they would 'probably' or 'definitely' attend a conference again if they were the victim of a young person's offending again, while only 5 per cent said they would 'definitely not' attend.

Table 6.1 reveals that over three-quarters of *property victims* (82 per cent) were satisfied with the outcome immediately after the conference and, 84 per cent of these were still satisfied at the time of the interview six weeks later. Over half of *violence victims* (53 per cent) were satisfied immediately after the conference, and 100 per cent of them remained satisfied at interview six weeks later. This apparent reversal in satisfaction levels over time may have been related to the nature of the offences and the characteristics of victims and offenders in the two offence categories. Typically, victims of property offences were middle class and middle aged while their offenders tended to be young and poor (see Chapter 4). The outcome agreement entailed undertakings made by the offender that were sometimes not complied with, and the drop in satisfaction levels some weeks after the conference usually reflected failure in compliance. By contrast, victims and offenders in violent cases had much more in common with each other in terms of age and background (see Chapter 4). The offences were usually intensely personal, and it was more difficult to reach an outcome agreement that was truly satisfactory to the victim: however, once that had been arrived at, there seemed to be less difficulty in achieving compliance and hence ultimately a higher satisfaction level. Findings by Pruitt *et al.* (1992) may be relevant here: that the best predictors of long-term success in mediation are joint problem solving by the parties during the discussion and the parties' perceptions that fair procedures were used.

6.3   Dissatisfaction: Court vs Conference

When *all victims* were asked whether 'the way your case was dealt with made you feel angry', 18 per cent of the conference-assigned said they felt angry, compared with 32 per cent of the court-assigned (Figure 6.3).

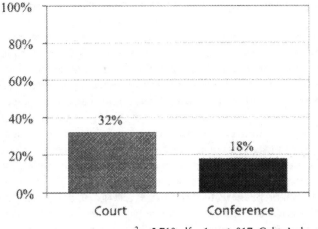

$\chi^2 = 5.710$, df = 1, p ≤ .017; Cohen's d = .408

FIGURE 6.3. The Way Case was Dealt With Made You Feel Angry—all victims

When *all victims* were asked whether 'you feel bitter about the way you were treated in the case'. A similar percentage of both the conference victims and court victims said they did (Figure 6.4), but

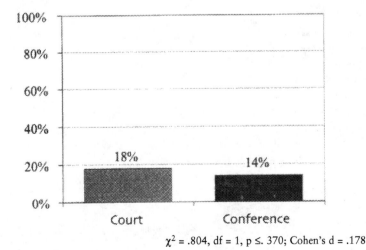

$\chi^2 = .804$, df = 1, p ≤. 370; Cohen's d = .178

FIGURE 6.4. You Feel Bitter about the Way You were Treated—all victims

violence victims agreed more often than *property victims* (Table 6.2).

Perhaps the ultimate indicator of dissatisfaction with the way the case was dealt with by the justice system is when victims are so unhappy that they wish to take the law into their own hands. To explore this, *all victims* were asked whether 'you would do some harm to your offender yourself if you had the chance'. Overall, 20 per cent of the court victims but only 7 per cent of the conference victims said that they would (p < 0.005) (Figure 6.5), suggesting that the conference setting and the opportunity it provides to gain an understanding of the offender and his or her circumstances significantly reduces the desire for revenge.

As might be expected, there are very great differences between the *violence victims* and *property victims* in their response to this question. Around 7 per cent of both the court and conference property victims agreed. For the violence victims the response was dramatic: fully 45 per cent of the court victims said they would do some harm to their offenders if they had the chance, compared with only 9 per cent of the conference victims (p < 0.01) (Table 6.2).

About a quarter of all victims said they were not satisfied (27

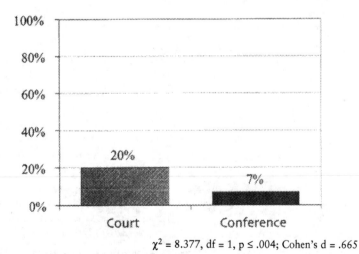

$\chi^2 = 8.377$, df = 1, p ≤ .004; Cohen's d = .665

FIGURE 6.5. You Would Harm the Offender if You had the Chance—all victims

TABLE 6.2   Dissatisfaction with Treatment, Property and Violence
Victims

	Court (n)	%	Conference (n)	%
The way my case was dealt with made me angry				
Property victims (n = 152)	(23)	29	(10)	14
Violence victims (n = 80)	(14)	39	(11)	24
'I feel bitter about the way I was treated'				
Property victims (n = 152)	(10)	13	(6)	9
Violence victims (n = 81)	(11)	31*	(10)	22*
'I would do some harm to my offender if I had the chance'				
Property victims (n = 152)	(7)	9	(4)	6
Violence victims (n = 81)	(16)	45**	(4)	9**
Dissatisfied with way case dealt with				
Property victims (n = 152)	(17)	21	(14)	20
Violence victims (n = 81)	(14)	39	(15)	33

* p < 0.005
** p < 0.01

per cent of the court-assigned and 25 per cent of the conference-assigned). *Violence victims* tended to be more dissatisfied than *property victims* both in court and in conference (Table 6.2).

6.4   Good and Bad Experiences

To illustrate the ways in which conferences can succeed and fail for victims, it is useful to look at some 'good' and 'bad' events, as measured by the reactions of the victims who experienced them.

Victims who were happy with their conferences described enthusiastically what it was about it that they liked.

The victim in JVC008 was an 8-year-old boy who had been knocked unconscious by the 14-year-old offender (the son of neighbours) on his way home from school. His parents were outraged by the assault which required an ambulance and hospital treatment, and were further upset about the matter being dealt with by a conference, which they anticipated would be a 'soft option'. At interview the mother said that the conference 'was very fair to everybody. As a result of the conference we've now become friends with Sam's [the offender's] parents. Sam had to come and do some gardening for us to make up for what he did. Barry [the victim] got very friendly with him and used to go out and help him with the work. . . . We are very pleased the case went to a conference because Barry could see what happened and that made him feel better. . . . He would never have known that Sam had to pay for what he did if it had gone to court.'

The victim in JVC003 (Jane) was a librarian in a public library where a number of young offenders had set a small fire. She said that some months after the conference a woman came into the library and put out her hand to touch her saying 'Do you remember me?' Jane did not know who she was at first but then realized she was the mother of one of the offenders. She told Jane how glad she was that her son had gone to a conference instead of court and that everything was all right. Jane said she was delighted that the woman had made contact, that it made her feel good that she had wanted to do so, and that it showed how worthwhile the conference had been.

The victim in JPP100 managed a sportsground where the offender had broken some windows and otherwise vandalized the facilities. She said that at the conference the offender had been sullen and uncommunicative at first but became more engaged as the conference proceeded. The outcome entailed his working at the sportsground on Saturday mornings. He had been complying with this undertaking and the victim was very pleased because she felt the offender was giving something back directly to the community for the damage he had caused.

However, throughout the data analysis it has been apparent that there are a minority of cases where the victims whose cases were assigned to conference have been extremely dissatisfied with their experiences. In order to identify the worst of these, so that we can see what we can learn from them, four key questions which are broadly measures of satisfaction have been selected, and all conference-assigned cases identified in which the victim responded with a score of less than three on a five-point 'strongly disagree . . . strongly agree' scale for at least three of the four questions (many victims whose cases were assigned to court also felt dissatisfied, but this analysis is restricted to the conference-assigned). The questions are:

- You are satisfied with the way your case was dealt with by the justice system;
- You are pleased your case was dealt with by conference rather than by court;

- If you were the victim of a young person's offending again, you would choose to attend a conference again;
- Immediately after the conference you were pleased with the outcome.

There are seven of these cases, two involving property victims and five involving violence victims. One of the violence cases (JVC011) was eventually dealt with in court when the offender withdrew his admissions prior to the conference; another (JVC020) was abandoned and no treatment eventuated when the offender withdrew his admissions during the conference.

- JPP032—*The missing letters of apology*
  This case involved the theft of wallets from three victims while they were exercizing at a gym one lunchtime. The offenders were cousins aged 12 and 9 who lived with their grandmother and who already were well known to the police for similar offences. None of the stolen cash was recovered. The conference agreement entailed the offenders writing a letter of apology to each victim, observing a 6 p.m. curfew for three months, cleaning up their grandmother's yard, 'especially the dog's poo', and 'doing what Nanna says for three months'.

  It is not known whether the boys complied with the outcomes relating to their grandmother, though the interviewer noted one month after the conference that they were 'finding the curfew a trial', so presumably the grandmother was enforcing it at that stage. It is known that they never wrote the letters of apology. Two of the three victims seemed philosophical about this, though they noted that they knew of no follow-up by the police, and they believed there should have been some effort to get the boys to comply. One of them commented that the gulf between her world and that of the offenders was so great that she could not say what would have been a more appropriate penalty, or one that they would more likely have complied with. However, the third victim was seriously dissatisfied with the conference, and especially with the failure of the police to follow up on the written apologies. He said he felt a lot less trusting in others as a result of the offence, and believed the outcome ought to have been more severe. When he was asked whether there had been any consequences of the conference which made him now regret taking part he replied: '[t]he fact that I haven't received the letter of apology and that I wasn't aware that non-first time offenders could take part in a conference rather than go to court.'

- JPP042—*From disengagement and pessimism to restoration and optimism*

  The victim in this case was the managing director of a retail business with a number of shops around Canberra. The offender was a 14-year-old boy who had thrown rocks at an illuminated business sign outside one of the shops when he was drunk and caused damage of over $3,000. Insurance covered all but $250 of this damage. The offender had scarcely participated at all in the conference and the victim felt frustrated at his lack of engagement. He was pessimistic about his complying with the outcome, which entailed payment to him of the $250 insurance excess and a written apology. He had been astonished to receive both the money and the apology and commented that if the case had been dealt with in court he would not have received either of them.

- JVC011—*Not guilty?*

  This case involved an assault in licensed premises late at night by a 23-year-old offender on the 22-year-old victim. The victim claimed it was an unprovoked attack resulting in his nose being broken, shortly after he had undergone reconstructive nose surgery. According to police records, the offender was removed by security staff and taken to the police station where he made full admissions about his responsibility for the offence, though he claimed that the victim had advanced on him in a threatening manner. The case was assigned to a conference and two attempts were made to hold a conference. On the first occasion the offender was absent; on the second occasion the offender would not clearly accept his responsibility for the incident and claimed it was self-defence. He was advised that the conference could not proceed unless he made full admissions; the offender said that he was willing to 'say whatever' to avoid court but at this point the victim said his preference was for the case to go to court. Given the lack of full admissions, it was decided to send the matter to court. The case was dealt with eighteen months later and the offender pleaded not guilty. The victim was called as a witness in court and freely admitted he had been drunk at the time of the incident. The case was dismissed on the grounds of self-defence.

The victim was incredulous at the court outcome and extremely unhappy about it. He said that he still had serious medical problems resulting from the assault, and that he had lost his job over the incident and his injuries. He said he never went out socially any more because he had lost all confidence, trust, and self-esteem, that he still felt very embarrassed over the incident, and was angry and afraid of the offender.

- JVC012—*Nagging suffering and nagging retribution*
Three friends were all in a nightclub when one of them was punched in the head by the offender. His friend, Janet, intervened and was punched in the head and had her finger broken as well. Then her brother intervened too and was also punched. The offender was apprehended by police and admitted the assaults. The case was assigned to a conference. The apprehending officer contacted the police gay liaison officer, who agreed to conduct the conference because all parties were members of the gay community. The outcome of the conference was that the offender would perform forty hours of voluntary work for the AIDS Council and make a $400 donation to AIDS research. The police report states: 'All participants very satisfied with conference and results.'

Two of the three victims did indeed express high levels of satisfaction with the conference process. They felt it had been fair to all parties, that the apology the offender had offered at the conference was sincere, that they were happy with the outcome agreement, and that they felt they could put the whole thing behind them. Janet felt very differently, however. On the positive side, at her interview four weeks after the conference she said that the conference had 'helped a little' in overcoming all the fears, loss of confidence, and increased distrust she felt as a result of the incident, that the apology had been 'somewhat sincere', and that the conference had been procedurally fair to her. She even agreed that the conference had taken adequate account of the effects of the offence on her, that her anger toward the offender had diminished after the conference, and her sympathy increased. However, she had been dissatisfied with the outcome and believed that she should have received money from the offender to compensate her for the harm she had experienced.

Janet's injury had been more serious and long-lasting than that inflicted on her brother and friend, but it is difficult to know whether this accounted for her markedly different attitudes. Two years later she believed that the way the case had been dealt with was very unfair to her, and she was very unhappy that the case had been dealt with by a conference rather than in court. She still was experiencing some medical problems with her broken finger, and had received $9,000 in criminal injuries compensation. She said that she felt bereft of confidence and a sense of security as a result of the incident and hardly went out any more. She complained that 'there is no record of the crime committed by this person—they get off too lightly' and indicated that she felt bitter and retributive towards the offender.

What we learn from this case is the sometimes unpredictable way that victims may decide whether or not they were happy about what happened in their conferences. Certainly Janet's injury was more severe than her companions', but this does not necessarily explain her very different attitude and the fact that she seemed to feel worse about it as time went by. She seemed to attribute to the conference unfortunate events which had happened subsequently, whereas her co-victims seemed to have put the offence and the conference behind them.

- JVC020—*Scapegoating, procedural injustice, and the forgotten victim*
  Matthew, the 24-year-old victim in this assault matter, was drinking on licensed premises when a fight broke out involving one of his friends. He said that in the general melee he tried to pull his friend out of the fight, when one of the security staff hit him over the head and ejected him into the car park, where the fighting continued, involving both patrons and security staff. Subsequently Charlie, aged 18 and employed on security at the pub, attended the police station

and made full admissions about having punched Matthew in the face. In the view of the apprehending officer, other staff were directing blame at Charlie and it appeared that he had been offered as the sole offender because he was young with no prior convictions, and likely not to be prosecuted.

The conference was attended by a large number of supporters of both Matthew and Charlie. As soon as it began, Matthew said that Charlie could not have been the person who assaulted him because he did not look anything like that person. Charlie's employer and workmates insisted that it was Charlie who was the assailant (though his family did not appear to believe that he had been involved). There were many claims and counter-claims in the course of the conference flowing from poor police investigation into the incident, including allegations that the victim and his friends had provoked the brawl. It was complicated by poor and untrusting relations between the licensee and the police, who frequently attended incidents at his premises and who believed that the licensee was exploitative and irresponsible towards his patrons. After about an hour of acrimonious discussion, the conference was abandoned as it was apparent that there was no agreement on what had happened and no likelihood of reaching an outcome acceptable to all the parties.

The licensee subsequently made a complaint to the ACT Ombudsman concerning the conduct of the conference. This resulted in an internal police investigation of the facilitator, who ultimately was fully exonerated but who never conducted another conference. It also led to formal 'counselling' of the investigating officer for the sloppiness of his investigation: he had wanted to send the case to court after the conference broke down, but the internal inquiry decided, thirteen months after the original incident, that no further action would be taken in the case.

Matthew was very angry and disappointed at what had happened in this case. His rage at the injustice of having effectively nothing happen following the assault had led to his carrying a knife for several months, and in fact to pull it out when the same friend again got into a fight. He spontaneously said that if he 'ran into' his assailants from the original incident he would probably attack them in revenge for what happened to him. He had been very upset at the way the conference unfolded, although he believed that the police had been fair and that he had had an opportunity to express his views. He wished the case had gone to court because he believed that that way all the co-offenders would have been prosecuted and punished (in fact this could not have happened as only Charlie had been identified as being involved). Two years after the incident he remained extremely angry because he saw the licensee and his security staff as having 'got away' with assaulting him.

- *JVC032—A facilitator who failed a cross-cultural challenge*
  The victim in this incident, James, was 16 at the time of the incident. He had been nominated by his school as a 'bus prefect' to maintain order on the school bus, which carried children of all ages to various schools. His mother said at interview that he had had trouble over a long period with an 11-year-old Asian boy who persistently misbehaved on the bus. One day after telling him off, James pushed him, causing him to fall and bruise his chest. James told one of the teachers at his school about it right away and admitted that he should not have done this. Two days later the child's uncle, aged 24, came looking for James, boarded the school bus, and punched him twice in the face. James went to hospital casualty for his injuries to be attended to: three months later he still could not breathe through one side of his nose and required surgery for a deviated septum. The medical bills were extensive and continuing.

James said that when he and his parents and other supporters arrived at the police station for the conference they felt extremely uncomfortable, as they were required to share the very small foyer area with the offender and his supporters. James and his family were given very little information about what was expected of them. The offender's family and friends spoke little English, and most of what they had to say was conveyed through a bilingual supporter attending with them. The victim's side felt intimidated by not knowing what was being said between the offender's supporters, and at one point James said that he wanted to hear what was being said in English or he would leave the conference. The communication problem was compounded by the very poor facilities at the police station where the conference was held: James's mother said that it was sometimes difficult to hear what was being said owing to the noise from other parts of the station.

The offender felt some degree of justification for his actions because of the assault on his nephew, and several times through the conference said that he wanted James charged and that he was as guilty as he (the offender) had been. The facilitator said that this prior matter was 'ancient history', that James was the victim here, and they were not there to discuss anything other than the assault on James. The discussion meandered fruitlessly for almost three hours until the facilitator called on James to say what he wanted to come out of the conference. James said that he had not expected this and could not think of what would be appropriate. Finally he said he wanted a written apology. (This was complied with: James's mother said that they had received a very nice letter, but she assumed the offender had not written it himself.)

James's mother said that having to say what they wanted was a very difficult thing for them as they had no idea what was appropriate. For example, they did not ask for any financial restitution for medical expenses because they did not know whether this would be acceptable. The family felt very uncomfortable about being placed in this position. They left the conference feeling extremely dissatisfied, especially after James's father had asked the offender how he felt about what had happened, and he replied 'Well I got out of that lightly didn't I'.

After the conference the parents talked at some length to the facilitator about what had happened. The facilitator told them that he did not agree with conferencing, 'so don't blame me'; he also said that it was not the fault of the police that the offender had been dealt with by a conference, but rather the fault of the government for introducing the programme. James's mother reiterated several times at interview that she did not blame the facilitator or the police generally for what had happened—in fact she felt that the facilitator had been 'very good'. The facilitator also told the parents that they were lucky James had not been more seriously hurt as Vietnamese youths commonly carry knives (this offender was Cambodian). James's mother is now thoroughly upset and suspicious about 'all Asians', and his father plans to write to 'somebody' and complain about what happened. The parents have a high level of regard and trust for the police and James's mother said she was grateful for the advice about staying away from Asians.

As a coda, James's mother remarked at the end of the interview that she realized that 'you can view the police differently when you're on the other side'. Their 11-year-old son had recently been involved in a car accident: he had caused it by careless bicycle riding, and in avoiding him the driver had written off her car. The police had spoken to them several times about what had happened and their son's culpability in the accident. Finally, they had told them that he would not be charged. She said she was very upset that the police could even consider charging an 11-year-old for this, but she spontaneously commented that the school bus incident had probably looked very different from her son's offender's point of view. A skilled facilitator could probably have used these feelings as the basis for building a bridge of understanding between James's family and his assailant, instead of leaving them more divided and antipathetic than they had been at the outset.

- JVC057—*A tiny crime with massive victimization unacknowledged*
  Dianne was a store detective for a large retailer. She noticed Alice, the 16-year-old offender, take some goods and leave the store without paying for them. She approached Alice and asked her to return to the store with the stolen goods; Alice swore at her and turned away. Dianne took her by the wrist, and a brief struggle ensued in which Dianne was very slightly injured. In the month preceding this incident she had been assaulted on two other occasions when apprehending shoplifters. A month after the present incident she had 'made a mistake' regarding the apprehension of a store customer which she attributed to the assaults she had experienced immediately beforehand. She recognized her culpability in this 'mistake' and was extremely anxious about it, to the

extent that she failed to appear for a disciplinary meeting with her employer and was dismissed from her job. She had been undergoing psychological counselling since that time and had been told that she should not work. As a result of the incidents she scarcely left her house for several months, though she decided ultimately that both for financial and health reasons she needed to work and had found another job just prior to her interview.

Dianne says she did not wish to take part in the conference but said she was 'hounded' by the police until she agreed. But most of all she was unhappy with the way the conference was conducted because she felt Alice was not obliged to confront her behaviour or take responsibility for it. Soon after the conference began Alice had become extremely upset and left the room, saying she was not prepared to continue. She agreed to stay after discussion with the facilitator and one of her supporters outside the room. Dianne felt that thereafter she was treated 'with kid gloves, as if she was a little girl not a 16-year-old who should take responsibility for what she had done'.

Dianne felt that throughout the conference all the attention was on Alice and almost none given to what she had suffered. She said that she did not especially want anything from Alice other than a genuine expression of remorse. This had been her main reason for attending, but she felt she was worse off after the conference than before it because she had had to talk about the incident all over again and got nothing out of it. She was particularly upset that after being 'hounded' to take part she was not aware of any follow-up by the police regarding the outcome (which entailed undertakings for Alice to live at home for certain periods each week). All Dianne knew was that nothing had come of the invitation she had made to Alice to ring if she wanted to meet for coffee and say she was really sorry. However, she was very familiar with the shortcomings of the court route and did not believe there would have been any better outcome, either for the offender or herself, if the case had gone to court.

Dianne had been seriously traumatized by a series of prior incidents and she readily admitted that she did not blame all her health problems on this particular matter. At no time did Dianne indicate that she sought any material restitution from the offender. However, she attached a great deal of significance to the idea of a sincere apology; she saw that because the offender was so engulfed by her supporters there was no possibility of the offender apologizing to her in that setting, but she was extremely disappointed that she did not take up her offer to meet her privately.

6.5 Lessons From Failed Conferences

There are several lessons we can learn from these cases in terms of improving aspects of the process and the outcome from the victim's perspective:

- *Poor investigative police work*, especially concerning the question of offenders' accepting responsibility for the offence, will always have dire consequences in the conference when attention is turned to the minutiae of what really happened. This problem was very evident in JVC011 and in JVC020. Some of these problems would be alleviated by having a different threshold of responsibility for the offence from the present requirement of 'full admissions': for example, in JVC011, while the offender refused to take the complete blame for the assault, he possibly would have 'declined to deny' responsibility. This is the standard required in New Zealand, where it is written into the legislation and appears to circumvent some of the difficulties surrounding a requirement for full admissions.
- *Insufficient preparation of victims* (and of offenders) regarding their role in the conference, their expectations about the outcome, and their rights in terms of requesting reparation can all have serious negative consequences for victims. It is plain that a face-to-face meeting with their offenders has the potential to be traumatic rather than restorative for victims. Victims need to feel confident about their participation in the process, they need to have given thought to what they want to come out of it and to feel confident about the legitimacy of their pursuing that outcome. This preparation also entails emphasizing to victims the need to bring supporters with

them. The isolation and vulnerability felt by the victim in JVC057 was compounded by the fact that she brought only her husband with her, who contributed very little to the discussion, whereas the offender was accompanied by eight voluble supporters. This case also illustrates the risk of revictimization for victims in the conference setting: the offender was shielded by her supporters from bearing responsibility for what had occurred and the facilitator gave far too little attention to the victim's point of view. It is also vital that victims are given realistic expectations about what can be achieved with a restorative process: over-optimistic assessments of likely outcomes can lead to disappointment and feelings of being let down if those expectations are not met (see Reeves & Mulley 2000; Erez 2000).

- *Poor conference organization* can also have devastating consequences for victims. Obliging victim parties and offender parties to share the same limited space prior to the conference is patently unacceptable, and requires only a moderate degree of forethought to avoid. If both must use the same reception area, then one party or the other can be asked to arrive in advance of the other and be taken to the conference room. This is absolutely essential, as victims can otherwise begin the process seriously intimidated by the offender party in the absence of any mediating authority. Likewise, poor facilities with lack of privacy, interruptions, and noise all contribute to a negative atmosphere in which to hold a conference. Attention should also be given to the issue of interpreting services when not all participants speak fluent English: in JVC032, communication difficulties contributed to feelings of distrust and suspicion between the participants.

- *Inadequate training of facilitators* can have serious consequences in numerous ways. The facilitator in JVC032 had personal prejudices inappropriate for a police officer in any role, but in addition was poorly trained and ill-disposed towards the programme. His comments after the conference was over left the members of the victim party more anxious and angry than they had felt at the beginning. Facilitators should be trained to ensure that 'ancient history', that is, precursors to the offence, is not ignored when that history is the emotional heart of the current offence.

- *Follow-up of conference agreements* must be carried out rigorously to monitor compliance by offenders, particularly with letters of apology. Victims must be notified that agreements have been honoured so that they can feel a sense of closure about the offence and the conference.
- *Excessive focus on the offender* and insufficient attention being given to the victim's perspective clearly disadvantage victims. JVC057 illustrated the dangers here. Placing victims under pressure to attend so that they feel bullied and coerced is plainly no basis on which to conduct a conference. Brown (1994) has expressed concerns about the possibility of victims being coerced in this way:

> If the victim is approached by law enforcement officials, the fact that the state or its surrogate initiates the discussion may create pressure to take part. . . . In addition . . . the victim may feel some moral or psychological pressure to participate. The very rhetorical appeal of the program may induce a sense of guilt in a reluctant victim. . . . This could be traumatizing to victims who may already be experiencing a sense of vulnerability and loss of control. (p. 1266)

The main issue in JVC057 was not so much how to dispose of a minor shoplifter, but rather how to help a victim who had suffered disproportionately and who ultimately was revictimized by the conference, but the conference failed to focus on this.

In summary, victims may be poorly served by conferencing when there is sloppy police investigation of the offence, when facilitators are inadequately trained, when the actual conference is badly organized with insufficient facilities for the participants, and when victims are not sufficiently clear about their roles and legitimate expectations.

6.6 Summary

The experience of victims in restorative justice programmes in the past has not often been a happy one. Where their views have been examined at all, victims have sometimes said they felt they have played 'second fiddle' to the offender in terms of both process and outcome. Chapter 3 canvassed some of the very offender-oriented mediation programmes of the early 1980s in Britain where the victim was produced mainly as an object for the offender to ponder in facing up to his or her culpability, with little effort made to repair the harm that had been suffered. Marshall and Merry (1990) suggested that when reparation and offender diversion were sought within the one forum, the victim usually lost out because diversion tends to override all other goals. They concluded that in these British programmes it was almost always the case that the offender's interests were promoted and the victim's interests were neglected. Maxwell and Morris (1993), in their evaluation of the New Zealand Family Group Conferencing programme, stated: '[i]t is our view that this has occurred in the New Zealand system of youth justice too' (p. 189). Brown (1994) went even further in proposing that:

[G]iven the vital emotional issues at stake for most victims, [restorative justice] may actually harm victims recovering from crime. . . . [A] victim's recovery in the wake of crime is a delicate process and generalizing about what is best for victims is very difficult and dangerous. (p. 1273)

The data discussed in this chapter are mixed. They tend to indicate that victims usually had a better experience with a conference than with court, but that sometimes a conference was a much worse experience than court. Most of the victims whose cases were dealt with in court effectively had no experience of the court process because they had no role to play in the disposition and had little opportunity to observe it. For some victims, this was a relief— for example, most of the small shopkeepers and shop managers in this data set (15 per cent of the total) who are repeatedly victimized by shoptheft (but who often experience real trauma around both their victimization and their involvement in apprehending their offenders) have no desire to take up their evenings attending the conferences of those offending against them. They frequently said that they were happy to hand the matter to the police and the courts, and wanted no further involvement. For victims of more personal crimes, this lack of participation in the process was a source of annoyance and frustration, as we have seen, and many of those with no prior experience of the justice system were incredulous that this was the normal experience for victims in our court process.

Most of the victims whose cases were dealt with by a conference had definite opinions: this tended more often than court to be either very satisfactory or very unsatisfactory. As well, victims of violent crime tended to have more definite opinions than did property victims and fewer were indifferent; this seems to be associated with the more personal nature of the crime.

So conferences are by no means superior to court for victims on every occasion. It may be that they are more satisfying for victims who are highly emotionally engaged with the offence, but these are the very same people for whom conferences can be most risky. Court may not help victims of uncontested cases very much, but neither does it harm a great deal. When victims expose themselves to the conference forum they may sometimes suffer victimization over again. But this occurred only in a minority of cases, and the data show that on most measures victims whose cases went to conference were more satisfied than those whose cases were dealt with in court.

7

Victims and Offenders: A Relational Analysis by Heather Strang and Daniel J. Woods*

7.1 Introduction

Over the past thirty years or so, there have been challenges in Western criminal justice to traditional views about both the victims of crime and their offenders. Chapter 2 described the rise of the victim movement world-wide, which led to increasing attention being given to fairness and justice for these forgotten third parties in the contest between the offender and the state. At the same time, issues relating to increased protection of offenders' rights and the 'due process' model of criminal justice (Packer 1968) have been just as much a matter for debate. Both of these well-justified concerns were soured, however, almost from the outset, by conservatives on both sides who characterized them as moves in a zero-sum game, where any enhancement in the rights of one was assumed to be at the expense of the other (Elias 1986).

7.2 The Zero-sum Analysis

Now we consider the relationship between the outcomes for victims and the outcomes for offenders in the justice system. Table 7.1 shows four logical possibilities in respect of victims and offenders winning and losing on any interest they have.

For certain victim advocates and for many conservative politicians who advance a straightforward pro-victim, anti-offender position, Cell 3 is the concern. They believe that any right or benefit

* My sincere thanks to Daniel J. Woods of the University of Pennsylvania who carried out all the statistical analysis in this chapter.

TABLE 7.1   Outcome Possibilities for Victims and Offenders

		Offenders	
		Win	Lose
Victims	Win	1	2
	Lose	3	4

given to offenders will be at the expense of the rights or interests of victims. A win for offenders will always mean a loss for victims.

Youth advocates and adversarial defence lawyers sometimes argue that their concern is the win/lose outcome in Cell 2. Sandor (1994), for example, in referring to various legislative changes proposed for dealing with young offenders, argued that criticisms of the changes were dealt with by cloaking them as enhanced victims' rights; '[t]he prominence of the victim discourse makes it possible for their schemes to be presented as pivoting on the rights of the victim rather than infringing the rights of the alleged offender' (p. 154). The implied argument here is that any move to give victims rights or serve victim interests in the criminal process will result in victim interests being asserted against offender interests. We also see this perspective commonly in arguments against victim impact statements (see, for example, Rubel 1986). Erez (1990) commented that '[j]udges and defense attorneys equate sensitivity to victims' problems with lack of fairness to the defendant' (p. 24). The concern is that victims will use their right to speak only to pressure the court for heavier punishment of the offender. A win for victims becomes a loss for offenders.

Critiques of restorative justice also often make assumptions about the inevitable win/lose character of victim–offender transactions. They usually refer to inherent dangers for both parties, but most often the offenders—an irony, given that offenders tend to indicate higher levels of satisfaction with restorative processes than victims do (Strang et al. 1999; Maxwell & Morris 1993). Levant et al. (1999), for example, suggested that 'conservatives endorse restorative justice as a means of securing more justice for victims. In doing so, they often attempt to increase the punishment of offenders' (p. 6). Likewise Wundersitz (2000) writes: '[b]ecause of such factors as the central role accorded to victims in the process, the focus on restitution and the individualised nature of their outcomes, conferences could become a highly punitive arm of the state-centred justice system' (p. 116). From the victim standpoint, criticism has been made of the limited attention given to the victim's perspective in early victim–offender mediation programmes discussed in Chapter 3 that were focused so specifically on diverting offenders from prosecution (Dignan 1992).

Thus both victim advocates and offender advocates often adopt a zero-sum analysis of the criminal justice game, whether it is played out in the traditional adversarial system or in a restorative setting—any win for one side means a loss for the other side. In summary, the zero-sum hypothesis is that most encounters in both court and conference will fall in cells 2 and 3 of Figure 1.

7.3 The Non-zero-sum Restorative Justice Analysis

Notwithstanding the critiques, the restorative justice theoretical position is that win/lose can be avoided and transformed to win/win. This is because the opportunity for confronting one another directly in a restorative setting ought more often to provide opportunities for synergy of emotion than court. In addition, the restorative justice critique of traditional courtroom justice is that what we get is something worse than win/lose. We get lose/lose. This is because of the relational nature of hurting and healing. Hurt tends to lead to more hurt. We see this lose/lose relational claim in the theorizing of Thomas Scheff (1994) on shame–rage spirals. Obversely, in the writing of Howard Zehr (1985) we get the notion that healing leads to healing. This is why some restorative justice theorists actually prefer the label 'relational justice' (Burnside & Baker 1994). Schluter (1994) argues that this is a preferable term because one of its foundations is to regard crime as a 'breakdown in relationships; even in those cases where the offender does not personally know the victim, a relationship can be said to exist by virtue of their being citizens together, bound together by rules governing social behaviour' (p. 24). This view is close to that expressed by Zehr (1985) who believes that crime should be seen as 'a wound in human relationships. The feelings that victim and offender have toward one another are not peripheral issues, as assumed by our justice system, but are the heart of the matter. Relationships are central' (no page numbers).

At the root of this relational claim is the view that hate and love are socially contagious emotions. Practices where one party hurts another creates emotions in the hurt person that may cause them to want to hurt as well. Generous acts of healing, on the other hand, may engender generous feelings in the healed person, which make them want to reciprocate with their own gestures of healing. For example, there may be more opportunity for empathy and understanding to develop between victims and their offenders when they interact directly with each other. On the offender side, Harris (1999) has shown more offender empathy in conferences than in court. Data in Chapter 5 show more victim empathy in conferences than in court. So now the question is whether empathy on one side elicits or reinforces empathy on the other side. Do the dynamics of restorative justice present an opportunity for victims and offenders to act directly upon one another in ways impossible in the formal justice setting? If Zehr and other theorists are right that relationships are central to restoration, then victims and offenders ought to influence each other through the character of their interaction in this setting. We postulate that this influence will be positive and that both parties win. Theoretically the influence can equally well be negative, enhancing the likelihood of lose/lose, but this outcome is as empirically testable as win/win in both adversarial and restorative settings, as we shall see.

We can reach the same theoretical conclusion about the enhanced potential for restorative justice to deliver win/win outcomes by game theoretic analysis. Von Neumann and Morganstern in their 1944 classic postulated that all games could be classified into singular (such as investing on the stock market), dual, or zero-sum (like chess, or poker, or, as the victim and offenders advocates claim, the adversarial court system) and plural games: the last could be further sub-divided into co-operative and non-co-operative. In all plural games, the players have more than one active interest at stake, and in co-operative plural games, which are based on coalition behaviour, parties to the coalition may distribute their 'payments' to maintain the coalition. In a restorative setting such as a conference, parties have a number of 'payments' at their disposal: apologies, forgiveness, empathy, restitution, avoiding a criminal record: everything that both sides stand to gain by reaching an agreement and everything that both invest in achieving the agreement. The claim, therefore, once again is that the conference presents a superior opportunity compared with court for a win/win outcome, given that the players have so many more 'payments' available to play with, compared with what is available for them in court. By pluralizing the interests of the parties, more degrees of freedom are in play for constituting an outcome favourable to each party, simultaneously.

This phenomenon can be observed in the realm of international diplomacy, especially in trade negotiations. Often agreement between countries on a particular issue becomes impossible. But when this happens, the strategy often employed is to broaden the negotiation agenda. Braithwaite and Drahos (2000) illustrate this with a hypothetical example of a dispute between Italy and Greece about Italian air pollution, which might be resolved by the Greeks undertaking to move on a Greek–Italian impasse on olive markets. Broadening the agenda, and therefore increasing the likelihood of reaching fair and just outcomes to all parties is theoretically much more feasible in restorative justice settings which provide opportunities for more to be placed on the table than courts can do. The most crucial difference between the two institutions here is that courts narrow the issues only to legally relevant ones, while restorative processes expand the interests at stake to all that is emotionally and materially relevant to the parties.

In summary, while the zero-sum hypothesis (win/lose) is that win/win will not occur (or, in weaker form, will rarely occur) in criminal justice games, the restorative justice hypothesis is that victim–offender win/win will be common in restorative justice, and much more common in restorative justice than courtroom justice. In addition, the theory of restorative justice, also contrary to the zero-sum hypothesis, is that lose/lose will be common in the adversarial climate of the courtroom, and much more common than in restorative justice conferences.

In this research we define a variety of different kinds of win/win and lose/lose comparisons for victims and offenders. Then we test whether, in accordance with the restorative justice theory, win/win is common in conferences and more common than in court. After that we test whether lose/lose is common in court and more common in court than in conferences. Finally, we examine the propensity for win/lose outcomes in both settings.

We find that the restorative justice theory is strongly supported on all counts. Contrary to the claims of zero-sum advocates, criminal justice is found to be rife with win/win and lose/lose, with win/win being more common in conferences and lose/lose more common in courtroom justice. We also find that win/lose occurs in both settings, though much more often in court than in conference, and much less often than win/win.

7.4   Testing the Relational Hypothesis

But more is required for the relational hypothesis to be correct as the explanation for this pattern. There may be non-relational reasons for win/win to be more common in conferences. For example if there are more good things to give away to both victims and offenders, then win/win is more likely for non-relational reasons. For example, if conferences are in general a procedurally fairer process than court, fairer for anyone and everyone, then there is win/win on fairness that is driven by the procedures of the institution rather than by relationships between people within it.

If the relational hypothesis is the explanation for why win/win is more common in conferences, it will also be true that a win for the victim will increase the odds of the offender winning and vice versa. A strong win/win result will not be simply a result of victims having good chances of winning and offenders having good chances of winning, so that the odds of both winning are statistically high. If it is true that one of them winning has a relational effect on the odds of the other winning, then the probability of win/win will be higher than the probability of the victim winning multiplied by the probability of the offender winning.

If what conferences do is simply to make it independently more likely that offenders win and victims win, that is, if there is no relational effect, then expected win/win is the probability of one winning times the probability of the other winning. But if the relational hypothesis is right, a win for one produces an emotional contagion and behavioural reciprocity that increases the odds of a win for the other. Obversely with lose/lose, when one hurts or is hurt, the other is more likely to hurt and to be hurt. If the concordance between victim and offender that we observe is greater than the concordance we expect statistically, then we can conclude that one party is influencing the other.

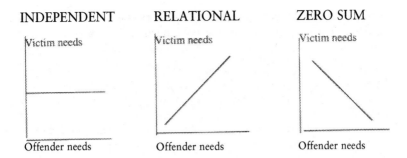

FIGURE 7.1. Independent, Relational, and Zero-sum Models of Victim and Offender Needs

Figure 7.1[1] helps show the three possibilities we are exploring in this second section of the data analysis. The first panel shows the independence hypothesis—the satisfaction of victim needs has no effect on the satisfaction of offender needs and vice versa. The expected win/win frequency will be a simple multiple of the odds of the victim winning times the odds of the offender winning.

The second panel shows the relational outcome. When the victim's needs are met, this increases the prospects that the offender's needs will be met and vice versa. Win/win is more likely than the unconditional joint probability of each winning.

The third panel shows the zero-sum outcome. When a victim wins, this reduces the odds of the offender winning, and vice versa.

7.5 Method

We use RISE data about what victims and offenders say of their experiences in court and, in the restorative justice setting of conferences, to test the extent of win/win outcomes for victims and offenders. We also explore a relational theory of restorative justice, by looking at whether and how they react to each other and the way they have been treated. Four areas have been selected for this investigation, on the basis that each of them is important for testing the possibilities for win/win outcomes, and that each provide plausible opportunities

---

[1] Thanks go to Philip Pettit for suggesting this model.

for one party to influence the feelings and attitudes of the other in ways that may be beneficial for both (or harmful for both):

1. Emotional harm and restoration;
2. Participation in the process;
3. Perceptions of procedural justice;
4. Perceptions of the legitimacy of the process.

The questions and statements selected for this analysis concern victims' and offenders' attitudes towards the other party in the incident in each of these areas, and feelings about what happened to them in the disposition of their cases.[2] They were chosen because either identical matching or reciprocal matching of questions and statements from the victim and offender interviews could be achieved:

- Identical matching—where both victims and offenders have been asked to respond to the same statement, for example, 'you were treated with respect in the court/conference'.
- Reciprocal matching where victims and offenders have been asked about the same feelings or experience from their own perspective. For example, offenders are asked 'were you treated in the conference/court case as though you were likely to commit another offence?', and victims are asked 'do you anticipate the offender will repeat the offence on you or another victim?'.

Wherever possible, the responses of victims and offenders whose cases went to conference are compared with the responses of victims and offenders whose cases went to court, to show how often win/win occurred in each treatment. However, victims whose cases went to court rarely attended their court cases and were therefore unable to answer questions or make comment about what happened in the disposition of their cases. In these instances only the responses of victims and offenders who went to conference are presented. These data will show how common win/win is in conferences without reference to a court comparison.

The victim–offender pairs in the analysis that follows consist of all victims in the data set described in Chapter 5, paired with each

---

[2] These questions are abbreviated in Tables 7.3–7.16 for reasons of space. They are listed in full in Appendix 2.

of their offenders, making a total of 194 pairs (Table 7.2). There were varying numbers of both victims and offenders: the maximum number of victims in any one case was eight and the maximum

TABLE 7.2   Number of Victims and Offenders in All Property and Violence Cases

Offender Number

Victim Number	1	2	3	4	6	Total
1	141 (72.7%)	22 (11.3%)	9 (4.6%)	1 (0.5%)	1 (0.5%)	174 (89.7%)
2	7 (3.6%)	4 (2.1%)	1 (0.5%)	0	0	12 (6.2%)
3	2 (1.0%)	2 (1.0%)	0	0	0	4 (2.1%)
4	0	1 (0.5%)	0	0	0	1 (0.5%)
5	0	0	1 (0.5%)	0	0	1 (0.5%)
7	0	0	1 (0.5%)	0	0	1 (0.5%)
8	0	0	1 (0.5%)	0	0	1 (0.5%)
Total	150 (77.3%)	29 (14.9%)	13 (6.7%)	1 (0.5%)	1 (0.5%)	194 (100.0%)

number of offenders was six. Where there was more than one offender in a case, all were co-offenders who had acted together in one or more offences being dealt with at the same time in their court or conference dispositions. Where there are multiple victims, each may have experienced different offences committed by the same offender(s) on different occasions (e.g. serial house burglary) but 'bundled' by the police and dealt with at the one disposition, or they may be victims of the same offence committed serially against them on the one occasion (e.g. multiple victims of assault by the same offender(s) on the same occasion).

It is important to note in the analysis that follows that not all of these victims and offenders were able to respond to every question or statement. Some victims could not respond to questions about what happened in their case because they did not attend the disposition and therefore did not know what took place. In general, victims could comment only if the questions were relevant to them.

For example, only victims who had received apologies could respond to the statement: 'you felt the apology [you received] was sincere.' Because there were varying numbers of victims and offenders able (or willing) to answer each question, the completion rate for each pair of questions (for every victim with each of Offender 1 and, where relevant, Offender 2) is noted in Appendix 3.

Completion rate refers to the percentage of all possible victim–offender pairs where both parties responded to the question or statement.

7.6 Data

The tables that follow show the extent of concordance between victims and offenders in their responses; that is, the percentage of cases where both parties responded 'strongly agree' or 'agree' or 'neither agree nor disagree'. The third category, 'neither agree nor disagree', was added to increase the number of cases which could reasonably be included in this analysis.[3] This concordance is recorded as 'win/win' when both parties responded positively to a positive question or statement: for example, where the offender 'agreed' in response to the statement '[t]he conference/court case allowed you to make up for what you did', and the victim 'agreed' in response to the statement '[y]ou felt the apology you were offered was sincere'. The concordance is recorded as 'lose/lose' where both parties responded positively to a negative question or statement: for example, where both the offender and victim 'agreed' in response to the statement 'you feel bitter about the way you were treated in the case'.

To check the effect of using this means of increasing n, all analyses have been re-run excluding the 'neither agree nor disagree' responses. This cuts the sample size substantially (by about one third). These results were substantively the same, and all in the same direction even though, as expected because of the smaller n,

---

[3] In some instances, available responses were not the 'strongly agree . . . strongly disagree' scale. E.g. Table 7.3 contains an analysis of responses to the victim question: 'how helpful to you did you find attending the conference/court case?' Available responses to this question were: 1. Very unhelpful 2. Unhelpful 3. Neither helpful nor unhelpful 4. Helpful 5. Very helpful. In this case, response 3 was treated as the equivalent of 'neither agree nor disagree'. For simplicity, the term 'agree' will be used throughout to include responses 3–5 on all five-point scales used in the interviews. Appendix 4 notes how the scaled responses were treated in the analysis.

there were fewer differences that reached statistical significance (those occasions when they did reach statistical significance are noted on the tables). In no instance did this more conservative analysis result in a significant difference between treatment groups that was not replicated with the larger analysis; in no instance were there significant differences between observed and expected values that were not replicated with the larger analysis. Items in the tables are asterisked when this analysis resulted in a significant difference between the two treatment groups or between observed and expected values. They have a double asterisk when the difference is also significant in the more conservative analysis where 'neither agree nor disagree' cases were excluded.

7.7   Who Wins, Who Loses in Court and Conference?

7.7.1   Emotional restoration post-treatment: the 'healing gives rise to healing' hypothesis

Victims assessing their offenders' apologies as sincere is postulated to be associated with their offenders feeling empathy towards them, a powerful indicator of healing rather than hurt and emotional restoration generally. All victims who said they had received an apology were asked about the sincerity of the apology. This question was paired with six questions asked of offenders which explore facets of empathy. Win/win occurred when both parties said they 'agreed' in response to the question.

Table 7.3 shows that win/win was far more common in conference than in court for items signalling emotional restoration. Consistently across all items, when positive emotions flowed from offenders, more of the victims in the conference group than the court group perceived the apology they were offered as sincere. For items 1, 2, 3, and 4 this difference was statistically significant ($p < .01$). The opportunity the restorative setting of the conference provides for this kind of interaction is illustrated by the following exchange between two young men, one a taxi driver and the other his intoxicated passenger who assaulted him after a misunderstanding between them (JVC071):

Offender: Now I can see things from [your] point of view. I thought you were totally different, I thought you wanted to fight me. I've been keeping an eye out for you in case you wanted to run me down.
Victim: I have to sympathise with you. Everything you've said I've

TABLE 7.3 Emotional Restoration Post-treatment: Victim–Offender Pairs, Court vs Conference

Offender Question/Victim Question	Conference			Court			Conference/ Court Ratio	
	win/win %	lose/lose %	win/lose %	win/win %	lose/lose %	win/lose %	win/win	lose/lose
1) Understood how others felt/ Felt apology was sincere (n = 101)	62	10	28	15	25	60	4.13**	.40
2) Others said you had learned lesson/ Felt apology was sincere (n = 101)	65	9	26	32	16	53	2.03*	.56
3) People indicated you were forgiven/ Felt apology was sincere (n = 101)	54	10	36	20	25	55	2.70*	.40
4) Felt allowed to make up for actions/ Felt apology was sincere (n = 101)	69	2	28	30	10	60	2.30*	.20
5) Affected by emotions of victims/ Felt apology was sincere (n = 101)	43	12	44	25	25	50	1.72	.48

* $p < .01$.
** Significant for the more limited data set which excluded 'neither agree nor disagree' ($p < .05$).

experienced as well since it happened—feeling guilty, how this is going to affect my career.

Offender: It shouldn't have happened should it—such foolish behaviour.

Table 7.3 also suggests that on emotional restoration almost always lose/lose may be more common in court than in conference, and usually around twice as common. But even in court, win/win happens as often as lose/lose. However, when we look at win/lose, we find that there is some support for the zero-sum hypothesis in court where across each of the items in the table more than half the victim–offender pairs indicated win/lose, and even in conferences this happened about one third of the time.

In summary, we find in terms of emotional restoration experienced after the treatment:

- Consistently more win/win in conference than in court;
- Consistently more win/lose in court than in conference;
- Consistently more lose/lose in court than in conference.

7.7.2 Emotional harm post-treatment: the 'hurt gives rise to hurt' hypothesis

Victims assessing that their offenders are likely to repeat the offence is postulated to be associated with the interaction being a harmful rather than a healing one. This is the realm of hurt giving rise to hurt. A lose/lose outcome occurs when feelings of contempt, anger, or vengefulness are shared by the parties.

In Table 7.4, items 1–10 look at the links between victims *expecting the worst* (that is, anticipating their offenders will re-offend) and offenders being angry and vengeful. An apparently trivial case involving the theft of a pet rabbit (JPP052) illustrates this sort of interaction. This theft, just one minor incident in an ongoing poisonous feud between neighbours, was dealt with in court in a perfunctory way, as might be expected. When interviewed after the court case, the victim said that the offender 'keeps telling me she'll steal the rabbit again and bash me up as well, and her parents say it too'.

For all items relating to 'expecting the worst', there was more lose/lose in court than in conference. For three of the ten items (items 1, 2, and 5) the lose/lose difference was statistically significant ($p < .05$). The court pairs consistently expected the worst of each other more often than the conference pairs did.

TABLE 7.4 Emotional Harm Post-treatment: Victim–Offender Pairs, Court vs Conference

| | Conference | | | | Court | | | Conference/ Court Ratio | |
Offender Question–Victim Question	win/win %	lose/lose %	win/lose %	win/win n %	lose/lose %	win/lose %		win/win	lose/lose
Expecting the worst									
1) Treatment made you angry/ Anticipate will repeat offence on another victim (n = 220)	45	10	45	27	24	49		1.67*	0.42*
2) Accusers more wrong than you/ Anticipate will repeat offence on another victim (n = 220)	44	8	48	30	20	50		1.46	0.4
3) Treated like you would reoffend/ Anticipate will repeat offence on another victim (n = 220)	43	9	48	36	16	48		1.19	0.56
4) Wish could get back at accusers/ Anticipate will repeat offence on another victim (n = 220)	53	4	42	44	10	46		1.20	0.40
5) Treatment made you angry/ Anticipate will repeat offence on you (n = 219)	66	0	34	53	7	40		1.25	0*
6) Accusers were more wrong than you/ Anticipate will repeat offence on you (n = 219)	69	2	29	59	7	34		1.17	0.28
7) Treated like you would reoffend/ Anticipate will repeat offence on you (n = 219)	65	0	35	66	5	28		0.98	0
8) Wish could get back at accusers/ Anticipate will repeat offence on you (n = 219)	83	1	17	78	2	20		1.06	0.50

9) Cannot decide whether act was wrong/Anticipate will repeat offence on another victim (n = 218)	53	12	35	36	14	50	1.47	0.85
10) Cannot decide whether act was wrong/Anticipate will repeat offence on you (n = 218)	72	1	27	66	3	31	1.09	0.33

Hitting back

11) Wish could get back at accusers/ Would harm offender if you could (n = 228)	71	1	28	75	8	17	0.95	.13* **
12) Accusers more wrong than you/ Would harm offender if you could (n = 228)	59	4	38	55	13	32	1.07* **	.31* **
13) Glad you committed offence/Would harm offender if you could (n = 239)	78	0	22	71	7	22	1.09	0*
14) Treatment made you angry/Would harm offender if you could (n = 228)	63	6	31	49	11	40	1.28	.55

Anger

15) Accusers were more wrong than you/ Treatment made you angry (n = 226)	69	4	27	63	8	30	10	.50
16) Glad you committed the offence/ Treatment made you angry (n = 237)	81	1	18	68	4	28	1.19* **	.25
17) Treatment made you angry/ Treatment made you angry (n = 225)	76	3	22	54	6	40	1.41* **	.50
18) Wish you could get back at accusers/ Treatment made you angry (n = 225)	79	1	20	69	3	28	1.14	.33
19) Feel bitter about your treatment/ Feel bitter about your treatment (n = 229)	69	2	29	68	6	26	1.01	.33

* $p < .05$.
** Also significant for the more limited data set which excluded 'neither agree nor disagree' ($p < .05$).

Next we look at *hitting back*, that is, victims' and offenders' feelings of vengefulness towards each other. In Table 7.3, items 11–14 explore interactions where victims were so angry that they said they would harm their offenders if they had the chance, and where offenders expressed feelings of defiance and anger. In JPP110, for example, a court case involving the theft of motorcycles by two young boys, who expressed their defiance by continuing harassment of the victim's family for 'dobbing them in', the victim said that if he knew where they lived 'I'd go down to their place and punch their lights out'. When victims and offenders jointly shared these harmful feelings towards one another they were consistently more often in cases assigned to court rather than to conference, and for three of the four items (items 11–13) the difference between treatment groups on lose/lose was statistically significant ($p < .05$).

Items 15–19 in Table 7.3 explore the *anger* of both victims and offenders. Victims and offenders both being angry was more common in court than in conference. This was consistently true across the items: for two of the items (items 16 and 17) the differences were statistically significant.

In summary, we find that in terms of emotional harm experienced after the treatment:

- Consistently more lose/lose in court than in conference;
- Consistently more win/win in conference than in court;
- Little difference in win/lose between court and conference except in anger where there tended to be more in court than conference.

7.7.3   Perceptions of legitimacy

The way conferences are designed to nurture democratic participation and respect the citizenship of everyone taking part might be expected to enhance citizen perceptions of the legitimacy of government and, more specifically, of the criminal justice system. The seven statements which make up the items in Table 7.4 were devised to explore feelings about legitimacy, as manifested in expressions of trust and respect, and were put to victims and offenders in both treatment groups.

Significantly more of the conference-assigned victims and offenders said that they felt they could trust the police during their

TABLE 7.5 Legitimacy: Victim–Offender Pairs, Court vs Conference

Offender Question/Victim Question	Conference win/win %	lose/lose %	win/lose %	Court win/win %	lose/lose %	win/lose %	Conference/Court Ratio win/win	lose/lose
1) Felt you could trust police during your case/Felt you could trust police during your case (n = 240)	81	1	18	60	3	37	** 1.35*	.33
2) As a result of treatment your respect for the police has increased/As a result of treatment your respect for the police has increased (n = 239)	78	3	19	50	5	45	1.56*	.60
3) As a result of treatment your respect for the law has increased/As a result of treatment your respect for the law has increased (n = 230)	82	2	16	70	1	29	1.17***	2.00
4) Police enforce law fairly/Police enforce law fairly (n = 237)	79	1	20	73	4	23	1.08	.25
5) As result of treatment your respect for justice system has increased/As result of treatment your respect for justice system has increased (n = 228)	78	3	19	69	2	30	1.13	1.50
6) Treatment will help prevent reoffending/Treatment will encourage you to obey the law (n = 226)	90	1	9	82	2	17	1.10	.50
7) Treatment will encourage you to obey the law/Treatment will encourage you to obey the law (n = 227)	90	1	9	89	0	11	1.01	0

* $p < .01$.
** Also significant for the more limited data set which excluded 'neither agree nor disagree' ($p<.05$).
*** $p < .05$.

cases (item 1) (p < .01); that their respect for the police had increased (item 2) (p = .01), and that their respect for both the law and the justice system had increased (items 3 and 5) (p < .05). Evidently the opportunity that conferences presented for participants to interact at close quarters and for an extended time with the police, both at the preparatory stage and during the conference itself, encouraged them to feel more positively towards them, compared with victims and offenders whose cases were dealt with in court and whose contact with the police was relatively brief. The same trend was apparent when participants were asked whether the police were generally fair in the way they enforce the law (item 4).

Victim and offender optimism about the law, the justice system, and the police went together consistently more often in conferences than in court (that is, win/win). Both expressed more trust and respect, and felt they had been treated better, if they had gone to a conference rather than to court. Trust giving rise to trust, confidence giving rise to confidence, respect giving rise to respect, seem much more a feature of conferences than of court. In conferences both parties report the greater trust, respect, fairness, and legitimacy available in conference proceedings in comparison with court proceedings.

However, when we look at the lose/lose picture, it turns out that there is very little difference between the two treatment groups. In fact very few victims and offenders responded negatively to the statements on legitimacy, and there was almost no difference between court and conference: in both types of justice, lose/lose is a rare event.

In summary we find concerning perceptions about the legitimacy of the process:

- Consistently more win/win in conference than in court;
- Lose/lose is rare both in court and in conference;
- Consistently more win/lose in court than in conference.

7.8   Who Wins, Who Loses in Conferences?

There were three dimensions of victim–offender experience where only conference data were collected: emotional harm and restoration occurring within the treatment; participation in the process;

and views on procedural justice. In each of these win/win occurred commonly. On every item for each of these dimensions, more than half the victim–offender pairs were win/win.

7.8.1   Emotional restoration in treatment: the 'healing gives rise to healing' hypothesis

In Table 7.6, some facets of offenders' empathy in the conference are explored and paired with statements about victims' perceptions of their offenders' understanding of the harm they caused. These give us some measure of the extent of emotional restoration the parties achieved in conferences. For every item relating to empathy between the parties, the extent to which they saw the conference as being helpful to them and the sense of closure the conference had given them, around 60 per cent was win/win. Lose/lose across these measures was uncommon, but around a quarter were win/lose.

7.8.2   Emotional harm in treatment: the 'hurt gives rise to hurt' hypothesis

Table 7.7 reveals the minimal extent of emotional harm which victims and offenders report arising from a conference. On average only 6 per cent of victim–offender pairs reported lose/lose from their conferences. Although the majority reported that they had not suffered on these indicators of emotional harm, about one third reported win/lose.

7.8.3   Participation in conferences

Table 7.8 shows the extent to which both parties win on participation in the conference process. On average, two-thirds (66 per cent) of the victim–offender pairs reported win/win on these measures of the extent of their participation and nearly one-third (31 per cent) reported win/lose. Item 4 about feeling awkward is telling: around half reported win/lose and most of those feeling awkward were offenders.

7.8.4   Procedural justice in conferences

Included in Table 7.9 are all the statements on perceptions of procedural justice which were put to both victims and offenders who had attended their treatment. In Chapters 1 and 6 the social psychology of procedural justice was reviewed from the victim perspective (Tyler 1988, 1990). This work and other research as

TABLE 7.6 Emotional Restoration in Treatment—Victim–Offender Pairs, Conference Only

Offender Question/Victim Question	Conference win/win %	lose/lose %	win/lose %
Empathy			
1) Understood how others felt/Offender understood harm caused to you (n = 89)	57	16	27
2) Felt bad about hurting others/Offender understood harm caused to you (n = 89)	56	17	27
3) Felt ashamed of actions/Offender understood harm caused to you (n = 89)	54	15	31
4) Think what you did was stupid/Felt offender had learned lesson (n = 84)	80	2	18
5) Victim was hurt as a result of your offence/Offender understood harm caused to you (n = 87)	60	6	34
Helpfulness			
6) Treatment helped to solve problems/Found it helpful to attend treatment (n = 86)	76	2	29
7) Treatment helped to solve problems/Treatment helped to solve problems (n = 89)	52	10	38
8) Felt allowed to clear conscience/Found it helpful to attend treatment (n = 86)	72	1	27
Closure			
9) People said you had learned lesson/Felt offender had learned lesson (n = 85)	64	7	29
10) People indicated forgiveness/Felt forgiving towards offender (n = 89)	56	6	38
11) People said you could put incident behind you/Able to put incident behind you (n = 89)	56	3	40

TABLE 7.7 Emotional Harm in Treatment—Victim–Offender Pairs, Conference Only

Offender Question/Victim Question	Conference		
	% win/ win	% lose/ lose	% win/ lose
1) Felt accusers were more wrong than you/After conference felt angry with offender (n = 86)	50	8	42
2) Felt victims were just sorry for themselves/ After conference felt angry with offender (n = 87)	57	8	34
3) Glad you committed the offence/After conference felt angry with offender (n = 87)	63	3	33

well (Lind & Tyler 1988; Makkai & Braithwaite 1996) hypothesized that when offenders believe that they have been treated fairly by the criminal justice system, they will be more likely to comply with the law in future. So perceptions of the fairness of the process may be important both in terms of satisfaction and in terms of future behaviour. On almost all items, relating to the facets of control, impartiality, ethicality, and correctability, there was win/win for both parties in over 75 per cent of cases and lose/lose

TABLE 7.8 Participation in the Process—Victim–Offender Pairs, Conference Only

Offender Question/Victim Question	Conference		
	% win/ win	% lose/ lose	% win/ lose
1) Had influence over conference outcome/ Conference took account of what you said (n = 87)	77	1	33
2) People spoke up for me in the conference/ Attended because you wanted to have a say (n = 86)	83	1	16
3) Disagree too intimidated to speak in conference/Disagree too intimidated to speak in conference (n = 89)	66	7	27
4) Disagree felt awkward in the conference/ Disagree felt awkward in the conference (n = 88)	39	14	47

TABLE 7.9 Procedural Justice—Victim_Offender Pairs, Conference Only

Offender Question/Victim Question		Conference	
	win/win %	lose/lose %	win/lose %
Control facet			
1) Had enough control over the way conference was run/Had enough control over the way conference was run (n = 82)	70	2	28
2) Disagree felt pushed into things you did not agree with/Disagree felt pushed into things you did not agree with (n = 82)	76	2	23
3) Conference took account of what you said re outcome/Conference took account of what you said re outcome (n = 88)	83	2	14
4) Understood what was going on in the conference/Understood what was going on in the conference (n = 91)	87	5	8
5) Had opportunity to express your views in the conference/Had opportunity to express your views in the conference (n = 89)	76	1	22
Impartiality facet			
6) Disagree that outcome was too severe/Conference was fair to offender (n = 85)	64	1	35
7) Disagree that you were judged unfairly/Conference was fair to you (n = 88)	83	1	16
8) All sides got a chance to bring out facts in conference/All sides got a chance to bring out facts in conference (n = 89)	85	1	13
9) Police were fair during the conference/Police were fair during the conference (n = 89)			
Ethicality facet			
10) Conference respected your rights/Conference respected your rights (n = 88)	89	1	10
11) Disagree disadvantaged by age, income, sex, race/Disagree disadvantaged by age, income, sex, race (n = 89)	85	1	14
12) Treated with respect in the conference/Treated with respect in the conference (n = 88)	84	0	16
	83	0	17
Correctability facet			
13) If treated unfairly, could have got complaint heard/If treated unfairly, could have got complaint heard (n = 89)	64	3	33
14) Wrong facts were correctable in the conference/Wrong facts were correctable in the conference (n = 89)	71	3	26

was negligible. However, on all facets a substantial minority (on average 20 per cent) were win/lose.

7.9 Testing the Relational Hypothesis: Is Win/Win More Common than the Joint Probability of each Winning?

Even though our analysis shows that restorative justice is almost always more likely than the adversarial system to provide a win/win outcome for victims and offenders, we cannot assume that this outcome is a result of their acting positively upon one another. It is possible that they independently reach the same view of the outcome. For the relational hypothesis to be supported, we must show that the positive feelings of one party influenced the other party also to feel positively.

So, to test the relational hypothesis as an explanation for the concordance observed between victims and offenders, we must compare the observed frequency of win/win with the expected frequency of win/win, that is the frequency we would find if there were no influence by one party on the other (offender and victim responses were independent).[4] Expected frequencies are calculated as follows.

The unconditional probability of an offender 'agreeing' (that is, independently of what the victim said) is equal to the number of offenders who 'agreed' divided by the total number of offenders. This is called Event A. Likewise, the unconditional probability of a victim 'agreeing' (that is, independently of what the offender said) is equal to the number of victims who 'agreed' divided by the total number of victims. This is called Event B. To calculate the unconditional probability of both parties agreeing, we multiply the probability of Event A and the probability of Event B. That is:

$$P(A \text{ and } B) = P(A) \times P(B).$$

The expected frequency of both Event A and Event B occurring if they were independent of each other is:

$$P(A) \times P(B) \times n \text{ of cases.}$$

---

[4] Depending on the way the questions are worded, this result may be lose/lose, e.g. if the observed frequency of pairs who respond 'agree' to the question 'the treatment made me angry' exceeds the expected frequency.

- When the *observed* and *expected* percentages of victim–offender pairs who respond win/win in answering their question are the *same* (or not significantly different), then the agreement of one party is having no effect on the likelihood of the agreement of the other party (see 'independent' model in Figure 7.2);
- When the *observed* percentage is *greater* than the *expected* percentage, then a win by one party is *increasing* the likelihood of a win by the other party. If the difference between observed and expected values is statistically significant, the relational hypothesis is supported (see 'relational' model in Figure 7.2);
- When the *observed* percentage is *less* than the *expected* percentage, then a win by one party is *decreasing* the likelihood of a win by the other party. If the difference between observed and expected values is statistically significant, the zero-sum hypothesis is supported (see 'zero-sum' model in Figure 7.2).

Contingency tables are used to calculate the probability of the difference between observed and expected values being statistically significant (usually Chi-square, but when the *n* of any cell in the calculation was less than five, Fisher's Exact Test[5] was used).

While this method provides a good opportunity to refute the independence, relational, and zero-sum models, it cannot confirm their causal claims because we have only associational data at one point in time. For example, we cannot confirm that what happens with the relational hypothesis is that an offender gets less angry and then the victim gets less angry, or vice versa.

As before, the analysis concerns four dimensions of victim–offender experience: emotional harm and restoration, participation in the process, views on procedural justice, and views on the legitimacy of the criminal justice process. Tables 7.10–7.16 show for each item the expected and observed percentages of victim–offender win/win (or, in the case of items about emotional

---

[5] Fisher's exact distribution calculates the difference between observed and expected data, considering the given marginals and the assumptions of the model of independence, in exactly the same way as the Chi-square for two by two tables. However, Chi-square gives only an estimate of the true probability value which may be unreliable with cell values less than five: in this case Fisher's Exact is a preferable technique.

harm, victim–offender lose/lose). When there is a significant difference between expected and observed values (p > .05), the p value is noted. Wherever possible, conference results are compared with court results, but, as before, only conference data are available for items concerning emotional harm and restoration in the treatment, participation in the process, and perceptions of procedural justice.

7.9.1 Emotional restoration: the 'healing gives rise to healing' hypothesis

Table 7.10 sets out the percentages of victim–offender pairs with win/win on these items. For neither conference nor court were there any significant differences between the expected and observed values. This indicates that victims and offenders in both treatment groups were most often independent of each other in their responses on these items.

When we compare the treatment groups on win/win, we find that conferences are consistently superior to court in providing opportunities for emotional restoration for both parties. This finding is supported when we examine items concerning emotional restoration in the treatment, as opposed to post-treatment (conference-only data). Table 7.11 reveals statistically significant differences between observed and expected values for four of the five items relating to feelings of *empathy* experienced by victims and offenders in conferences. The significantly higher observed than expected values suggest that in conferences there was a strong tendency for the empathic feelings of one party to influence the other party to experience empathy. This result supports the relational hypothesis.

In items 6–8 of Table 7.11, offenders and victims were asked about the *helpfulness* of attending the conference and especially whether it helped to solve any problems. There was little difference here between the observed and expected values. These findings indicate that victims and offenders were independent of each other regarding the helpfulness of their conference.

Items 9–11 of Table 7.11 relate to issues of *closure*. Offenders were asked about what people said to them or how they acted towards them at the end of the conference. These responses were paired with the responses of victims about their feelings towards their offenders after the conference. There was no significant difference between these observed and expected values.

TABLE 7.10 Emotional Restoration Post-treatment—Victim–Offender Pairs, Court vs Conference, Treatment Differences

Offender Question/Victim Question	Conference		Court	
	% win/win Expected*	Observed*	% win/win Expected*	Observed*
1) Understood how others felt/ Felt apology was sincere (n = 101)	58	62	20	15
2) Others said you had learned lesson/ Felt apology was sincere (n = 101)	61	65	23	20
3) People indicated you were forgiven/ Felt apology was sincere (n = 101)	52	54	23	20
4) Felt allowed to make up for actions/ Felt apology was sincere (n = 101)	69	69	34	30
5) Affected by emotions of victims/ Felt apology was sincere (n = 101)	42	43	25	25

* No significant difference between any expected/observed values in either conference or court.

TABLE 7.11 Emotional Restoration in Treatment—Victim/Offender Pairs, Conference Only, Expected and Observed Values

Offender Question/Victim Question	Conference % win/win	
	Expected	Observed
1) Understood how others felt/Offender understood harm caused to you (n = 89)	50**	57**
2) Felt bad about hurting others/Offender understood harm caused to you (n = 89)	48**	56**
3) Felt ashamed of actions/Offender understood harm caused to you (n = 89)	48*	54*
4) Think what you did was stupid/Felt offender had learned lesson (n = 84)	78*	80*
5) Victim was hurt as a result of your offence/Offender understood harm caused to you (n = 87)	59	60
Helpfulness		
6) Treatment helped to solve problems/Found it helpful to attend treatment (n = 86)	70	76
7) Treatment helped to solve problems/Treatment helped to solve problems (n = 89)	49	52
8) Felt allowed to clear conscience/Found it helpful to attend treatment (n = 86)	73	72
Closure		
9) People said you had learned lesson/Felt offender had learned lesson (n = 85)	61	64
10) People indicated forgiveness/Felt forgiving towards offender (n = 89)	56	56
11) People said you could put incident behind you/Able to put incident behind you (n = 89)	58	56

* Significant difference between expected and observed values $p < .05$.
** Significant difference between expected and observed values $p < .001$.

TABLE 7.12 Emotional Harm Post-treatment—Victim–Offender Pairs, Court vs Conference, Treatment Differences

Offender Question/Victim Question	Conference % lose/lose		Court % lose/lose	
	Expected	Observed	Expected	Observed
1) Treatment made you angry/Anticipate will repeat offence on another victim (n = 220)	10	10	23	24
2) Accusers more wrong than you/Anticipate will repeat offence on another victim (n = 220)	10	8	20	20
3) Treated like you would reoffend/Anticipate will repeat offence on another victim (n = 220)	9	11	14	16
4) Wish could get back at accusers/Anticipate will repeat offence on another victim (n = 220)	5	4	7	10
5) Treatment made you angry/Anticipate will repeat offence on you (n = 219)	1	0	6	7
6) Accusers were more wrong than you/ Anticipate will repeat offence on you (n = 219)	1	2	4	7
7) Treated like you would reoffend/Anticipate will repeat offence on you (n = 219)	1	0	3	5
8) Wish could get back at accusers/Anticipate will repeat offence on you (n = 219)	0	1	1	2
9) Cannot decide whether act was wrong/Anticipate will repeat offence on another victim (n = 218)	9	12	13	14
10) Cannot decide whether act was wrong/Anticipate will repeat offence on you (n = 218)	1	1	3	3
Hitting back				
11) Wish could get back at accusers/Would harm offender if you could (n = 228)	2	1	3	8 ** +
12) Accusers more wrong than you/Would harm offender if you could (n = 228)	4	4	7	13*
13) Glad you committed offence/Would harm offender if you could (n = 239)	0	0	3	7 **
14) Treatment made you angry/Would harm offender if you could (n = 228)	4	6	8	11

TABLE 7.12 (continued):

Offender Question/Victim Question	Conference % lose/lose		Court % lose/lose	
	Expected	Observed	Expected	Observed
Anger				
15) Accusers were more wrong than you/Treatment made you angry (n = 226)	3	4	5	8
16) Glad you committed offence/Treatment made you angry (n = 237)	1	1	3	4
17) Treatment made you angry/Treatment made you angry (n = 225)	2	3	7	6
18) Wish you could get back at accusers/Treatment made you angry (n = 225)	3	3	1	1
19) Feel bitter about your treatment/Feel bitter about your treatment (n = 229)	2	2	3	6

* Significant difference between expected and observed values $p < .05$.
** Significant difference between expected and observed values $p < .001$.
\+ Also significant for the more limited data set which excluded 'neither agree nor disagree' responses $p < .05$.

TABLE 7.13 Emotional Harm in Treatment—Victim–Offender Pairs, Conference Only, Expected and Observed Values

Offender Question/Victim Question	Conference % lose/lose	
	Expected*	Observed*
1) Felt accusers were more wrong than you/After conference felt angry with offender (n = 86)	8	8
2) Felt victims were just sorry for themselves/After conference felt angry with offender (n = 87)	6	8
3) Glad you committed the offence/After conference felt angry with offender (n = 87)	3	3

* No significant difference between any expected/observed values $p > .05$.

In summary, these data suggest independence of victim and offender perceptions on helpfulness and closure, but that they influence each other positively on empathy.

7.9.2 Emotional harm: the 'hurt gives rise to hurt' hypothesis

Table 7.12 sets out the observed and expected lose/lose values for both treatment groups. For the conference group, the values were usually small and similar to each other; in fact many had both expected and observed values near zero, so rare was lose/lose in this treatment.

For the court group, lose/lose outcomes were much more common than for the conference group, and for several items the difference between observed and expected values reached statistical significance. For three of the four items about the desire to 'hit back' (items 11–14), the observed values were significantly higher than expected values. Consistently with the 'hurt gives rise to hurt' hypothesis, the victims who felt vengeful towards their offenders influenced those offenders to feel vengeful, defiant, and angry (or vice versa, as we cannot tell the direction of the influence). These results support the relational hypothesis.

We also looked at some aspects of emotional harm in the treatment (Table 7.13). Victims' anger with offenders as a result of the conference was explored in relation to offenders' attitudes of anger and contempt toward their victims. Expected and observed results were very similar, but the number of cases was too small to make the analysis meaningful. The results are presented for completeness.

7.9.3 Perceptions of legitimacy

When we examine whether victims and offenders influence one another in their perceptions of the legitimacy of the process, we find that neither in court nor in conference is there any significant difference between observed and expected win/win. The data in Table 7.14 suggest that victims and offenders independently reached similar views, rather than influencing each other towards those views.

7.9.4 Participation in the process (conference data only)

Table 7.15 shows that differences between the expected and the

TABLE 7.14 Legitimacy—Victim–Offender Pairs, Court vs Conference, Treatment Differences

Offender Question/Victim Question	Conference % Victim–Offender Agreement		Court % Victim–Offender Agreement	
	Expected*	Observed*	Expected*	Observed*
1) Felt you could trust police during your case/Felt you could trust police during your case (n = 240)	80	81	61	60
2) As a result of treatment your respect for the police has increased/As a result of treatment your respect for the police has increased (n = 239)	77	78	52	50
3) As a result of treatment your respect for the law has increased/As a result of treatment your respect for the law has increased (n = 230)	81	82	72	70
4) Police enforce the law fairly/Police enforce the law fairly (n = 237)	80	79	72	73
5) As result of treatment your respect for justice system has increased/As result of treatment your respect for justice system has increased (n = 228)**	77	78	70	69
6) Treatment will help prevent reoffending/Treatment will encourage you to obey the law (n = 226)	89	90	81	82
7) Treatment will encourage you to obey the law/Treatment will encourage you to obey the law (n = 227)	89	89	90	90

* No significant difference between any expected/observed values in either conference or court $p > .05$.
** Also significant for the more limited data set which excluded cases in which victims or offenders responded 'neither agree nor disagree' $p < .05$.

TABLE 7.15 Participation in the Process—Victim–Offender Pairs, Conference Only, Expected and Observed Values

Offender Question/Victim Question	Conference % Victim/Offender Agreement	
	Expected*	Observed*
1) Had influence over conference outcome/Conference took account of what you said (n = 87)	77	77
2) People spoke up for me in the conference/Attended because you wanted to have a say (n = 86)	82	83
3) Too intimidated to speak in conference/Too intimidated to speak in conference (n = 89)	4	7
4) Felt awkward in the conference/Felt awkward in the conference (n = 88)	38	39

* No significant difference between any expected/observed value $p > .05$.

observed values here are small and unremarkable. On all these items, the parties tend to be independent of each other in their feelings about their participation in the process.

7.9.5   Perceptions of procedural justice (conference data only)

Table 7.16 reveals that for most items, the differences between observed and expected values hover around zero, and none of them approach significance. However, in this kind of analysis, such consistent findings of no difference are important in their support for the independence hypothesis. The interesting result is, for example, that it is *not* true that offenders' feeling that the police were fair during the conference causes victims to feel they were treated unfairly (item 9—Impartiality facet). Indeed, this was consistently untrue across all items for the various facets of procedural justice identified by Tyler. However, the very small expected/observed differences for all items indicate that victims and offenders influenced one another's views very little in perceptions of procedural justice in their conferences but arrived independently at the same conclusions.

7.10   Summary

The aim of this chapter has been twofold. First, it set out to investigate the claim of certain victim advocates and offender advocates that criminal justice is a zero-sum game in which any gain by one side must be at the cost of the other side (win/lose). We hypothesized that the dynamics of the restorative justice model would provide more opportunities than the traditional court system for both sides to win. Secondly, having demonstrated that, indeed, win/win occurs to some extent in both conference and court settings, but far more often in conference than in court, we tested the relational hypothesis, this is, whether victims and offenders influence each other towards similar positive (or negative) views. The direction of causality on these data cannot be tested, that is whether it was victims influencing offenders or offenders influencing victims, but the existence of any kind of positive synergy can be explored. We also investigated whether victims and offenders arrive independently at the same conclusions, because support for the 'independence' hypothesis set out in Figure 7.2, that is, that

TABLE 7.16 Procedural Justice—Victim–Offender Pairs, Conference Only, Expected and Observed Values

Offender Question/Victim Question	% Victim–Offender Agreement	
	Expected*	Observed*
Control facet		
1) Had enough control over the way conference was run/Had enough control over the way conference was run (n = 82)	69	70
2) Felt pushed into things you did not agree with/Felt pushed into things you did not agree with (n = 82)	2	2
3) Conference took account of what you said re outcome/Conference took account of what you said re outcome (n = 88)	82	83
4) Understood what was going on in the conference/Understood what was going on in the conference (n = 91)	82	87
5) Had opportunity to express your views in the conference/Had opportunity to express your views in the conference (n = /89)	77	76
Impartiality facet		
6) Disagree that outcome was too severe/Conference was fair to offender (n = 85)	63	64
7) Disagree that you were judged unfairly/Conference was fair to you (n = 88)	83	83
8) All sides got a chance to bring out facts in conference/All sides got a chance to bring out facts in conference (n = 89)	85	85
9) Police were fair during the conference/Police were fair during the conference (n = 89)	88	89
Ethicality facet		
10) Conference respected your rights/Conference respected your rights (n = 88)	85	85
11) Disadvantaged by age, income, sex, race/Disadvantaged by age, income, sex, race (n = 89)	1	0
12) Treated with respect in the conference/Treated with respect in the conference (n = 88)	83	83
Correctability facet		
13) If treated unfairly, could have got complaint heard/If treated unfairly, could have got complaint heard (n = 89)	64	64
14) Wrong facts were correctable in the conference/Wrong facts were correctable in the conference (n = 89)	70	71

* No significant difference between any expected/observed value p > .05.

they do not influence each other at all, would also refute the win/lose perspective of the rights' advocates.

Win/win occurs commonly in conferences and much more commonly in conference than in court. Lose/lose is more common in court than in conference. Both of these findings are strongest for the dimensions of emotional harm, especially anger and vengefulness in the court, and emotional restoration, especially empathy in conferences. Win/lose occurs in a minority of cases in both court and conference, but more commonly in court than in conference.

In terms of the relational hypothesis, in most cases victims and offenders did not influence each other, even though they frequently expressed similar views both about their treatment and about each other. When they did influence each other, it was most often in the dimensions of *emotional harm and restoration*. There turned out to be little influence by the parties on each other in terms of *participation* in the conference process: victims' and offenders' views were largely independent of each other on measures concerning their willingness to speak and their feelings of nervousness and intimidation. Likewise, victims and offenders appeared to influence each other very little in terms of their perceptions of *procedural justice*. On all procedural justice facets examined, victim and offender perceptions appeared to be independent of one another. Finally, the measures of *legitimacy* of the justice process also reveal that even though victims and offenders had apparently not influenced each other, once again they had independently arrived at the same views.

It is important to note that, given the small size of the available data, these interaction effects have to be large to be statistically significant. Inadequate sample size haunts this analysis, despite the decision to include the victims who gave 'middle' responses ('neither agree nor disagree') in the 'agree' category as a device for increasing the number of available cases. As expected, only a relatively small number of the comparisons were statistically significant, both between court and conference when looking at win/win and between the expected and observed values when looking at the relational hypothesis. Nevertheless, many of the responses tended in the same direction.

All these findings largely negate the arguments of both victim rights and offender rights proponents about the inevitability of a win/lose scenario in any justice disposition. Win/lose occurs far less frequently in conferencing than in court, while win/win occurs much more frequently in conferencing than in court and is overwhelmingly the majoritarian result in the restorative justice process. On this small sample, it is only on the dimension of empathy in emotional restoration, and of vengefulness in emotional harm, that we can show that victims and offenders are influencing each other towards these outcomes. The strongest support is for the 'independence' hypothesis, that is that victims and offenders do not usually influence each other: while in restorative justice processes they may both reach the 'win' position, the 'win' for one does not seem in most dimensions to increase the odds of a 'win' for the other. From the perspective of restorative justice theory, however, which gives such a prominent place to emotion, the findings in support of relational hypothesis on empathy in emotional restoration and vengefulness in emotional harm are extremely important exceptions.

In summary we conclude that restorative justice indeed does appear to have the potential to allow both parties to benefit more often than adversarial justice. The data indicate that, at least for the areas chosen for this analysis, win/lose is not inevitable, and in fact in the conferences occurred in only a minority of cases. The analysis contains some limited support for a relational theory of restorative justice, that the character of the restorative setting has the potential to influence participants in positive directions and towards win/win outcomes for both parties. These findings deserve further exploration with a larger data set.

8

Repair or Revenge?

8.1 Introduction

The momentum of the restorative justice movement over the past decade has given rise to some extravagant claims for its superiority to formal justice processes in dealing with crime. Most of those claims relate to benefits for offenders and, to a lesser extent, to communities which will profit from the lower offending rates which, it is hoped and sometimes assumed, will follow from restorative interventions. Less attention has been paid to the way victims feel about restorative programmes and many victim advocates have remained suspicious about the motivations behind such programmes, their focus, and the likely benefit to victims from taking part.

In this book I have asked whether restorative justice offers better outcomes for victims in the terms they say matter. Much more needs to be done in exploring the potentials and pitfalls of restorative justice for different kinds of victims in different kinds of circumstances, but the data gathered through the present study provide a basis upon which to build more knowledge.

This final chapter begins by retracing the course of the book. It then considers some theoretical critiques of restorative justice from the victim's perspective in the context of the empirical findings, and suggests some policy implications that may follow from the shortcomings for victims of the court system. It then addresses the limitations and the strengths of the experiments from which the empirical findings are drawn, and finally suggests some future directions for research.

8.2 Summary of Findings

8.2.1 Victims' discontents

A review of the victimological literature over the past twenty years reveals dissatisfactions widely shared by victims caught up in an adversarial justice system. However, their role was not always so debased: restorative justice has historically been the dominant paradigm of criminal justice, by which I mean that the response to crime until the rise of the modern state involved offenders making amends to their victims, so as to restore order and peace as quickly as possible and to avoid vengeful blood feuds. The diminished role for victims in criminal justice which now obtains began in Europe in the late Middle Ages as the Crown increasingly assumed the right of both adjudication and compensatory benefit for wrong-doing. This decline continued through the centuries in the West, until victims retained almost no rights in the justice process, which became exclusively a struggle between the offender and the state.

Victims have not lost their importance in the matter of bringing offenders to justice. Their co-operation is still essential in reporting offences and providing evidence in court. Nevertheless, they seem to be undervalued by every sector of the criminal justice system—police, prosecution, and the court itself—and the system remains inflexibly unresponsive to their perspective (Shapland 2000), despite more than two decades of victim movement activism (discussed in Chapter 2). Considerable effort has been made in improving victim *services* in most Western countries, but it has been argued (see, for example, Elias 1986) that the politics of victim *rights* have been captured by law-and-order forces, especially in the United States, which perceive criminal justice as a zero-sum game where the enhancement of victims' rights can be achieved only by circumscribing the rights of offenders (a subject considered in Chapter 7).

So what is it that victims want? Chapter 1 concluded that victim research shows clearly that victims want:

- a less formal process where their views count;
- more information about both the processing and outcome of their cases;
- participation in their cases;
- fair and respectful treatment;
- material restoration;
- emotional restoration, including an apology.

It is plain that to achieve these objectives victims need the opportunity for much greater engagement with the justice system. Success has been claimed in responding to some of these issues: legislation has been passed in many countries requiring victims to be kept informed about their cases and for victim impact statements to be considered in the sentencing of offenders, while state-financed compensation arrangements now exist in many jurisdictions around the world. Yet victims still often believe they are not given the attention they deserve. An important question is whether, in terms of what victims want, the limits of the formal justice system have been reached.

8.2.2   The restorative justice alternative

Chapter 3 took up this question with a comprehensive examination of the theory and practice of another way of 'doing justice', restorative justice. Restorative justice is old, but only recently have ancient practices been rediscovered by the West and adapted to contemporary conditions. Dissatisfaction by both victim and offender advocates with aspects of the dominant models of criminal justice—rehabilitation and retribution—accounts in part for the interest in this third model, in which the moral, social, economic, and political contexts of crime are taken into account. Instead of offenders and offending being viewed in isolation, they are placed in a conceptual framework where the needs of victims for restoration and of communities for protection and safety are given priority as well. This 'balanced' approach aims to make the justice system more responsive to the needs of all the players (Bazemore & Umbreit 1994).

Chapter 3 discussed what is understood by the term 'restorative justice' and then described some of its forms. These include victim–offender reconciliation and mediation programmes now found in great numbers in North America and Europe, and Canadian sentencing circles, which incorporate traditional First Nation ways of responding to offenders. Also discussed were the Family Group Conferencing programmes established in New Zealand, which draw on traditional Maori strategies for resolving disputes and dealing with criminal behaviour, and the conferencing programmes developed in Australia over the past decade.

I then turned to what is known from empirical studies about the value of restorative justice in addressing the shortcomings of the adversarial justice system from the victim's point of view. Research results so far are mixed: while advantages are evident, a different set of problems sometimes arise. These include cases of increased levels of fear resulting from victims confronting their offenders, the replication of power imbalances between victims and offenders known to one another, and the excessive offender-focus of some programmes, which has at times resulted in coercion and revictimization. The chapter concludes that the next logical step is to compare in a systematic way the effectiveness for victims of the traditional formal, court-based justice system with the restorative alternative.

The Reintegrative Shaming Experiments (RISE) in Canberra were designed with victim satisfaction as a major outcome measure in comparing court with a restorative alternative in the form of a police-led programme of restorative justice conferencing. Chapter 4 explains that a randomized controlled trial was chosen as the research protocol for RISE, despite the practical difficulties inherent in conducting field experiments of this kind, because only random assignment of subjects to treatment and control groups with equal probability ensures that prior to treatment the groups are equivalent within known statistical limits. The reason that this research design is regarded as the most rigorous of evaluation methods is its capacity to ensure equivalence, not only on known variables, but also on variables which the researcher has not considered and may not even have imagined. This means that differences which emerge between the groups may be attributed, with greater confidence than any other research design would permit, to the effect of the different treatments they have received.

In two of the four experiments the offences involved direct victims (the other two involved only indirect or unidentified victims, who were not part of this analysis). These experiments concerned middle-range property and violent crimes committed by young offenders who had made full admissions about their responsibility for the offence. All cases were serious enough that they would normally have been dealt with in court, but in the study were randomly assigned either to court or to a conference.

Ideally in testing on victims the effectiveness of the experimental treatment compared with the control treatment, the sampling frame would consist of victims randomly assigned to each treatment. However, this was not feasible because the great majority of randomly selected victims would have no identified offenders, owing to the small percentage of offences which result in an apprehension, and there could be no 'treatment' for the victim unless there were 'treatment' for an identified offender. A design involving the screening of eligible victims prior to case assignment was not employed, partly because offender recidivism was the primary outcome measure, and partly because of the extra time and expense that would have been involved. Thus, rather than a randomized controlled trial of victim effects, the study is a randomized controlled trial of offender and victim effects, where not all cases have victims. There were no significant differences between the victims assigned to conference and those assigned to court on any pre-assignment characteristic.

Structured interviews were conducted with 232 victims of property and violent crime. The interviews aimed to find out whether these victims concurred with what the literature says that victims want, and the extent to which court and conference delivered these outcomes.

Internal and external validity of the experiments are important measures of the adequacy of the design. High scores were achieved in the experiments on the key measures of treatment observation rates (90 per cent), treatment as assigned (97 per cent), and post-treatment interview response rates (89 per cent for victims and 69 per cent for offenders), so internal validity is very satisfactory. How generalizable the results are to other samples at other times or in other places—the external validity of the study—is more difficult to assess but can be tested by replicating the methodology in other locations.

8.2.3   Comparing court and conference

All analyses reported were conducted on the basis of treatment randomly assigned to cases, rather than the treatment victims actually experienced. The reasons for this are explained in Chapters 4, 5, and 6. In brief, this permits the views to be heard of victims who had expected to have a conference but it did not take place. Analysing in this way means that the findings relating to various dimensions of victim satisfaction with the conference process appear to be depressed, because those who actually experienced a conference were nearly always more positive than those assigned to a conference who did not experience it.

Chapter 5 explored the lived experiences of the property and violent crime victims who are the subject of the experiments. As expected in a randomized design, the court and conference groups were very similar in their demographic characteristics and in the amount of harm they had experienced. There was no significant difference between the groups in either experiment on age, education, sex, Aboriginality, place of birth, marital status, or employment status. On material harm, there was no significant difference between the groups in the harm suffered for property damage, loss of goods or cash, security improvements or lost wages in the case of property victims, nor in the extent of injury or associated financial costs for violence victims. These similarities give great confidence that any difference in outcomes between the treatment groups is due solely to the treatment they received.

Chapter 5 then examined the responses of all the victims to questions on the issues the literature identifies as important for victims and neglected by the formal court-based system. On some of these questions only conference data were available: too few court-assigned victims attended the disposition of their cases to question them about their opportunities for participation in their cases, whether they thought their views had been counted, or whether they felt they had been treated fairly and respectfully. On all these dimensions conference victims usually reported high levels of satisfaction.

One of the areas of persistent complaint for victims about court is the inadequate way that they are kept informed about the progress of their cases. Court victims in this study felt the same way, with many criticisms about failures in communication at every stage of the justice process. Many were amazed that their cases had progressed through the entire system without their being told anything at all. Conference victims, by contrast, needed to be consulted about both the process and the outcome of their cases because their participation was central to a successful resolution. Consequently they expressed high levels of satisfaction about the information they received.

On material restoration these victims said that they did not receive as much as they thought they should, either in court or in conference (though court victims felt this was more important than conference victims did). Few in either group received financial restitution, but conference victims more often received other forms of restitution, such as work by the offender either for them or for others.

However, the biggest differences between the groups related to emotional restoration. These were some of the notable findings:

- On safety and fear of victimization, three times as many of the court-assigned property victims and five times as many of the violence victims believed the offender would repeat the offence on them, compared with their conference-assigned counterparts. When asked whether they thought their offenders would reoffend with a different victim, their responses were also striking: more than half of both the property and violence victims whose cases were assigned to court believed this would happen, compared with only around one third of those assigned to a conference.

- Conference victims reported that their feelings of fear, anger, and anxiety fell markedly after the conference while feelings of sympathy and security rose (no comparable court data available).

- Conference victims also reported that their treatment most often had a beneficial effect on feelings of dignity, self-respect, and self-confidence. Two thirds of them reported that the conference experience had given them a sense of closure about the offence (no comparable court data available).

- Almost all victims, regardless of the offence they had suffered or their treatment assignment, believed that their offenders should have apologized to them. Four times as many conference-assigned as court-assigned victims actually received an apology.

- Most striking of all were the responses of violence victims about feelings of vengefulness and unresolved anger towards their offenders: almost half of the court-assigned said they would harm their offenders if they had the chance, compared with only 9 per cent of the conference-assigned, a compelling measure of the power of the conference to allay victims' desire for revenge.

In reviewing various measures of satisfaction in Chapter 6, I conclude that victims usually had a better experience with conference than with court. In answer to the question: 'you were satisfied with the way your case was dealt with by the justice system' (strongly disagree ... strongly agree), significantly more of the conference-assigned victims than court-assigned victims were satisfied. An even higher proportion of those who *actually* went to a conference expressed satisfaction on this measure compared with those whose cases were dealt with in court.

But attending a conference is an inherently riskier experience: whereas many of the court victims were indifferent about what had happened in the disposition of their cases, most of the conference victims felt strongly, usually positively, but in a minority of cases very negatively. Throughout the study, it was evident that around one fifth of conference-assigned victims were unhappy with their experience. In some cases this was because, despite their being assigned to a conference, the conference never took place and victims were angry and disappointed as a result. Sometimes the cause of dissatisfaction lay in the way the conference was conducted or its aftermath. So as to learn more about the experience of the victims who were dissatisfied with their conferences, Chapter 6 concluded with a close examination of seven conferences which had gone badly wrong from the victim's point of view. The failure of conferencing for these victims turned out to be much more a failure of practice than of principle. Victims' dissatisfaction flowed mainly from the incompetent way in which the process was delivered—poor police investigation, inadequate facilitator training, poor conference organization, insufficient knowledge about the victim's role, and legitimate expectations from the process. Dissatisfaction was expressed in terms of process failures rather than negative attitudes towards the principles of restorative justice.

8.2.4   Zero-sum justice?

In Chapter 7 I returned to the claim of many victim and offender advocates that criminal justice is a zero-sum game, in which any benefit by one side must be at the cost of the other side (win/lose). This claim has been made both about formal court-based justice and about restorative justice. I hypothesized that the restorative justice setting of conferences would provide more opportunities than court for both sides to win. This is because the restorative setting ought theoretically to provide more opportunities for emotional synergy than the court process does.

I examined the responses of victim and offender pairs (that is, the victim(s) and offender(s) involved in any one incident) to identical or reciprocal questions asked in their structured interviews.

When both parties responded positively to the question, the response was rated as win/win; when both responded negatively it was rated lose/lose; and when one party was positive and the other negative it was rated as win/lose. Four areas were chosen for this study, on the basis that each provides plausible opportunities for one party to influence the other. These areas were: participation in the process; perceptions of procedural justice; perceptions of the legitimacy of the process; emotional harm and restoration.

For the dimensions of participation in the process and perceptions of procedural justice, only conference data were available: in each of these win/win occurred commonly—in around two-thirds of all cases—and win/lose infrequently (lose/lose was negligible). On legitimacy of the process, there was significantly more win/win in conference than in court and significantly more win/lose in court than in conference (again, lose/lose was negligible). On emotional harm too, there was significantly more win/win in conference than in court and significantly more lose/lose in court than conference, but similar results for both treatments in win/lose. The differences were most striking in the dimension of emotional restoration: win/win occurred here significantly more often in conference than in court—in fact, depending on the question asked, between one and a half times and four times more often—while win/lose occurred significantly more often in court than in conference (there was more lose/lose in court than conference but the difference was not statistically significant).

The analysis showed that the restorative alternative of conference was almost always more likely than court to produce a win/win result for both victims and offenders. However, it cannot be assumed that this was a consequence of their influencing each other in the same direction. It was equally possible that both parties independently reached the same view. Contingency tables were used to calculate the probability of the difference between observed and expected win/win responses being statistically significant. No difference was found for the dimensions of participation in the process, perceptions of procedural justice, legitimacy of the process, or emotional harm: in all these cases it appeared that victims and offenders independently tended towards the same views. However, on the dimension of emotional restoration there was a strong tendency in conferences for empathy felt by one party to influence the other party to feel empathy as well. The analysis revealed no evidence to support the zero-sum (win/lose) hypothesis of the rights advocates and it appears that restorative justice has the potential to allow both parties to 'win' more often than court justice does.

8.3 Critiques of Restorative Justice from the Victim Perspective

This book demonstrates that there are often substantial advantages to victims in the restorative approach. However, some principled concerns have been raised about their closer engagement in the justice process, based on jurisprudential considerations. Other objections are based on explanatory theory and can be partially answered by drawing on the empirical findings of this study.

8.3.1 Principled problems with focusing on harm to the victim

Ashworth (1986) argued that the restorative approach:

> ignores one cardinal element in serious crimes—the offender's mental attitude. . . . Criminal liability and punishment should be determined primarily according to the wickedness or danger of the defendant's conduct . . . on what he was trying to do or thought he was doing, not upon what actually happened in the particular case. (p. 97)

Ashworth asserts that focusing on harm to the individual victim rather than the criminal intent of the offender (thus substituting the quantum of harm for the quantum of intent as the central determinant of liability and making restitution to the victim a principal goal of criminal justice) would require a major rethink of both criminal law and traditional punitive responses to these transgressions. He is concerned that sanctions agreed to in a restorative setting would not be proportionate to the severity of the offence, and that offenders who have committed similar offences would not be sanctioned in the same way.

Restorative justice does raise the prospect of a fundamental repositioning of victim and offender interests and concerns in the way we 'do justice' on the basis, as Barnett (1977) argued, that 'equality of justice means equal treatment of victims' (p. 259). But the problem may be that equal treatment of victims inevitably compromises equal treatment of offenders, and vice versa. Choosing either equality of treatment of victims or of offenders as a policy goal is bound to result in disappointingly unequal outcomes in a world where most offenders are not apprehended. The deepest inequality will remain between apprehended and unapprehended offenders, to the point where equality among those apprehended would be a comparatively trivial accomplishment, even if it could be attained. Similarly, the deepest inequality for victims is between those whose crimes are and are not solved. Dignan and Cavadino (1996) noted that only 7 per cent of offenders are caught and punished, so all victim-oriented measures that require an identified offender can benefit only a very small proportion of victims. These are the grounds for objection to restorative approaches by victim advocates such as Reeves and Mulley (2000) and Herman (2000), who fear the reallocation of scarce resources from more general forms of victim assistance. It remains true that equal justice for offenders and for victims are incompatible objectives. However, inconsistent outcomes for either victims or offenders may in fact be fairer if they are the result of genuine, undominated, consensual decision-making between all the key parties—victims, offenders, and their communities of concern. Braithwaite and Strang (2000) suggested that instead of consistency the aim should be to ensure minimum guarantees of justice for both parties instead of the impossible reconciliation of equal justice for victims and equal justice for offenders. For example, one possible compromise is to constrain unequal treatment of offenders only by a guarantee that none will be punished above a maximum specified for each offence, and to guarantee victims a hearing where their needs are considered. Another option may be the infusion of restorative justice into court-based criminal justice processing, so that agreements reached between victims and offenders in conferences may be taken into account in the sentencing of the offenders.[1]

8.3.2 Principled problems with focusing on private wrong rather than public interest

Another sticking point is the essentially irreconcilable and conflicting view of the public/private dimensions of crime. The restorative paradigm is based on a view of crime as not only a transgression against society but also, even perhaps primarily, a private wrong

---

[1] Research into the viability and effectiveness of this approach is underway in the United Kingdom (www.crim.upenn.edu/jrc).

against the specific victim; further, that the principal objective of the justice system should be to focus on the repair of that private wrong. Critics object that restorative justice gives insufficient attention to the broader social dimension, that is, the harm society as a whole suffers through the harm experienced by any individual within it. For example, Ashworth (1992: 3) argued that 'the provisions of the criminal law set out to penalise those forms of wrongdoing which . . . touch public rather than merely private interests' and that 'punishment is a function of the state, to be exercised in the public interest' (1993: 284). This is because the state's concern is not only with the case at hand but also with the interests of other potential future victims and of the community as a whole. The complexity of the competing issues of private wrong and public interest were illustrated in a case which came before the New Zealand Court of Appeal (R. v. *Clotworthy* (1998) 15 CRNZ 651), where a beneficial conference outcome from the victim's point of view was overturned because the Court found that it contained too little consideration of the public interest in denunciation and general deterrence (see Morris & Young 2000; Mason 2000). However, this problem too may be resolved by finding a means for taking agreements reached in conferences into account in judicial sentencing.

The issue of punishment in restorative justice has recently been the subject of lively debate (see Daly 2000; Barton 2000) on whether the two concepts are irreconcilable, either on grounds of principle—that restorative processes ought never result in retributive outcomes—or on the moral and ethical grounds that punishment should remain the preserve of the state. Cavadino and Dignan (1997) supported the latter view—that punishment *per se* requires the sanction of the state or its representative with power of veto—but depart from Ashworth in arguing that the wishes of the victim of *this* particular crime should carry special weight in determining appropriate reparation. Watson *et al.* (1989) also held the view that because the offence against victims has entailed an infringement or denial of their rights in ways not shared with the general public, victims have a special status that entitles them to a say about reparation. Morris and Young (2000) describe how in New Zealand family group conferences victims and all the other participants not only discuss reparation but also take deterrence, incapacitation, denunciation, and retribution into account in deciding on the outcome. Arguably, punishment as an outcome is not irreconcilable with restorative values, provided all participants agree about the sanction and have arrived at that agreement through an uncoerced, restorative process (see Braithwaite & Strang 2000).

In balancing the personal interests of victims and the wider public interest, it is also important to remember that the restorative approach avoids the court's exclusive preoccupation with 'public interest' and provides an accessible forum for victims to participate in the disposition of their cases and secure both emotional and material restoration. And according to the theory of reintegrative shaming, the opportunities for reintegration of victims into their 'communities of care' which is provided through restorative processes is just as important as for offenders: indeed, the one is seen as an important means of accomplishing the other (Braithwaite & Mugford 1994).

8.3.3   Problems with victim fear

At the end of Chapter 3 I discussed some speculations about problems for victims which can result from facing their offenders in the restorative setting. Certainly the potential must be acknowledged, and much depends on the skill of the conference facilitator and other participating citizens in addressing this concern (see Chapter 6 for discussion of the various consequences of poorly run conferences). However, the empirical evidence from this study is that both property and violence conference victims feel safer and less fearful of their offenders than court victims do. It seems that the opportunity to meet their offenders and make their own personal assessments is usually far more reassuring than fear-inducing, at least for these offences and these offenders. When this fails and victims are left feeling worse after a conference than they did before, it is most often because of the poor quality of the conference rather than a result of their objection to the principles of restorative justice (see Chapter 6).

8.3.4   Problems with power imbalance

It remains true that to date there had been little research on how to achieve equal treatment of the disputing parties when one is much less powerful or articulate than the other. Much of this debate has centred on concerns about using restorative interventions in cases of domestic and sexual violence. Here Braithwaite and Daly (1994) have argued that victims may in fact be better served by a restorative approach than by the court because of the potential for involving more and less powerful supporters associated with each party. But Astor (1994) and Stubbs (1995, 2002), for example, believe that restorative interventions are most likely to fail and to leave women victims more vulnerable than they were before. The problem of power imbalance is not, in any case, limited to domestic violence: any dispute involving people known to each other may bring with it pre-existing power relationships, while young people in general may find themselves dominated by their elders, indigenous people by whites and so on.

There is much we need to learn about the possibilities and limitations for restorative justice in all these settings. But what we have learned from this study gives grounds for optimism: for example, women victims of offences other than domestic violence overwhelmingly reported that their conference experience was procedurally fair, that they felt able to assert and express themselves in the presence of their offenders, and that they had not been disadvantaged because of gender, age, race, or any other reason. Much of this debate must remain open to empirical investigation, rather than subjected to premature closure on purely normative grounds.

8.3.5   Problems with 'using' victims

Chapter 3 discussed some of the programmes used in the past which were so completely offender-focused that victims emerged from these encounters feeling angry and revictimized. Ashworth (2000) believes that the emphasis in more recent programmes on anticipated reductions in re-offending rather than on their value to victims may lead to victims being transformed from 'court fodder' under the traditional court system to 'agents of offender rehabilitation', under restorative justice. Victims' rights and support organizations also worry about this (see, for example, George 1999). Reeves and Mulley (2000) comment that initiatives introduced to give victims an enhanced role in the disposition of their cases may amount in reality to little more than new obligations. They point to the Crime and Disorder Act 1998 in England and Wales as an example: under this Act victims have the right to be informed and consulted at almost every stage of the disposition of their cases, but they are concerned that this may be experienced as 'a burden in the form of unwanted contact with, or even responsibility for, the offender. . . . They may feel guilty if they choose not to participate yet anxious if they do' (p. 139).

It is a shortcoming of this study that victims were not explicitly asked whether they ever felt like 'props' in the service of an offender-oriented show: indeed, this question has not yet been asked of victims in restorative interventions anywhere so it is a truly speculative issue. Nevertheless, we know that a significant minority of victims in this study felt dissatisfied with their experience. I identified some of the sources of this dissatisfaction in Chapter 6 when I looked at the elements of those conferences where most dissatisfaction was evident. Perhaps implicit among the problems to do with poor facilitation, insufficient preparation, unrealistic expectations, and unsatisfactory constitution of the conference (especially an unbalanced mix of victim and offender supporters) was a sense that far too much focus was placed on the offender at the victim's expense. All these problems derive from a failed understanding of what a restorative process entails. Restorative justice is not value-free: it begins with a presumption that victims have been harmed and that their restoration is a priority. It involves an ethical commitment to justice, not merely to conflict resolution. If this principle is paramount, then using victims in this damaging way is proscribed.

8.4 Policy Implications

Although this analysis has concentrated on examining the comparative advantages of court and conferences for victims, it is important to look as well at where either of them absolutely fails. We have explored what the data tell us about when conferences fail victims; we need to consider too the shortcomings of court which prevail in spite of more than two decades of victim activism. In Canberra, for example, opting for principles rather than rights has not worked, even on such an apparently straightforward dimension as keeping victims informed of the progress and outcomes of their cases, a major focus of the Victims of Crime Act (1994). Victim advocates doubt the Act will ever be complied with in this regard because there, as in many other places, the justice system is not administered in a way that makes it feasible to meet this obligation.

It is possible that a full-blown rights approach, of the kind prevailing in the United States (see Chapter 2), may be more successful in achieving what victims want. A US Department of Justice report (Kilpatrick *et al.* 1998) compared the experiences of victims in states in which legal protection of victims' rights was strong with those in states in which such protection was weak. It found that strong victims' rights laws made a difference and that victims from 'strong protection' states had better experiences with the justice system. However, there have been serious limitations to the success of even a strong rights approach: the same report found that in the states with strong protection, still more than one in four victims were very dissatisfied with the criminal justice system. Further, we must presume substantial costs in credibly enforcing a rights approach.

It may be the case that the structures of formal justice are so inflexible that their limits have been reached in terms of providing victims with better justice. What we have been exploring in the restorative alternative is a paradigm shift which bypasses the issues of marginal change and improvement in the way victims are treated, controversial as many of them have turned out to be. Restorative justice may be risky for victims because it asks more of them, but this study shows that the potential gains are considerable.

8.5   Future Research

Restorative justice is a term covering a multitude of ideological, theological, and public policy principles and processes. Much has been written to clarify what the concept means, accompanied by much theorizing about its potential, but only slow progress has been made in determining empirically whether this promise can be realized.

Some would maintain that restorative justice, if it is to be successful in the mainstream of criminal justice, will have to be shown to 'work' for offenders—that it is successful in reducing recidivism and preventing crime (see, for example, Braithwaite 1998), whether alone or in conjunction with usual court-based justice. But others believe that if we can be satisfied that it is at least as successful as court justice alone on those measures, then the issue of victim satisfaction with the process becomes paramount in public policy decisions about the widespread use of restorative alternatives.

We are just beginning to piece together a knowledge base about victims and restorative justice. We know that there is some heterogeneity in their reaction to conferences. We suspect that they react differently depending on the emotional harm they have suffered: that conferences are most satisfying in absolute terms to those who have experienced much emotional harm because of the offence and have derived emotional restoration from them. Obversely, we suspect that conferences are most unsatisfying in absolute terms for those who experienced much emotional harm and who are revictimized by poor conferences which have provided no emotional restoration for them. But neither of these suspicions has been confirmed conclusively by this study. In the same vein, we suspect that victims would prefer offences with little personal content, such as the majority of shoplifting matters, to be dealt with in court, but this too has not been demonstrated conclusively: indeed, there remains a great deal we do not know about when conferences are most beneficial for victims and when the formal court response is preferable. We also know very little in a systematic way about the potential for conferencing with adult offenders or with more serious offences, including domestic and sexual violence (with the exception of the work of Burford and Pennell (1998) in Northern Canadian communities).

8.6   'An Experience of Justice'?

Howard Zehr (1995), a seminal thinker in restorative justice, has suggested that victims need first and foremost what he calls 'an experience of justice', an experience that he says is almost never available to them in the formal court-based system. He believes that while vengeance is often assumed to be a part of this need, that in fact vengeful feelings may more often be the result of justice denied. Findings in this study about the anger felt by victims whose conferences were never held, for example, and the desire for revenge of nearly half the victims of violence whose cases went to court, go to support this view. He also believes that because victims have experienced a fundamental disrespect for their property and their person through their victimization, what they want from justice is an experience of respect. This too accords with findings here about feelings of loss of dignity, respect, and other emotional harm caused by the offence, which were repaired for the majority of victims who had the restorative alternative of a conference.

We should be careful though in guarding against seeing victims in some 'ideal' way (Christie 1986). The 232 victims upon whose experiences and views this study is based were highly varied. Some of them fitted the stereotype of victims' rights organizations—the innocent young, the frail elderly, victims of unprovoked attacks on their right to safety and security. Others did not fit the stereotype at all, even though every victim survey shows that young males are the most victimized sector of the population. We must not be deluded into thinking that only 'ideal' victims deserve a better deal from our justice system. All of the different kinds of people who contributed to this study wanted the outcomes identified at the outset of the book: participation in their case, information, fair and respectful treatment, material and, especially, emotional restoration.

Likewise, we must be conscious of the limiting consequences of portraying crime simply as a violation of one individual by another (Wundersitz & Hetzel 1996). Young (2000) argues that it is more meaningful to see crime as typically affecting multiple victims—individuals, groups, communities, and society as a whole—in many different ways. Besides the fact that crime is often committed by organized groups, corporate entities, or the state itself (Nelken 1997; Lacey & Wells 1998), much 'street' crime also does not meet conventional views of crime as harm inflicted by one party upon another. In this study there were a number of offences for which it was impossible to identify a single victim, but which had undoubtedly caused harm; these included discharging a weapon in a public place, burglary in schools, and criminal damage perpetrated against public buildings or buses. Likewise, conspiracy, incitement, and attempted offences of various kinds are all difficult to fit within the conventional framework. Even in apparently clear-cut cases of harm-infliction such as assault, the labels of 'victim' and 'offender' may be socially constructed, which is to say 'the product of a complex interaction of personal and group perception of events and the contexts in which they take place' (Miers 1987: 9). Young suggests that in all these circumstances the formulation that 'crime involves one individual violating another, thus giving rise to a duty to repair the violation, fails rather miserably to capture the murky morality of many offender–victim interactions' (2000: 233).

The flexibility of the restorative approach means that the complexities of criminal activity and of social life can be accommodated more easily than the structure of the formal justice system could ever allow, giving an opportunity for everyone affected by the crime—direct and indirect victims, offenders' 'communities of care', and the offenders themselves—to explain the harm and seek repair.

Nor should we limit our imaginations about where a restorative response to injustice is possible. Desmond Tutu (1999) has written movingly about the need of victims of South African state terror to forgive and about their extraordinary willingness to do so. He shares Hannah Arendt's belief that forgiveness actually releases the victim from revenge. Laura Blumenfeld (2002) has written movingly about her redemptive meeting with the Palestinian who tried to kill her Jewish father. The restorative approach gives victims and offenders the chance for a crucial transaction to take place—the offering of an apology and the granting of forgiveness. In this study in an Australian city we find the same reactions by victims as Tutu, Arendt, Blumenfeld, and others have found in the wider world of victims' suffering on scales almost unimaginable.

This research has explored systematically and scientifically many questions raised about the potential for restorative justice in repairing harm to victims. It does indeed offer promise for victims in delivering the justice they seek. We must be wary of claiming too much and raising expectations too far. Nevertheless, what has been learned from this study answers many of the fears of restorative justice critics and gives grounds for optimism for a better deal for victims through the restorative alternative.

Appendices

Appendix 1

ACT Justice Survey

Victim Questionnaire

Interviewer Preparation

Was the respondent's case disposed of by conference or court case? (Circle whichever is applicable)

conference / *court case*

Did the respondent attend the conference or court case? (Circle whichever is applicable)

yes / *no*

Is the respondent a juvenile? (Circle whichever is applicable)

juvenile / *non-juvenile*

(Get the respondent to read and sign the Consent Form. If the respondent is a juvenile, the Consent Form must be filled in by a parent or guardian.)

First I want to ask you a few questions about how you found the processing of your case.

1. Were you informed in good time about when your case was to be dealt with ?

Yes 1

No.. 2

☞ Card 1

For Conference Victims only

2. Were you given information on what would happen at the conference?.....	None at all 1	Not much 2	Some 3	A lot 4
3. Were you given information on what was expected of you at the conference?	None at all 1	Not much 2	Some 3	A lot 4
4. Were you given information on possible outcomes?...................................	None at all 1	Not much 2	Some 3	A lot 4
5. Were you given time to discuss your case with the police?........................	None at all 1	Not much 2	Some 3	A lot 4

For Court Victims only

6a. Were you officially informed about what the offender(s) was charged with?

Yes 1

No.. 2

6b. **(If no above)** Do you feel you should have been informed of the charge?

Yes... 1

No.. 2

7a. Do you know what the outcome was from the offender's going to court?

Yes 1

No.. 2

7b. **(If no above)** Do you feel you should have been informed of the outcome?

Yes... 1

No.. 2

☞ Card 2

8. As a result of the way your case was handled, would you say your respect for the police has ....

| Gone down a lot 1 | Gone down a little 2 | Not changed 3 | Gone up a little 4 | Gone up a lot 5 |

I now want to read out some statements and ask you to respond by telling me how much you agree with each of them .

☞ Card 3

9. You felt you suffered a loss of dignity as a result of this offence............................

| Strongly disagree 1 | Disagree 2 | Neither agree nor disagree 3 | Agree 4 | Strongly agree 5 |

10. You felt you suffered a loss of self-respect as a result of this offence...............

| Strongly disagree 1 | Disagree 2 | Neither agree nor disagree 3 | Agree 4 | Strongly agree 5 |

11. You felt you suffered a loss of self-confidence as a result of this offence.........

| Strongly disagree 1 | Disagree 2 | Neither agree nor disagree 3 | Agree 4 | Strongly agree 5 |

12. You felt you could trust the police during your case...

| Strongly disagree 1 | Disagree 2 | Neither agree nor disagree 3 | Agree 4 | Strongly agree 5 |

13. In general, the police in Canberra enforce the law fairly ....

| Strongly disagree 1 | Disagree 2 | Neither agree nor disagree 3 | Agree 4 | Strongly agree 5 |

14. You are satisfied with the way your case was dealt with by the justice system...

| Strongly disagree 1 | Disagree 2 | Neither agree nor disagree 3 | Agree 4 | Strongly agree 5 |

15. The way your case was dealt with made you feel angry ....

| Strongly disagree 1 | Disagree 2 | Neither agree nor disagree 3 | Agree 4 | Strongly agree 5 |

16. You feel bitter about the way you were treated in the case..............................

| Strongly disagree 1 | Disagree 2 | Neither agree nor disagree 3 | Agree 4 | Strongly agree 5 |

17. You would do some harm to the offender(s) yourself if you had the chance ....

| Strongly disagree 1 | Disagree 2 | Neither agree nor disagree 3 | Agree 4 | Strongly agree 5 |

Now I would like to ask you some questions about the offender(s) in your case.

18a. Has the offender(s) apologised to you?

Yes 1

Some or one of them 2

No 3

18b. (If yes)   Was the apology part of the **conference**/*court case* outcome?

Yes 1

No 2

18c. Do you feel the apology you were offered was   ☞ Card 4

	Offender 1	Offender 2	Offender 3	Offender 4
Not at all sincere	1	1	1	1
Not very sincere	2	2	2	2
Somewhat sincere	3	3	3	3
Sincere	4	4	4	4
Don't know	5	5	5	5

18d. (**If no apology**) Do you think that an apology would have helped you to forgive the offender(s)? ....

☞ Card 5

Definitely not $_1$	Probably not $_2$	Unsure $_3$	Probably $_4$	Definitely yes $_5$

19. Do you anticipate that the offender(s) will repeat this offence?

For offender 1   On you .... Yes$_1$ No$_2$ DK$_3$

On another victim .... Yes$_1$ No$_2$ DK$_3$

For offender 2   On you .... Yes$_1$ No$_2$ DK$_3$

On another victim .... Yes$_1$ No$_2$ DK$_3$

For offender 3   On you .... Yes$_1$ No$_2$ DK$_3$

On another victim .... Yes$_1$ No$_2$ DK$_3$

For offender 4   On you .... Yes$_1$ No$_2$ DK$_3$

On another victim .... Yes$_1$ No$_2$ DK$_3$

20. Have you heard of diversionary conferencing?

Yes 1

No... 2

If no, tell respondent:
In the ACT some offences can be dealt with by a new procedure called diversionary conferencing. In these conferences, the offender(s) and the victim(s), together with their family and friends, meet face to face to discuss an arrangement for resolving the harm caused by the offence.

☞ **Card 6**

21. You are pleased that your case was dealt with by **conference** (*court*) rather than by **court** (*conference*)	Strongly disagree 1	Disagree 2	Neither agree nor disagree 3	Agree 4	Strongly agree 5

22. What happened in your case will encourage you to obey the law...................	Strongly disagree 1	Disagree 2	Neither agree nor disagree 3	Agree 4	Strongly agree 5

☞ **Card 7**

23. As a result of your experience with this case, has your respect for the justice system..	Gone down a lot 1	Gone down a little 2	Not changed 3	Gone up a little 4	Gone up a lot 5

24. As a result of your experience with this case, has your respect for the law	Gone down a lot 1	Gone down a little 2	Not changed 3	Gone up a little 4	Gone up a lot 5

For property offences only

Now I would like to ask you some questions about the actual loss and harm you experienced as a result of the offence.

25. What do you estimate were the financial costs to you resulting from the offence, before any insurance claim? (Whole dollar amounts)

Damage to property	$_____	None oooo
Loss of wages	$_____	None oooo
Medical costs	$_____	None oooo
Legal costs	$_____	None oooo
Repairs	$_____	None oooo
Improved security	$_____	None oooo
Other (specify)	$_____	None oooo
Total	$_____	

☞ Card 8

26. How much of these costs did you recover through insurance?

NA.. 1
None.. 2
Some of it... 3
Most of it.. 4
All of it... 5

27. Were your stolen goods recovered?

NA.. 1
No... 2
Partly 3
Yes 4

For Court Victims of property offences only

28a. **If no insurance cover or recovery** - Would you have been prepared to settle the case out of court if the offender(s) had returned the goods/cash and repaired damages?

Yes 1

Perhaps.. 2

No... 3

28b. **(If no above)** What compensation and/or action by the offender(s), in addition to the goods/cash returned, would you have required in order to settle the case out of court?

No amount... 1

$ amount.. 2

Other action (specify) _____ 3

29a. Were any of your possessions disarranged or otherwise interfered with during the incident ?

Yes 1

No.. 2

☞ **Card 9**

29b. **(If yes above)** Did this   **Not at all   Not very   Somewhat   Very**
make you feel................................   **upset   upset   upset   upset**
                                                       1   2   3   4

For violent crime only

30a. Did you suffer injury as a result of the offence which required medical attention?

Yes 1

No... 2

30b. **(If yes above)** Did you require

The attention of a doctor.. Yes₁   No₂

Hospital emergency-casualty assistance .... Yes₁   No₂

Admission to hospital .... Yes₁   No₂

☞ **Card 10**

31. How much of the financial costs associated with this injury have you recovered through Workers Compensation, Criminal Injuries Compensation or any other insurance?

NA.. 1

None 2

Some of it... 3

Most of it.. 4

All of it... 5

32. Have you experienced any of the following as a result of the offence:

☞ Card 11

			A fair amount	
a. Financial problems..................................	None 1	Little 2	amount 3	A lot 4

			A fair amount	
b. Housing difficulties................................	None 1	Little 2	amount 3	A lot 4

			A fair amount	
c. Employment difficulties	None 1	Little 2	amount 3	A lot 4

d. Any other difficulties? (specify)

_____

_____

33. Do you believe you should have received any of the following from the offender(s) to compensate you for loss and harm?

Money..	Yes$_1$	No$_2$
Offender(s) should do some work for you/family	Yes$_1$	No$_2$
Any other restitution...	Yes$_1$	No$_2$
An apology	Yes$_1$	No$_2$
Other (specify)...	Yes$_1$	No$_2$

_____

_____

34a. Were you awarded any of these through the **conference**/*court case*?

Yes 1

No.. 2

34b. **(If yes)** Which ones?

_____

_____

For Court Victims only

35. Have you thought about seeking compensation or restitution for the offence?

Yes 1

No.. 2

36a. Have you taken any precautions to minimise the risk of becoming a victim of crime again?

Yes 1

No... 2

36b. (If yes above). What are they?

For property offences:

Lock doors and windows...	Yes$_1$	No$_2$
More careful with valuables..	Yes$_1$	No$_2$
Security improvements	Yes$_1$	No$_2$
Leave lights and TV on, etc	Yes$_1$	No$_2$
Look out for suspicious people	Yes$_1$	No$_2$
Check behind the front door when you get home	Yes$_1$	No$_2$
Make special arrangements for your children..................	Yes$_1$	No$_2$
Anything else? (Keep probing until answer is negative) ..	Yes$_1$	No$_2$

_____

_____

For violent offences:

Don't go out as much	Yes$_1$	No$_2$
Avoid location of the offence and similar places.............	Yes$_1$	No$_2$
Self-defence classes......................................	Yes$_1$	No$_2$
Carry weapon of any kind (Specify) _____	Yes$_1$	No$_2$
More careful about what you say and do.......................	Yes$_1$	No$_2$
Control your own anger more	Yes$_1$	No$_2$
Anything else? (Keep probing until answer is negative) ..	Yes$_1$	No$_2$

....

....

Now I would like to ask you about any psychological or non-material harm that you have experienced as a result of the offence.

37a. Have you suffered from any of the following as a result of the offence

Fear of being alone	Yes₁	No₂
Sleeplessness/nightmares	Yes₁	No₂
Headaches or other physical symptoms	Yes₁	No₂
General increase in suspicion or distrust	Yes₁	No₂
Loss of confidence	Yes₁	No₂
Loss of self-esteem	Yes₁	No₂
Other problems (Specify)	Yes₁	No₂

_____

_____

☞ **Card 12**

37b. (If yes above) To what extent was the **conference**/*court case* helpful in your overcoming these difficulties? ....

Not helpful	Helped a little	Helped a lot	Did not attend conference/ court
1	2	3	4

38. Have you previously been the victim of this kind of offence?

Yes 1

No... 2

39a. Did you know the offender(s) before this offence occurred?

Yes 1

One/some of them... 2

No... 3

39b. (If yes or some of them above) What was the nature of your relationship with the principal offender?

Friend 1

Acquaintance 2

Neighbour... 3

Relative 4

Someone at work 5

Someone else who you have had trouble with before 6

Other (specify) _____7

40a. Have you previously been the victim of the same offender(s)?

Yes 1

No.. 2

40b. **(If yes, above)** Did you report these incidents to the police?

Yes... 1

Some of them... 2

No... 3

Thank you. Now I am going to read out some statements again and ask you to tell me how much you agree with them. Again, the possible answers are from Strongly agree to Strongly disagree.

☞ Card 13

41. You feel that whether you are a victim of crime again in the future is pretty much beyond your control	**Strongly disagree** 1	**Disagree** 2	**Neither agree nor disagree** 3	**Agree** 4	**Strongly agree** 5

42. The offence made you feel you were unworthy of respect...................................	**Strongly disagree** 1	**Disagree** 2	**Neither agree nor disagree** 3	**Agree** 4	**Strongly agree** 5

43. You sometimes think that the incident might have been prevented if you had been more careful or less provoking	**Strongly disagree** 1	**Disagree** 2	**Neither agree nor disagree** 3	**Agree** 4	**Strongly agree** 5

44. Did you attend the **<u>conference</u>/*court case*** concerning your case

Yes .... 1 ➜ go to question 46

No... 2

45. Do you now think you would have got some benefit from going to the **<u>conference</u>/*court case*?**

Yes 1

No.. 2

Don't know 3

SKIP TO QUESTION 112 on page 19

Now I would like to ask you about the reasons for your decision to attend the **<u>conference</u>/*court case*.** Could you please tell me how important each of the following reasons were for you?

☞ Card 14

46. You attended because you wanted to express your feelings and speak directly to the offender(s)..	**Not at all important** 1	**Not very important** 2	**Somewhat important** 3	**Quite important** 4	**Very important** 5

| 47. You attended because you wanted to help the offender(s)............................... | Not at all important 1 | Not very important 2 | Somewhat important 3 | Quite important 4 | Very important 5 |

| 48. You attended because you wanted to ensure that the penalty for the offence was appropriate.. | Not at all important 1 | Not very important 2 | Somewhat important 3 | Quite important 4 | Very important 5 |

| 49. You attended because you felt a duty to attend.. | Not at all important 1 | Not very important 2 | Somewhat important 3 | Quite important 4 | Very important 5 |

| 50. You attended because you wanted to have a say in how the problem was resolved... | Not at all important 1 | Not very important 2 | Somewhat important 3 | Quite important 4 | Very important 5 |

| 51. You attended because you wanted to ensure that you would be repaid for the harm you had experienced .... | Not at all important 1 | Not very important 2 | Somewhat important 3 | Quite important 4 | Very important 5 |

For Conference Victims only

| 52. You attended because you were curious and wanted to see how conferencing works.................................. | Not at all important 1 | Not very important 2 | Somewhat important 3 | Quite important 4 | Very important 5 |

53. Were there any other reasons? *(Probe respondent by asking for any other reasons until a negative reply is obtained)*

_____

_____

_____

(End of statements)

Now I would like to ask you a few questions about your **conference**/*court case*

54. Who attended the **conference**/*court case* with you? (*indicate number, if more than one*)

No one attended.. 1

The following people: 2

Relationship	Number
21 Victim's spouse/partner	
22 Victim's mother..	
23 Victim's father..	
24 Victim's stepmother/defacto mother	
25 Victim's stepfather/defacto father	
26 Victim's sibling(s)..	
27 Victim's child(ren)	
28 Victim's grandparent(s)	
29 Victim's other relative(s)	
30 Victim's friend(s)	
31 Victim's neighbour(s)	
32 Victim's co-worker(s)	
33 Victim's supervisor	
34 Co-victim..	
35 Other (specify relationship) _____ ...	

☞ Card 15

For Conference Victims only

55. How satisfied were you with the arrangements made by police to ensure that you could get along for the conference? ....

	Very dissatisfied 1	Quite dissatisfied 2	Neither satisfied nor dissatisfied 3	Quite satisfied 4	Very satisfied 5

56. Did anything go wrong with these arrangements?

Yes (*specify*) _____ 1

No... 2

☞ Card 16

I now want to read out some statements and ask you to respond by telling me how much you agree with each of them .

	Strongly disagree 1	Disagree 2	Neither agree nor disagree 3	Agree 4	Strongly agree 5
57. You were afraid of the offender(s) before the **conference**/*court case*	Strongly disagree 1	Disagree 2	Neither agree nor disagree 3	Agree 4	Strongly agree 5
58. Before the **conference**/*court case* you felt embarrassed over the whole incident..	Strongly disagree 1	Disagree 2	Neither agree nor disagree 3	Agree 4	Strongly agree 5
59. Before the **conference**/*court case* you felt ashamed about the whole incident..	Strongly disagree 1	Disagree 2	Neither agree nor disagree 3	Agree 4	Strongly agree 5
60. You understood what was going on in the **conference**/*court case*....................	Strongly disagree 1	Disagree 2	Neither agree nor disagree 3	Agree 4	Strongly agree 5
61. You feel you were treated with respect during the **conference**/*court case*	Strongly disagree 1	Disagree 2	Neither agree nor disagree 3	Agree 4	Strongly agree 5
62. The police were fair during the **conference**/*court case*..............................	Strongly disagree 1	Disagree 2	Neither agree nor disagree 3	Agree 4	Strongly agree 1
63. If the **conference**/*court case* got the facts wrong, you felt able to get this corrected	Strongly disagree 1	Disagree 2	Neither agree nor disagree 3	Agree 4	Strongly agree 3
64. If you had been treated unjustly by the **conference**/*court case* or the police, you believe you could have got your complaint heard	Strongly disagree 1	Disagree 2	Neither agree nor disagree 3	Agree 4	Strongly agree 5
65. At the **conference**/*court case* you had an opportunity to explain the loss and harm that resulted from the offence	Strongly disagree 1	Disagree 2	Neither agree nor disagree 3	Agree 4	Strongly agree 5
66. During the **conference**/*court case* you felt awkward and aware of yourself	Strongly disagree 1	Disagree 2	Neither agree nor disagree 3	Agree 4	Strongly agree 5
67. During the **conference**/*court case* you felt ashamed	Strongly disagree 1	Disagree 2	Neither agree nor disagree 3	Agree 4	Strongly agree 5

68. All sides got a fair chance to bring out the facts at the **conference**/*court case* ....

| Strongly disagree 1 | Disagree 2 | Neither agree nor disagree 3 | Agree 4 | Strongly agree 5 |

69. You felt you had the opportunity to express your views in the **conference**/*court case* ....

| Strongly disagree 1 | Disagree 2 | Neither agree nor disagree 3 | Agree 4 | Strongly agree 5 |

70. The **conference**/*court case* took account of what you said in deciding what should be done ....

| Strongly disagree 1 | Disagree 2 | Neither agree nor disagree 3 | Agree 4 | Strongly agree 5 |

71. After the **conference**/*court case* you felt the offender(s) had a proper understanding of the harm caused to you ..

| Strongly disagree 1 | Disagree 2 | Neither agree nor disagree 3 | Agree 4 | Strongly agree 5 |

72. The **conference**/*court case* took adequate account of the effects of the offence on you ....

| Strongly disagree 1 | Disagree 2 | Neither agree nor disagree 3 | Agree 4 | Strongly agree 5 |

73a. You were disadvantaged in the **conference**/*court case* by your age, income, sex, race or some other reason.....

| Strongly disagree 1 | Disagree 2 | Neither agree nor disagree 3 | Agree 4 | Strongly agree 5 |

73b. *If agree or strongly agree above*, What was the reason? *(Probe respondent by asking for any other reasons until a negative reply is given)*

Race/ethnicity 1

Sex. 2

Age 3

Income.. 4

Other (specify)_____5

74. You felt too intimidated to say what you really felt in the **conference**/ *court case* ....

| Strongly disagree 1 | Disagree 2 | Neither agree nor disagree 3 | Agree 4 | Strongly agree 5 |

For Conference Victims only					
75. You felt you had enough control over the way things were run in the conference...	Strongly disagree ₁	Disagree ₂	Neither agree nor disagree ₃	Agree ₄	Strongly agree ₅
76. During the conference you felt pushed into things you did not agree with	Strongly disagree ₁	Disagree ₂	Neither agree nor disagree ₃	Agree ₄	Strongly agree ₅
77. You felt pushed around in the conference by people with more power than you..	Strongly disagree ₁	Disagree ₂	Neither agree nor disagree ₃	Agree ₄	Strongly agree ₅
78. The conference only made you remember things you wanted to forget..	Strongly disagree ₁	Disagree ₂	Neither agree nor disagree ₃	Agree ₄	Strongly agree ₅
79. The government should use conferencing as an alternative to court more often...................................	Strongly disagree ₁	Disagree ₂	Neither agree nor disagree ₃	Agree ₄	Strongly agree ₅

80. After the **conference/court case** you felt afraid of the offender(s)	Strongly disagree ₁	Disagree ₂	Neither agree nor disagree ₃	Agree ₄	Strongly agree ₅
81. You felt the **conference/court case** allowed the harm done to you by the offender(s) to be repaired...........	Strongly disagree ₁	Disagree ₂	Neither agree nor disagree ₃	Agree ₄	Strongly agree ₅
82. Since the **conference/court case** you now think the offender(s) has learnt his lesson and deserves a second chance	Strongly disagree ₁	Disagree ₂	Neither agree nor disagree ₃	Agree ₄	Strongly agree ₅
83. The **conference/court case** made you feel you could put the whole thing behind you...................................	Strongly disagree ₁	Disagree ₂	Neither agree nor disagree ₃	Agree ₄	Strongly agree ₅
84. Since the **conference/court case**, in thinking about the offender(s), you have felt...	Very unforgiving ₁	Unforgiving ₂	Neither forgiving or unforgiving ₃	Forgiving ₄	Very forgiving ₅

☞ Card 17

Thank you. Now I would like to ask you a few questions about how you felt about your conference/court case.   ☞ Card 18

85. How nervous were you about attending the **conference**/*court case*? Would you say......................................

Not at all nervous	Not really nervous	Somewhat nervous	Very nervous
1	2	3	4

☞ Card 19

86. How fair did you feel the **conference**/ *court case* was for you? Would you say that it was ....

Very unfair	Somewhat unfair	Somewhat fair	Very fair
1	2	3	4

87. How fair do you think the **conference**/ *court case* was to the offender(s)? ....

Very unfair	Somewhat unfair	Somewhat fair	Very fair
1	2	3	4

☞ Card 20

88. How much did you feel the **conference**/ *court case* respected your rights? Would you say..............................

Not at all	A little	A fair bit	A lot
1	2	3	4

89. Do you think the **conference**/*court case* helped to solve any problems? Would you say..

Not at all	A little	A fair bit	A lot
1	2	3	4

☞ Card 21

90. Before the **conference**/*court case* how angry did you feel with the offender(s)? ....

Not at all angry	Not very angry	Quite angry	Very angry
1	2	3	4

91. After the **conference**/*court case* how angry did you feel with the offender(s)? ....

Not at all angry	Not very angry	Quite angry	Very angry
1	2	3	4

☞ Card 22

92. How sympathetic did you feel towards the offender(s) before the **conference**/*court case*?............................

Very unsympathetic	Not very sympathetic	A little sympathetic	Very sympathetic
1	2	3	4

93. How sympathetic did you feel
towards the offender(s) after the
conference/*court case*? ....

Very unsympathetic 1	Not very sympathetic 2	A little sympathetic 3	Very sympathetic 4

94. How sympathetic did you feel
towards the offender's family and
supporters before the conference/*court
case*? ....

Very unsympathetic 1	Not very sympathetic 2	A little sympathetic 3	Very sympathetic 4

95. How sympathetic did you feel
towards the offender's family and
supporters after the conference/*court
case*? ....

Very unsympathetic 1	Not very sympathetic 2	A little sympathetic 3	Very sympathetic 4

☞ Card 23

96. How helpful to you did you find
attending the conference/*court case*? ....

Very unhelpful 1	Unhelpful 2	Neither helpful nor unhelpful 3	Helpful 4	Very helpful 5

☞ Card 24

97. Did the conference/*court case*
make you feel more or less settled
emotionally about the offence? ....

A lot less settled 1	A little less settled 2	No different 3	A little more settled 4	A lot more settled 5

☞ Card 25

98. In the week after the
conference/*court case* did your family
and friends give you more support or
less support than they usually give you?....

Much less support 1	A little less support 2	About the same 3	A little more support 4	Much more support 5

☞ Card 26

99. Since the conference/*court case*
have you felt your sense of security has
been restored? ....

No 1	Yes, partly 2	Yes, completely 3	NA 4

☞ Card 27

100. The **conference**/*court case* has given you satisfaction that the offender(s) was caught	Not at all 1	A little 2	A fair bit 3	A lot 4	

☞ Card 28

101. Was your sense of dignity increased or reduced after the **conference**/*court case*?	Reduced a lot 1	Reduced a little 2	No different 3	Increased a little 4	Increased a lot 5

102. Was your sense of self-respect increased or reduced after the **conference**/ *court case*?	Reduced a lot 1	Reduced a little 2	No different 3	Increased a little 4	Increased a lot 5

103. Was your self-confidence increased or reduced after the **conference**/*court case*?	Reduced a lot 1	Reduced a little 2	No different 3	Increased a little 4	Increased a lot 5

☞ Card 29

104. If you were the victim of a young person's offending again, you would chose to attend a **conference**/*court case* again	Definitely not 1	Probably not 2	Unsure 3	Probably yes 4	Definitely yes 5

☞ Card 30

105a. Immediately after the **conference**/ *court case*, you were satisfied with the outcome	Strongly disagree 1	Disagree 2	Neither agree nor disagree 3	Agree 4	Strongly agree 5
105b. **(If agree or strongly agree above)**. You are still satisfied with the outcome	Strongly disagree 1	Disagree 2	Neither agree nor disagree 3	Agree 4	Strongly agree 5

Thank you. Now I would like to ask you some questions about your feelings before and after the **conference**/*court case*.

☞ Card 31

106. Before the **conference**/*court case*, what would you say the offence had done to your trust in others? Were you....	A lot less trusting 1	A little less trusting 2	No different 3	A little more trusting 4	A lot more trusting 5

107. After the **conference**/*court case*, how did you feel regarding your trust in others? Were you	A lot less trusting 1	A little less trusting 2	No different 3	A little more trusting 4	A lot more trusting 5

☞ Card 32

108. Before the **conference**/*court case*, how anxious were you about the offence happening again	Not anxious 1	A little anxious 2	Somewhat anxious 3	Anxious 4	Very Anxious 5

109. <u>After</u> the <u>**conference**</u>/***court case***, how anxious were you about the offence happening again ....

| Not anxious 1 | A little anxious 2 | Somewhat anxious 3 | Anxious 4 | Very Anxious 5 |

☞ Card 33

110. The <u>**conference**</u>/***court case*** has helped you in dealing with any feelings of embarrassment you might have about the offence.......................................

| NA 1 | Not at all 2 | Not much 3 | To some extent 4 | Quite a lot 5 |

111. The <u>**conference**</u>/***court case*** has helped you in dealing with any feelings of shame you might have about the offence.............

| NA 1 | Not at all 2 | Not much 3 | To some extent 4 | Quite a lot 5 |

FOR RESPONDENTS WHO ANSWERED QUESTION 45 ON PAGE 10, RECOMMENCE HERE

Thank you. Now, I am going to read a list of statements and I would like you to indicate how well you think each one describes you.

☞ Card 34

112. It takes a lot to make me mad ....

| Strongly disagree 1 | Disagree 2 | Agree 3 | Strongly agree 4 |

113. I frequently get upset ....

| Strongly disagree 1 | Disagree 2 | Agree 3 | Strongly agree 4 |

114. There are many things that annoy me...

| Strongly disagree 1 | Disagree 2 | Agree 3 | Strongly agree 4 |

115. All in all, I'm inclined to believe that I'm a failure ....

| Strongly disagree 1 | Disagree 2 | Agree 3 | Strongly agree 4 |

116. I am able to do things as well as most other people...

| Strongly disagree 1 | Disagree 2 | Agree 3 | Strongly agree 4 |

117. If I can't do a job the first time, I keep trying until I can ....

| Strongly disagree 1 | Disagree 2 | Agree 3 | Strongly agree 4 |

118. When I'm trying to learn something
new, I soon give up if I'm not initially
successful ....

Strongly disagree	Disagree	Agree	Strongly agree
1	2	3	4

119. I can tolerate frustration better
than most ....

Strongly disagree	Disagree	Agree	Strongly agree
1	2	3	4

120. Failure just makes me try harder ....

Strongly disagree	Disagree	Agree	Strongly agree
1	2	3	4

121. I give up easily................................

Strongly disagree	Disagree	Agree	Strongly agree
1	2	3	4

122. I feel that I don't have much to be
proud of...

Strongly disagree	Disagree	Agree	Strongly agree
1	2	3	4

123. Nothing much ever bothers me ....

Strongly disagree	Disagree	Agree	Strongly agree
1	2	3	4

Now, can you tell me:

☞ Card 35

124. To what extent do you believe
people try to be helpful? ....

Hardly ever	Sometimes	A lot of the time	Almost always
1	2	3	4

125. To what extent do you believe
people are mostly just looking out for
themselves? ....

Hardly ever	Sometimes	A lot of the time	Almost always
1	2	3	4

126. To what extent do you believe that
most people would try to take advantage
of you if they got the chance?......................

Hardly ever	Sometimes	A lot of the time	Almost always
1	2	3	4

127. To what extent do you believe
that most people try to be fair? ....

Hardly ever	Sometimes	A lot of the time	Almost always
1	2	3	4

128. To what extent do you believe
that most people can be trusted?................

Hardly ever	Sometimes	A lot of the time	Almost always
1	2	3	4

129. To what extent do you believe that
you can't be too careful in dealing with
people? ....

Hardly ever	Sometimes	A lot of the time	Almost always
1	2	3	4

Now I want to ask you some questions about your background. These are used for statistical purposes only in studies like this so that we can group the answers of similar people together.

130. (*Code respondent's sex*)

Male.. 1

Female 2

131. What is your date of birth   __ / __ / 19 __

132. In which country were you born?

Australia... 01

New Zealand 02

United Kingdom 03

Ireland.. 04

Italy.. 05

Germany... 06

Greece.. 07

Malta.. 08

Netherlands 09

Poland... 10

Former Yugoslavia 11

Vietnam.. 12

Laos.. 13

China... 14

Phillipines... 15

Hong Kong.. 16

Tonga.. 17

Macedonia... 18

Chile 19

Other (please specify) _____ 20

Don't know.. 21

133. Are you of Aboriginal or Torres Strait Islander heritage?

Yes 1

No.. 2

134. Apart from weddings, funerals and baptisms, about how often do you attend religious services?

At least once a week 1

At least once a month 2

Several times a year 3

At least once a year 4

Less than once a year 5

Never 6

135. Since you were born, how many years have you lived in the ACT?

_____ years   [_____ months]

(If length less than 1 year, specify months)

(If respondent can't remember - obtain year and month of arrival and calculate)

☞ **Card 36**

136. What is the highest grade or year of (primary or secondary) school <u>you</u> have completed?

No formal schooling... **00**

Primary .... Grade 1 .... **01**

Grade 2 .... **02**

Grade 3 .... **03**

Grade 4 .... **04**

Grade 5 .... **05**

Grade 6 .... **06**

Secondary................. Year 7 (Form 1).. **07**

Year 8 (Form 2).. **08**

Year 9 (Form 3).. **09**

Year 10 (Form 4)...................................... **10**

Year 11 (Form 5)...................................... **11**

Year 12 (Form 6)...................................... **12**

137. Have you obtained a trade qualification, a degree or a diploma, or any other qualification since leaving school? What is your <u>highest</u> qualification?

Non-trade qualification... **01**

Trade qualification... **02**

Associate Diploma... **03**

Undergraduate Diploma **04**

Bachelor Degree **05**

Postgraduate Diploma.. **06**

Higher degree - Masters or PhD **07**

Certificate.. **08**

No qualification since leaving school **09**

Not applicable / Still at school **10**

☞ **Card 37**

138. Looking at the answers on this card, which best describes you situation during the last 6 months?

Working full-time for pay **1**

Working part-time for pay... **2**

Unemployed and looking for work **3**

Unemployed and not looking for work...................................... **4**

Retired from paid work.. **5**

A full-time school or university student.................................... **6**

Home duties **7**

Other (please specify)_____ **8**

For respondents who are employed

139. What type of work do you do? (*Interviewer to code on basis of response to this question*)

Higher professional (examples: doctor, electrical engineer, university scientist, secondary school teacher, lawyer, clergy) 01

Higher administrator (examples: banker, executive in big business, high government official, union official) 02

Technical and lower professional (examples: nurse, artist, primary school teacher, lab technician) 03

Clerical (examples: secretary, clerk, office manager, public servant, bookkeeper) 04

Sales (examples: sales manager, shop owner, shop assistant, insurance agent) 05

Service (examples: restaurant owner, policeman, waitress, barber, janitor) 06

Skilled worker (examples: foreman, motor mechanic, printer, seamstress, electrician) 07

Semi-skilled worker (examples: bus driver, cannery worker, carpenter, metal worker, baker) .. 08

Unskilled worker (examples: labourer, porter, unskilled factory worker) 09

Farm (examples: farmer, farm labourer, jackeroo) 10

140. Is your job permanent or temporary?

Permanent 1

Temporary 2

141. In your job do you supervise other people?

Yes 1

No 2

142. How much authority do you have
in deciding how to do your work? ....

| Very little 1 | Not very much 2 | Moderate 3 | Great 4 | Very great 5 |

☞ Card 38

143. If I give you this card, can you tell me the number which indicates the total (gross) annual income from all sources, before tax or other deductions, for you and your family living with you?

Less than $3,000 per year   (Less than $58 per week)............................ 01

$3001 to $5,000 per year   ($58 to $96 per week)................................ 02

$5001 to $8,000 per year   ($96 to $154 per week)............................... 03

$8,001 to $12,000 per year   ($154 to $231 per week)......................... 04

$12,001 to $16,000 per year   ($231 to $308 per week)...................... 05

$16,001 to $20,000 per year   ($308 to $385 per week)...................... 06

$20,001 to $25,000 per year   ($385 to $481 per week)...................... 07

$25,001 to $30,000 per year   ($481 to $577 per week)...................... 08

$30,001 to $35,000 per year   ($577 to $673 per week)...................... 09

$35,001 to $40,000 per year   ($673 to $769 per week)...................... 10

$40,001 to $50,000 per year   ($769 to $962 per week)...................... 11

$50,001 to $60,000 per year   ($962 to $1,154 per week) 12

$60,001 to $70,000 per year   ($1,154 to $1,346 per week)............... 13

$70,001 to $80,000 per year   ($1,346 to $1,538 per week)............... 14

$80,001 to $90,000 per year   ($1,538 to $1,731 per week)............... 15

$90,001 to $100,000 per year   ($1,1731 to $ 1,923 per week)........... 16

More than $100,000 per year   (More than $1,923 per week)............... 17

Don't know 18

Refused 19

144. What is your current marital status?   '

Never married.. 1

Now married (including de facto relationships) 2

Widowed... 3

Divorced or separated 4

N/A.. 5

145. *(Interviewer to code - Is respondent under 18 years?)*

Yes 1

No.. 2 ➜ go to last page

146. Do you live with your mother or female guardian?................. Mother ₁   Female Guardian ₂   No ₃

147. Do you live with your father or male guardian? .... Father ₁   Male Guardian ₂   No ₃

148. In what country was your mother born?

Australia.. 01
New Zealand 02
United Kingdom 03
Ireland 04
Italy.. 05
Germany... 06
Greece.. 07
Malta... 08
Netherlands 09
Poland 10
Former Yugoslavia 11
Vietnam.. 12
Tonga.. 13
Other (please specify) _____ 14
Don't know.. 15

☞ **Card 39**

149. Looking at the answers on this card, which best describes what your mother has been doing during the last 6 months?

Working full-time for pay 1
Working part-time for pay... 2
Unemployed and looking for work 3
Unemployed and not looking for work.. 4
Retired from paid work.. 5
A full-time school or university student.. 6
Home duties 7
Other (please specify)_____ 8

150. What type of work does your mother do? (*Interviewer to code on basis of response to this question*)

Higher professional (examples: doctor, electrical engineer, university scientist, secondary school teacher, lawyer, clergy).. 01

Higher administrator (examples: banker, executive in big business, high government official, union official)... 02

Technical and lower professional (examples: nurse, artist, primary school teacher, lab technician) 03

Clerical (examples: secretary, clerk, office manager, public servant, bookkeeper) 04

Sales (examples: sales manager, shop owner, shop assistant, insurance agent)........................ 05

Service (examples: restaurant owner, policeman, waitress, barber, janitor) 06

Skilled worker (examples: foreman, motor mechanic, printer, seamstress, electrician) 07

Semi-skilled worker (examples: bus driver, cannery worker, carpenter, metal worker, baker). 08

Unskilled worker (examples: labourer, porter, unskilled factory worker)................................. 09

Farm (examples: farmer, farm labourer, jackeroo)... 10

151. In what country was your father born?

Australia... 01

New Zealand 02

United Kingdom 03

Ireland.. 04

Italy.. 05

Germany... 06

Greece.. 07

Malta.. 08

Netherlands 09

Poland 10

Former Yugoslavia 11

Vietnam.. 12

Tonga.. 13

Other (please specify) _____ 14

Don't know.. 15

☞ Card 40

152. Looking at the answers on this card, which best describes what your father has been doing during the last 6 months?

Working full-time for pay 1

Working part-time for pay.. 2

Unemployed and looking for work 3

Unemployed and not looking for work.. 4

Retired from paid work.. 5

A full-time school or university student... 6

Home duties 7

Other (please specify)_____ 8

For fathers who are employed

153. What type of work does your father do? *(Interviewer to code on basis of response to this question)*

Higher professional (examples: doctor, electrical engineer, university scientist, secondary
    school teacher, lawyer, clergy) 01

Higher administrator (examples: banker, executive in big business, high government
    official, union official) 02

Technical and lower professional (examples: nurse, artist, primary school teacher,
    lab technician) 03

Clerical (examples: secretary, clerk, office manager, public servant, bookkeeper) 04

Sales (examples: sales manager, shop owner, shop assistant, insurance agent)....................... 05

Service (examples: restaurant owner, policeman, waitress, barber, janitor)............................ 06

Skilled worker (examples: foreman, motor mechanic, printer, seamstress, electrician)............ 07

Semi-skilled worker (examples: bus driver, cannery worker, carpenter, metal worker, baker) . 08

Unskilled worker (examples: labourer, porter, unskilled factory worker)............................... 09

Farm (examples: farmer, farm labourer, jackeroo).. 10

154. Do you expect to move house sometime in the next 12 months -- just your best guess?

Probably not move house.. 1

Will probably move in the next year.. 2

Will definitely in the next year.. 3

155. We would very much like to get in touch with you again in a year or so. If that is OK, could you please give us the address of a relative or friend who will know your new address in case you have moved by then?

Person to be contacted: _____

Relationship to repondent: _____

Address: _____
Street

_____ _____
Suburb   Postcode

Phone Number: _____ _____
Work   Home

(Close interview and thank respondent)

Was the entire interview conducted in private? . . . . **Yes**   **No**

Interviewer to sign name to indicate true and correct interview

_____ —— / —— / 20—— —————— am / pm (circle)   ☐ ☐

Signature   Date   Time at end of interview   Interviewer code

Appendix 2
Full Text of All Questions Used in the Tables in Chapter 7

Table 7.3 and Table 7.10

1. In the conference/court I began to understand what it actually felt like for those who had been affected by my actions/Do you feel the apology you were offered was sincere?

2. Did others at the conference/court case say that you had learnt your lesson and now deserved a second chance?/ Do you feel the apology you were offered was sincere?

3. At the end of the conference/court case did people indicate that you were forgiven?/Since the conference/court case, in thinking about the offender(s) you have felt forgiving

4. The conference/court case allowed you to make up for what you did/ Do you feel the apology you were offered was sincere?

5. During the conference/court case I found myself really affected by the emotions of those who had been hurt in some way/ Do you feel the apology you were offered was sincere?

Table 7.4 and Table 7.12

1. The conference/court case just made you angry/Do you anticipate the offender(s) will repeat this offence on another victim?

2. You feel the people who accused you in the conference/court case were more wrong than you were/Do you anticipate the offender(s) will repeat this offence on another victim?

3. Were you treated in the conference/court case as though you were likely to commit another offence?/Do you anticipate the offender(s) will repeat this offence on another victim?

4.   You wish that you could get back at the people who were accusing you in the conference/court case/Do you anticipate the offender(s) will repeat this offence on another victim?

5.   The conference/court case just made you angry/Do you anticipate the offender(s) will repeat this offence on you?

6.   You feel the people who accused you in the conference/court case were more wrong than you were/Do you anticipate the offender(s) will repeat this offence on you?

7.   Were you treated in the conference/court case as though you were likely to commit another offence?/Do you anticipate the offender(s) will repeat this offence on you?

8.   You wish that you could get back at the people who were accusing you in the conference/court case/Do you anticipate the offender(s) will repeat this offence on you?

9.   Since the conference/court case have you found yourself unable to decide, in your own mind, whether or not what you did was wrong?/Do you anticipate the offender(s) will repeat this offence on another victim?

10.   Since the conference/court case have you found yourself unable to decide, in your own mind, whether or not what you did was wrong?/Do you anticipate the offender(s) will repeat this offence on you?

11.   You wish that you could get back at the people who were accusing you in the conference/court case/You would do some harm to the offender(s) yourself if you had the chance

12.   You feel the people who accused you in the conference/court case were more wrong than you were/ You would do some harm to the offender(s) yourself if you had the chance

13.   Now that it is all over you feel glad that you committed the offence that you did/ You would do some harm to the offender(s) yourself if you had the chance

14.   The conference/court case just made you angry/ You would do some harm to the offender(s) yourself if you had the chance

15.   You feel the people who accused you in the conference/court

case were more wrong than you were/The way your case was dealt with made you feel angry

16. Now that it is all over you feel glad that you committed the offence that you did/The way your case was dealt with made you feel angry

17. The conference/court case just made you angry/The way your case was dealt with made you feel angry

18. You wish that you could get back at the people who were accusing you in the conference/court case/The way your case was dealt with made you feel angry

19. You feel bitter about the way you were treated in the case/ You feel bitter about the way you were treated in the case

Table 7.5 and Table 7.14

1. You felt that you could trust the police during this case/ You felt that you could trust the police during your case

2. As a result of the way your case was handled would you say your respect for the police has [gone up]/As a result of the way your case was handled would you say your respect for the police has [gone up]

3. As a result of the way your case was handled would you say your respect for the law has [gone up]/As a result of the way your case was handled would you say your respect for the law has [gone up]

4. In general, the police in Canberra enforce the law fairly/In general, the police in Canberra enforce the law fairly

5. As a result of the way your case was handled would you say your respect for the justice system has [gone up]/As a result of the way your case was handled would you say your respect for the justice system has [gone up]

6. The conference/court case will help prevent you from breaking the law in future/What happened in your case will encourage you to obey the law

7. What happened in your case will encourage you to obey the

law/What happened in your case will encourage you to obey the law

Table 7.6 and Table 7.11

1. In the conference I began to understand what it actually felt like for those who had been affected by my actions/After the conference you felt the offender(s) had a proper understanding of the harm caused to you

2. I felt bad in the conference/court because my actions had hurt others/After the conference/court case you felt the offender(s) had a proper understanding of the harm caused to you

3. During the conference/court case I felt ashamed of what I did/After the conference/court case you felt the offender(s) had a proper understanding of the harm caused to you

4. You felt after the conference/court case that what you did was just plain stupid/Since the conference/court case you now think the offender(s) has learnt his lesson and deserves a second chance

5. As a result of your offence there was a victim hurt in some way/After the conference/court case you felt the offender(s) had a proper understanding of the harm caused to you

6. Do you think the conference/court helped to solve any problems/How helpful did you find attending the conference/court case?

7. Do you think the conference/court helped to solve any problems/Do you think the conference/court helped to solve any problems

8. The conference/court case allowed you to clear your conscience/How helpful did you find attending the conference/court case?

9. Did others at the conference/court case say you had learnt your lesson and now deserved a second chance?/After the conference/court case you felt the offender(s) had a proper understanding of the harm caused to you

10. At the end of the conference/court case did people indicate that you were forgiven?/Since the conference/court case, in thinking about the offender(s), you have felt forgiving

11. At the end of the conference/court case, or since then, have

people made it clear to you that you can put the whole thing behind you?/The conference/court case made you feel you could put the whole thing behind you

Table 7.7 and Table 7.13

1.   You feel the people who accused you in the conference/court case were more wrong than you/After the conference/court case how angry did you feel with the offender(s)?

2.   I felt in the conference/court case that those complaining about my actions were just sorry for themselves/ After the conference/court case how angry did you feel with the offender(s)?

3.   Now that it is all over you feel glad that you committed the offence that you did/ After the conference/court case how angry did you feel with the offender(s)?

Table 7.8 and Table 7.15

1.   How much influence did you have over the agreement reached in the conference/court case?/The conference/court case took account of what you said in deciding what should be done

2.   People in the conference/court spoke up on your behalf/You attended [the conference/court case] because you wanted to have a say in how the problem was resolved

3.   You felt too intimidated to say what you really felt in the conference/court case/You felt too intimidated to say what you really felt in the conference/court case

4.   During the conference/court case I felt awkward and aware of myself/During the conference/court case I felt awkward and aware of myself

Table 7.9 and Table 7.16

1.   You felt you had enough control over the way things were run in the conference/You felt you had enough control over the way things were run in the conference

2.   During the conference you felt pushed into things you did not

agree with/During the conference you felt pushed into things you did not agree with

3.   The conference/court case took account of what you said in deciding what should be done/ The conference/court case took account of what you said in deciding what should be done

4.   You understood what was going on in the conference/court case/You understood what was going on in the conference/court case

5.   You felt you had the opportunity to express your views in the conference/court case/ You felt you had the opportunity to express your views in the conference/court case

6.   How severe did you feel the outcome of the conference/court case was for you?/How fair do you think the conference/court case was to the offender(s)?

7.   Since the conference/court case have you found yourself continually bothered by thoughts that you were unfairly judged by people at the conference/court case?/How fair did you feel the conference/court case was to you?

8.   All sides got a fair chance to bring out the facts at the conference/court case/All sides got a fair chance to bring out the facts at the conference/court case

9.   The police were fair during the conference/court case/ The police were fair during the conference/court case

10.   How much did you feel the conference/court case respected your rights?/ How much did you feel the conference/court case respected your rights?

11.   You were disadvantaged in the conference/court case by your age, income, sex, race or some other reason/ You were disadvantaged in the conference/court case by your age, income, sex, race or some other reason

12.   You feel you were treated with respect in the conference/court case/ You feel you were treated with respect in the conference/court case

13.   If you had been treated unjustly by the conference/court case

or the police, you believe you could have got your complaint heard/
If you had been treated unjustly by the conference/court case or the
police, you believe you could have got your complaint heard

14.   If the conference/court case got the facts wrong, you felt able
to get this corrected/If the conference/court case got the facts
wrong, you felt able to get this corrected

Appendix 3
Completion Rates—Offender Question followed by Victim Question—for the Tables in Chapter 7

Tables 7.3 and 7.10: Emotional restoration post-treatment

1) Understood how others felt/Felt apology was sincere:
>> Overall completion is 75% (79/106) for Off 1
>> Overall completion is 58% (18/31) for Off 2
>> Overall completion is 38% (3/8) for Off 3
>> Overall completion is 100% (1/1) for Off 4

2) Others said you had learned lesson/Felt apology was sincere:
>> Overall completion is 75% (78/106) for Off 1
>> Overall completion is 58% (18/31) for Off 2
>> Overall completion is 25% (2/8) for Off 3
>> Overall completion is 100% (1/1) for Off 4

3) People indicated you were forgiven/Felt apology was sincere:
>> Overall completion is 75% (79/106) for Off 1
>> Overall completion is 58% (18/31) for Off 2
>> Overall completion is 38% (3/8) for Off 3
>> Overall completion is 100% (1/1) for Off 4

4) Felt allowed to make up for actions/Felt apology was sincere:
>> Overall completion is 75% (79/106) for Off 1
>> Overall completion is 58% (18/31) for Off 2
>> Overall completion is 38% (3/8) for Off 3
>> Overall completion is 100% (1/1) for Off 4

5) Affected by emotions/Felt apology was sincere
>> Overall completion is 75% (79/106) for Off 1
>> Overall completion is 58% (18/31) for Off 2
>> Overall completion is 38% (3/8) for Off 3
>> Overall completion is 100% (1/1) for Off 4

Tables 7.4 and 7.12: Emotional harm post-treatment

1) Treatment made you angry/Anticipate repeat offence on another

> Overall completion is 64% (149/232) for Off 1
> Overall completion is 70% (49/70) for Off 2
> Overall completion is 67% (20/30) for Off 3
> Overall completion is 100% (2/2) for Off 4

2) Accusers more wrong than you/Anticipate repeat offence on another

> Overall completion is 64% (149/232) for Off 1
> Overall completion is 70% (49/70) for Off 2
> Overall completion is 67% (20/30) for Off 3
> Overall completion is 100% (2/2) for Off 4

3) Treated like you would reoffend/Anticipate repeat offence on another

> Overall completion is 64% (149/232) for Off 1
> Overall completion is 70% (49/70) for Off 2
> Overall completion is 67% (20/30) for Off 3
> Overall completion is 100% (2/2) for Off 4

4) Wish could get back at accusers/Anticipate repeat offence on another

> Overall completion is 64% (149/232) for Off 1
> Overall completion is 70% (49/70) for Off 2
> Overall completion is 67% (20/30) for Off 3
> Overall completion is 100% (2/2) for Off 4

5) Treatment made you angry/Anticipate repeat offence on you

> Overall completion is 64% (148/232) for Off 1
> Overall completion is 70% (49/70) for Off 2
> Overall completion is 67% (20/30) for Off 3
> Overall completion is 100% (2/2) for Off 4

6) Accusers more wrong than you/Anticipate repeat offence on you

> Overall completion is 64% (148/232) for Off 1
> Overall completion is 70% (49/70) for Off 2
> Overall completion is 67% (20/30) for Off 3
> Overall completion is 100% (2/2) for Off 4

7)   Treated like you would reoffend/Anticipate repeat offence on you

> Overall completion is 64% (148/232) for Off 1
> Overall completion is 70% (49/70) for Off 2
> Overall completion is 67% (20/30) for Off 3
> Overall completion is 100% (2/2) for Off 4

8)   Wish could get back at accusers/Anticipate repeat offence on you

> Overall completion is 64% (148/232) for Off 1
> Overall completion is 70% (49/70) for Off 2
> Overall completion is 67% (20/30) for Off 3
> Overall completion is 100% (2/2) for Off 4

9)   Cannot decide what you did was wrong/Anticipate offender will repeat offence on another

> Overall completion is 64% (148/232) for Off 1
> Overall completion is 70% (49/70) for Off 2
> Overall completion is 67% (20/30) for Off 3
> Overall completion is 100% (2/2) for Off 4

10)   Cannot decide what you did was wrong/Anticipate offender will repeat offence on you

> Overall completion is 63% (147/232) for Off 1
> Overall completion is 70% (49/70) for Off 2
> Overall completion is 67% (20/30) for Off 3
> Overall completion is 100% (2/2) for Off 4

11)   Wish you could get back at your accusers/Would harm the offender if you had the chance

> Overall completion is 64% (149/232) for Off 1
> Overall completion is 74% (52/70) for Off 2
> Overall completion is 77% (23/30) for Off 3
> Overall completion is 100% (2/2) for Off 4
> Overall completion is 100% (1/1) for Off 5
> Overall completion is 100% (1/1) for Off 6

12)   Accusers more wrong than you/Would harm the offender if you had the chance

> Overall completion is 64% (149/232) for Off 1
> Overall completion is 74% (52/70) for Off 2
> Overall completion is 77% (23/30) for Off 3

Overall completion is 100% (2/2) for Off 4
Overall completion is 100% (1/1) for Off 5
Overall completion is 100% (1/1) for Off 6

13)   Glad you committed the offence/Would harm the offender if you had the chance

Overall completion is 68% (158/232) for Off 1
Overall completion is 77% (54/70) for Off 2
Overall completion is 77% (23/30) for Off 3
Overall completion is 100% (2/2) for Off 4
Overall completion is 100% (1/1) for Off 5
Overall completion is 100% (1/1) for Off 6

14)   Treatment made you angry/Would harm the offender if you had the chance

Overall completion is 64% (149/232) for Off 1
Overall completion is 74% (52/70) for Off 2
Overall completion is 77% (23/30) for Off 3
Overall completion is 100% (2/2) for Off 4
Overall completion is 100% (1/1) for Off 5
Overall completion is 100% (1/1) for Off 6

15)   Accusers more wrong than you/Treatment made you angry

Overall completion is 64% (148/232) for Off 1
Overall completion is 74% (52/70) for Off 2
Overall completion is 77% (23/30) for Off 3
Overall completion is 50% (1/2) for Off 4
Overall completion is 100% (1/1) for Off 5
Overall completion is 100% (1/1) for Off 6

16)   Glad you committed the offence/Treatment made you angry

Overall completion is 68% (157/232) for Off 1
Overall completion is 70% (49/70) for Off 2
Overall completion is 77% (23/30) for Off 3
Overall completion is 50% (1/2) for Off 4
Overall completion is 100% (1/1) for Off 5
Overall completion is 100% (1/1) for Off 6

17)   Treatment made you angry/Treatment made you angry

Overall completion is 64% (148/232) for Off 1
Overall completion is 74% (52/70) for Off 2
Overall completion is 77% (23/30) for Off 3

>Overall completion is 100% (2/2) for Off 4
>Overall completion is 100% (1/1) for Off 5
>Overall completion is 100% (1/1) for Off 6

18)　Wish you could get back at your accusers/Treatment made you angry

>Overall completion is 64% (148/232) for Off 1
>Overall completion is 74% (52/70) for Off 2
>Overall completion is 77% (23/30) for Off 3
>Overall completion is 50% (1/2) for Off 4
>Overall completion is 100% (1/1) for Off 5
>Overall completion is 100% (1/1) for Off 6

19)　Feel bitter about your treatment/Feel bitter about your treatment

>Overall completion is 64% (149/232) for Off 1
>Overall completion is 77% (54/70) for Off 2
>Overall completion is 77% (23/30) for Off 3
>Overall completion is 50% (1/2) for Off 4
>Overall completion is 100% (1/1) for Off 5
>Overall completion is 100% (1/1) for Off 6

Tables 7.4 and 7.13: Legitimacy

1)　Felt you could trust the police during case/Felt you could trust the police during case

>Overall completion is 69% (159/232) for Off 1
>Overall completion is 77% (54/70) for Off 2
>Overall completion is 77% (23/30) for Off 3
>Overall completion is 100% (2/2) for Off 4
>Overall completion is 100% (1/1) for Off 5
>Overall completion is 100% (1/1) for Off 6

2)　Respect for police has increased/Respect for police has increased

>Overall completion is 68% (158/232) for Off 1
>Overall completion is 77% (54/70) for Off 2
>Overall completion is 77% (23/30) for Off 3
>Overall completion is 100% (2/2) for Off 4
>Overall completion is 100% (1/1) for Off 5
>Overall completion is 100% (1/1) for Off 6

3)   Respect for law has increased/Respect for law has increased
> Overall completion is 64% (149/232) for Off 1
> Overall completion is 77% (54/70) for Off 2
> Overall completion is 77% (23/30) for Off 3
> Overall completion is 100% (2/2) for Off 4
> Overall completion is 100% (1/1) for Off 5
> Overall completion is 100% (1/1) for Off 6

4)   Police enforce law fairly/Police enforce law fairly
> Overall completion is 68% (157/232) for Off 1
> Overall completion is 76% (53/70) for Off 2
> Overall completion is 77% (23/30) for Off 3
> Overall completion is 100% (2/2) for Off 4
> Overall completion is 100% (1/1) for Off 5
> Overall completion is 100% (1/1) for Off 6

5)   Respect for justice system has increased/Respect for justice system has increased
> Overall completion is 64% (149/232) for Off 1
> Overall completion is 74% (52/70) for Off 2
> Overall completion is 77% (23/30) for Off 3
> Overall completion is 100% (2/2) for Off 4
> Overall completion is 100% (1/1) for Off 5
> Overall completion is 100% (1/1) for Off 6

6)   Treatment will prevent reoffending/Treatment will encourage you to obey law
> Overall completion is 64% (148/232) for Off 1
> Overall completion is 74% (52/70) for Off 2
> Overall completion is 77% (23/30) for Off 3
> Overall completion is 100% (2/2) for Off 4
> Overall completion is 100% (1/1) for Off 5
> Overall completion is 100% (1/1) for Off 6

7)   Treatment will encourage you to obey law/Treatment will encourage you to obey law
> Overall completion is 64% (148/232) for Off 1
> Overall completion is 74% (52/70) for Off 2
> Overall completion is 77% (23/30) for Off 3
> Overall completion is 100% (2/2) for Off 4
> Overall completion is 100% (1/1) for Off 5
> Overall completion is 100% (1/1) for Off 6

Tables 7.6 and 7.11: Emotional restoration in treatment (Conference only)

1) Understood how others felt /Offender understood harm
   - Overall completion is 58% (67/116) for Off 1
   - Overall completion is 74% (14/37) for Off 2
   - Overall completion is 27% (3/11) for Off 3
   - Overall completion is 100% (1/1) for Off 4
   - Overall completion is 100% (1/1) for Off 5
   - Overall completion is 100% (1/1) for Off 6

2) Felt bad about hurting others/Offender understood harm
   - Overall completion is 58% (67/116) for Off 1
   - Overall completion is 74% (14/37) for Off 2
   - Overall completion is 27% (3/11) for Off 3
   - Overall completion is 100% (1/1) for Off 4
   - Overall completion is 100% (1/1) for Off 5
   - Overall completion is 100% (1/1) for Off 6

3) Felt ashamed of actions/Offender understood harm
   - Overall completion is 58% (67/116) for Off 1
   - Overall completion is 74% (14/37) for Off 2
   - Overall completion is 27% (3/11) for Off 3
   - Overall completion is 100% (1/1) for Off 4
   - Overall completion is 100% (1/1) for Off 5
   - Overall completion is 100% (1/1) for Off 6

4) Think what you did was stupid/Felt offender had learned his lesson
   - Overall completion is 56% (65/116) for Off 1
   - Overall completion is 74% (14/37) for Off 2
   - Overall completion is 18% (2/11) for Off 3
   - Overall completion is 100% (1/1) for Off 4
   - Overall completion is 100% (1/1) for Off 5
   - Overall completion is 100% (1/1) for Off 6

5) Victim was hurt as a result of your offence/Offender understood harm
   - Overall completion is 58% (67/116) for Off 1
   - Overall completion is 74% (14/37) for Off 2
   - Overall completion is 18% (2/11) for Off 3
   - Overall completion is 100% (1/1) for Off 4

Overall completion is 100% (1/1) for Off 5
Overall completion is 100% (1/1) for Off 6

6)   Treatment helped solve problems/Found it helpful to attend
Overall completion is 57% (66/116) for Off 1
Overall completion is 74% (14/37) for Off 2
Overall completion is 27% (3/11) for Off 3
Overall completion is 100% (1/1) for Off 4
Overall completion is 100% (1/1) for Off 5
Overall completion is 100% (1/1) for Off 6

7)   Treatment helped solve problems/Treatment helped solve problems
Overall completion is 58% (67/116) for Off 1
Overall completion is 74% (14/37) for Off 2
Overall completion is 27% (3/11) for Off 3
Overall completion is 100% (1/1) for Off 4
Overall completion is 100% (1/1) for Off 5
Overall completion is 100% (1/1) for Off 6

8)   Felt allowed to clear conscience/Found it helpful to attend conference
Overall completion is 57% (66/116) for Off 1
Overall completion is 74% (14/37) for Off 2
Overall completion is 27% (3/11) for Off 3
Overall completion is 100% (1/1) for Off 4
Overall completion is 100% (1/1) for Off 5
Overall completion is 100% (1/1) for Off 6

9)   People said you had learned your lesson/Felt offender had learned his lesson
Overall completion is 56% (65/116) for Off 1
Overall completion is 74% (14/37) for Off 2
Overall completion is 27% (3/11) for Off 3
Overall completion is 100% (1/1) for Off 4
Overall completion is 100% (1/1) for Off 5
Overall completion is 100% (1/1) for Off 6

10)   People indicated forgiveness/Felt forgiving towards offender
Overall completion is 58% (67/116) for Off 1
Overall completion is 74% (14/37) for Off 2
Overall completion is 27% (3/11) for Off 3

Overall completion is 100% (1/1) for Off 4
Overall completion is 100% (1/1) for Off 5
Overall completion is 100% (1/1) for Off 6

11)   People said could put incident behind you/Able to put incident behind you

Overall completion is 58% (67/116) for Off 1
Overall completion is 74% (14/37) for Off 2
Overall completion is 27% (3/11) for Off 3
Overall completion is 100% (1/1) for Off 4
Overall completion is 100% (1/1) for Off 5
Overall completion is 100% (1/1) for Off 6

Tables 7.7 and 7.13: Emotional harm in treatment (Conference only)

1)   Felt accusers were more wrong than you/After conference, angry with offender

Overall completion is 58% (67/116) for Off 1
Overall completion is 74% (14/37) for Off 2
Overall completion is 27% (3/11) for Off 3
Overall completion is 100% (1/1) for Off 4
Overall completion is 100% (1/1) for Off 5
Overall completion is 100% (1/1) for Off 6

2)   Felt victims were sorry for themselves/After conference, angry with offender

Overall completion is 58% (67/116) for Off 1
Overall completion is 74% (14/37) for Off 2
Overall completion is 27% (3/11) for Off 3
Overall completion is 100% (1/1) for Off 4
Overall completion is 100% (1/1) for Off 5
Overall completion is 100% (1/1) for Off 6

3)   Glad committed the offence/After conference, angry with offender

Overall completion is 58% (67/116) for Off 1
Overall completion is 74% (14/37) for Off 2
Overall completion is 27% (3/11) for Off 3
Overall completion is 100% (1/1) for Off 4
Overall completion is 100% (1/1) for Off 5
Overall completion is 100% (1/1) for Off 6

Tables 7.8 and 7.15: Participation in the process (Conference only)

1) Had influence over conference outcome/Conference took account of what I said

> Overall completion is 56% (65/116) for Off 1
> Overall completion is 74% (14/37) for Off 2
> Overall completion is 27% (3/11) for Off 3
> Overall completion is 100% (1/1) for Off 4
> Overall completion is 100% (1/1) for Off 5
> Overall completion is 100% (1/1) for Off 6

2) People spoke for me in the conference/Attended b/c wanted to have a say

> Overall completion is 57% (66/116) for Off 1
> Overall completion is 74% (14/37) for Off 2
> Overall completion is 27% (3/11) for Off 3
> Overall completion is 100% (1/1) for Off 4
> Overall completion is 100% (1/1) for Off 5
> Overall completion is 100% (1/1) for Off 6

3) Too intimidated to speak in conference/Too intimidated to speak in conference

> Overall completion is 58% (67/116) for Off 1
> Overall completion is 74% (14/37) for Off 2
> Overall completion is 27% (3/11) for Off 3
> Overall completion is 100% (1/1) for Off 4
> Overall completion is 100% (1/1) for Off 5
> Overall completion is 100% (1/1) for Off 6

4) Felt awkward in the conference/Felt awkward in the conference

> Overall completion is 57% (66/116) for Off 1
> Overall completion is 74% (14/37) for Off 2
> Overall completion is 27% (3/11) for Off 3
> Overall completion is 100% (1/1) for Off 4
> Overall completion is 100% (1/1) for Off 5
> Overall completion is 100% (1/1) for Off 6

Tables 7.9 and 7.16: Procedural justice (Conference only)

1)   Had enough control how conference ran/Had enough control how conference ran

Overall completion is 53% (62/116) for Off 1
Overall completion is 74% (14/37) for Off 2
Overall completion is 27% (3/11) for Off 3
Overall completion is 100% (1/1) for Off 4
Overall completion is 100% (1/1) for Off 5
Overall completion is 100% (1/1) for Off 6

2)   Felt pushed into things didn't agree with/Felt pushed into things didn't agree with

Overall completion is 53% (62/116) for Off 1
Overall completion is 74% (14/37) for Off 2
Overall completion is 27% (3/11) for Off 3
Overall completion is 100% (1/1) for Off 4
Overall completion is 100% (1/1) for Off 5
Overall completion is 100% (1/1) for Off 6

3)   Took account of your say in the outcome/Took account of your say in the outcome

Overall completion is 57% (66/116) for Off 1
Overall completion is 74% (14/37) for Off 2
Overall completion is 27% (3/11) for Off 3
Overall completion is 100% (1/1) for Off 4
Overall completion is 100% (1/1) for Off 5
Overall completion is 100% (1/1) for Off 6

4)   Understood what was going on /Understood what was going on

Overall completion is 58% (67/116) for Off 1
Overall completion is 74% (14/37) for Off 2
Overall completion is 27% (3/11) for Off 3
Overall completion is 100% (1/1) for Off 4
Overall completion is 100% (1/1) for Off 5
Overall completion is 100% (1/1) for Off 6

5)   Had opportunity to express views/Had opportunity to express views

Overall completion is 58% (67/116) for Off 1

Overall completion is 74% (14/37) for Off 2
Overall completion is 27% (3/11) for Off 3
Overall completion is 100% (1/1) for Off 4
Overall completion is 100% (1/1) for Off 5
Overall completion is 100% (1/1) for Off 6

6)   Disagree that outcome was too severe/Conference was fair for offender

Overall completion is 56% (65/116) for Off 1
Overall completion is 74% (14/37) for Off 2
Overall completion is 27% (3/11) for Off 3
Overall completion is 100% (1/1) for Off 4
Overall completion is 100% (1/1) for Off 5
Overall completion is 100% (1/1) for Off 6

7)   Disagree that you were judged unfairly/Conference was fair to you

Overall completion is 57% (66/116) for Off 1
Overall completion is 74% (14/37) for Off 2
Overall completion is 27% (3/11) for Off 3
Overall completion is 100% (1/1) for Off 4
Overall completion is 100% (1/1) for Off 5
Overall completion is 100% (1/1) for Off 6

8)   All sides got a chance to bring out facts/All sides got a chance to bring out facts

Overall completion is 58% (67/116) for Off 1
Overall completion is 74% (14/37) for Off 2
Overall completion is 27% (3/11) for Off 3
Overall completion is 100% (1/1) for Off 4
Overall completion is 100% (1/1) for Off 5
Overall completion is 100% (1/1) for Off 6

9)   Police were fair during conference/Police were fair during conference

Overall completion is 58% (67/116) for Off 1
Overall completion is 74% (14/37) for Off 2
Overall completion is 27% (3/11) for Off 3
Overall completion is 100% (1/1) for Off 4
Overall completion is 100% (1/1) for Off 5
Overall completion is 100% (1/1) for Off 6

10)   Conference respected your rights/Conference respected your rights

> Overall completion is 57% (66/116) for Off 1
> Overall completion is 74% (14/37) for Off 2
> Overall completion is 27% (3/11) for Off 3
> Overall completion is 100% (1/1) for Off 4
> Overall completion is 100% (1/1) for Off 5
> Overall completion is 100% (1/1) for Off 6

11)   Disadvantaged by age, income, sex, race/Disadvantaged by age, income, sex, race

> Overall completion is 58% (67/116) for Off 1
> Overall completion is 74% (14/37) for Off 2
> Overall completion is 27% (3/11) for Off 3
> Overall completion is 100% (1/1) for Off 4
> Overall completion is 100% (1/1) for Off 5
> Overall completion is 100% (1/1) for Off 6

12)   Treated with respect in conference/Treated with respect in conference

> Overall completion is 57% (66/116) for Off 1
> Overall completion is 74% (14/37) for Off 2
> Overall completion is 27% (3/11) for Off 3
> Overall completion is 100% (1/1) for Off 4
> Overall completion is 100% (1/1) for Off 5
> Overall completion is 100% (1/1) for Off 6

13)   If treated unfairly, complaint was heard/If treated unfairly, complaint was heard

> Overall completion is 58% (67/116) for Off 1
> Overall completion is 74% (14/37) for Off 2
> Overall completion is 27% (3/11) for Off 3
> Overall completion is 100% (1/1) for Off 4
> Overall completion is 100% (1/1) for Off 5
> Overall completion is 100% (1/1) for Off 6

14) Wrong facts were correctable in/Wrong facts were correctable

> Overall completion is 58% (67/116) for Off 1
> Overall completion is 74% (14/37) for Off 2
> Overall completion is 27% (3/11) for Off 3

Overall completion is 100% (1/1) for Off 4
Overall completion is 100% (1/1) for Off 5
Overall completion is 100% (1/1) for Off 6

Appendix 4
Treatment of Questions with Other than 'Agree–Disagree' Five-Point Response Scale in Tables in Chapter 7

For the majority of the questions used in Chapter 7, victims and offenders responded on a five-point scale, namely, 'strongly disagree', 'disagree', 'neither agree nor disagree', 'agree', 'strongly agree'. However, the questions listed below required responses to a five-point scale other than 'disagree/agree'. In general, negative responses (usually 1 and 2) were coded as 'disagree' and positive or indifferent responses (usually 3, 4, and 5) were coded as 'agree': the only exception was the question concerning the sincerity of the apology offered in Table 7.2, where responses 1, 2, and 5 were coded 'disagree' and responses 3 and 4 were coded 'agree'.

Table 7.3

'Do you feel the apology you were offered was . . .'
Not at all sincere/Not very sincere/Somewhat sincere/Sincere/Don't know

Table 7.5

'As a result of the way your case was handled would you say your respect for the police/justice system/law has . . .'
Gone down a lot/Gone down a little/Not changed/Gone up a little/Gone up a lot

Table 7.6

'Since the conference/court case, in thinking about the offender(s), you have felt'

Very unforgiving/Unforgiving/Neither forgiving nor unforgiving/ Forgiving/Very forgiving

'How helpful to you did you find attending the conference/court case?'
Very unhelpful/Unhelpful/Neither helpful nor unhelpful/Helpful/ Very helpful

Table 7.8

'You attended [the conference/court case] because you wanted to have a say in how the problem was resolved'
Not at all important/Not very important/Somewhat important/ Quite important/Very important

'During the conference/court case I felt awkward and aware of myself'
Not at all/A little/Quite a bit/A lot/Felt overwhelmed by it

When the responses were for a four-point, rather than five-point, scale: Responses 1 and 2 were coded as 'Disagree' and responses 3 and 4 were coded as 'Agree'.

Table 7.3

'At the end of the conference/court case did people indicate you were forgiven?'
Not at all/A little/Somewhat/A lot

Table 7.4

'Before/After the conference/court case how angry did you feel with the offender(s)?'
Not at all angry/Not very angry/Quite angry/Very angry

'Were you treated in conference/court as though you were likely to commit another offence?'
Not at all/A little/Somewhat/A lot

Table 7.6

'At the end of the conference/court case did people indicate that you were forgiven?'
Not at all/A little/Somewhat/A lot

'Do you think the conference/court helped to solve any problems?'
Not at all/Not really/Somewhat/Definitely

'At the end of the conference/court case, or since then, have people made it clear to you that you can put the whole thing behind you?
Not at all/A little/Somewhat/A lot

'Did others at the conference/court case say that you had learnt your lesson and now deserved a second chance?'
Not at all/A little/Somewhat/A lot

Table 7.7

'After the conference/court case how angry did you feel with the offender(s)?'
Not at all angry/Not very angry/Quite angry/Very angry

Table 7.8

'How much influence did you have over the agreement reached in the conference/court?'
None at all/Not much/Some/A lot

'How nervous were you about attending the conference/court case?'
Not at all nervous/Not really nervous/Somewhat nervous/Very nervous

Table 7.9

'How fair do you feel the conference/court case was for you?'
Very unfair/Somewhat unfair/Somewhat fair/Very fair

'How fair do you feel the conference/court case was to the offender(s)?'
Very unfair/Somewhat unfair/Somewhat fair/Very fair

'How severe did you feel the outcome of the conference/court case was for you?
Not tough at all/A bit tough/Tough/Very tough

'How much did you feel the conference/court case respected your rights?'
Not at all/Not really/Somewhat/A lot

For two questions, the responses were for a three-point scale only:
(both in Table 7.4)
'Do you anticipate the offender(s) will repeat this offence on you?'
Yes/No/Don't know

'Do you anticipate the offender(s) will repeat this offence on another victim?'
Yes/No/Don't know

Bibliography

Abel, R. (1982), 'The Contradictions of Informal Justice', in R. Abel (ed.), *The Politics of Informal Justice: Volume One: The American Experience.* New York: Academic Press.

Alder, C. and Wundersitz, J. (1994), *Family Conferencing and Juvenile Justice: The Way Forward or Misplaced Optimism?* Canberra: Australian Institute of Criminology.

Angrist, J., Imbens, G., and Rubin, D. (1996), 'Identification of Causal Effects Using Instrumental Variables', *Journal of the American Statistical Assocation*, 91 (June): 444–455.

Arendt, H. (1958), *The Human Condition*, Chicago, Ill.: University of Chicago Press.

Ashworth, A. (1986), 'Punishment and Compensation: Victims, Offenders and the State', *Oxford Journal of Legal Studies*, 6(1): 86–122.

—— (1992), 'What Victims of Crime Deserve', paper presented to the Fulbright Colloquium on Penal Theory and Penal Practice, University of Sterling, 1992.

—— (1993), 'Some Doubts about Restorative Justice', *Criminal Law Forum*, 4: 277–299.

—— (2000), 'Victims' Rights, Defendants' Rights and Criminal Procedure', in A. Crawford and J. Goodey (eds.), *Integrating a Victim Perspective within Criminal Justice.* Aldershot: Ashgate.

—— and von Hirsch, A. (1993), 'Deserts and the Three Rs', *Current Issues in Criminal Justice*, 5(1): 9–12.

Astor, H. (1994), 'Swimming Against the Tide: Keeping Violent Men out of Mediation', in J. Stubbs (ed.), *Women, Male Violence and the Law.* The Institute of Criminology Monograph Series No. 6, Sydney.

Balint, J. (2002), *Genocide and the Law: A Holistic Approach to State Crime*, unpublished doctoral dissertation, Australian National University.

Barnett, R. (1977), 'Restitution: A New Paradigm of Criminal Justice', *Ethics: An International Journal of Social, Political and Legal Philosophy*, 87(4): 279–301, reprinted in B. Galaway and J. Hudson (eds.) (1981), *Perspectives on Crime Victims.* St Louis, Miss.: C. V. Mosby Company.

Barton, C. (1996), *Revenge and Victim Justice: A Philosophical Analysis and Evaluation*, unpublished doctoral dissertation, Australian National University.

—— (2000), 'Empowerment and Retribution in Criminal Justice' in H. Strang and J. Braithwaite (eds.), *Restorative Justice: Philosophy to Practice*. Aldershot: Ashgate.

Bazemore, G. (1997), 'After Shaming, Whither Reintegration: Restorative Justice and Relational Rehabilitation' in G. Bazemore and L. Walgrave (eds.), *Restoring Juvenile Justice*. Amsterdam: Kugler International Publications.

—— and Umbreit, M. (1994), *Balanced and Restorative Justice: Program Summary: Balanced and Restorative Justice Project*. Washington, DC: Department of Justice, Office of Juvenile Justice and Delinquency Prevention.

—— and Washington, C. (1995), 'Charting the Future of the Juvenile Justice System: Reinventing Mission and Management', *Spectrum*, Spring, 51–66.

Bentham, J. (1838, 1975), 'Political Remedies for the Evil of Offences' in *The Works of Jeremy Bentham, Now First Collected: Under the Superintendence of His Executor, John Bowing, Part 11*, reprinted in J. Hudson and B. Galaway (eds.), *Considering the Victim: Readings in Restitution and Victim Compensation*. Springfield, Ill.: Charles C. Thomas, 29–42.

Berk, R., Boruch, R., Chambers, D., Rossi, P., and Witte, A. (1985), 'Social Policy Experimentation: A Position Paper', *Evaluation Review*, 9(4): 387–429.

Beurskens, A. and Boers, K. (1985), 'Attitudes of Victims and Nonvictims Towards Restitution, Crime and Punishment: Tables', paper presented at the 5th International Symposium on Victimology, Zagreb, August.

Biderman, A., Johnson, L., McIntyre, J., and Weir, A. (1967), Report on a Pilot Study in the District of Columbia on Victimization and Attitudes towards Law Enforcement, *President's Commission on Law Enforcement and Administration of Justice, Field Surveys 1*, Washington, DC: US Government Printing Office.

Blackstone, Sir William (1778), *The Sovereignty of Law*, ed. by Gareth Jones from 7th edition (1973), London: Macmillan.

Blagg, H. (1985), 'Reparation and Justice for Juveniles: The Corby Experience', *British Journal of Criminology*, 25(7): 267–279.

Blumenfeld, L. (2002), 'The Apology', *The New Yorker*, 4 March 2002.

Boruch, R. (1997), *Randomized Experiments for Planning and Evaluation: A Practical Guide*, Applied Social Research Methods Series vol. 44. Thousand Oaks, Cal.: Sage Publications.

Braithwaite, J. (1989), *Crime, Shame and Reintegration*. Cambridge: Cambridge University Press.

—— (1996), 'Restorative Justice and a Better Future' paper presented at the Dorothy J. Killiam Memorial Lectures, Dalhousie University, 17 October.

—— (1998), 'Linking Crime Prevention to Restorative Justice' in T. Wachtel (ed.), *Conferencing: A New Approach to Wrongdoing*. Pipersville, Penn.: Real Justice.

—— (1999), 'Restorative Justice: Assessing Optimistic and Pessimistic Accounts' in M. Tonry (ed.), *Crime and Justice: A Review of Research*, vol. 25, Chicago, Ill.: University of Chicago Press.

—— and Daly, K. (1994), 'Masculinities, Violence and Communitarian Control' in T. Newburn and E. Stanko (eds.), *Just Boys Doing Business*. London and New York: Routledge.

—— and Drahos, P. (2000), *Global Business Regulation*. Cambridge: Cambridge University Press.

—— and Mugford, S. (1994), 'Conditions of Successful Reintegration Ceremonies: Dealing with Juvenile Offenders', *British Journal of Criminology*, 34(2): 139–171.

—— and Parker, C. (1997), 'Restorative Justice is Republican Justice in L. Walgrave and G. Bazemore (eds.), *Restoring Juvenile Justice: An Exploration of the Restorative Paradigm for Reforming Juvenile Justice*. Amsterdam/New York: Kugler Publications.

—— and Pettit, P. (1990), *Not Just Deserts: A Republican Theory of Criminal Justice*. Oxford: Oxford University Press.

—— and Strang, H. (2000), 'Connecting Philosophy to Practice' in H. Strang and J. Braithwaite (eds.), *Restorative Justice: Philosophy to Practice*, Aldershot: Ashgate.

Brown, J. (1994), 'The Uses of Mediation to Resolve Criminal Cases: A Procedural Critique', *Emory Law Journal*, 43: 1247–1309.

Brown, M. and Polk, K. (1996), 'Taking Fear of Crime Seriously: The Tasmanian Approach to Community Crime Prevention', *Crime and Delinquency*, 42(3): 398–420.

Brown, S. and Yantzi, M. (1980), *Needs Assessment for Victims and Witnesses of Crime*. Ontario: Mennonite Central Committee.

Brownmiller, S. (1975), *Against Our Will: Men, Women and Rape*. New York: Simon & Schuster.

Burford, G. and Pennell, J. (1998), *Family Group Decision Making: After the Conference—Progress in Resolving Violence and Promoting Well-Being*, Outcome Report vols 1 and 2. St John's:

St John's Newfoundland School of Social Work, Memorial University of Newfoundland.

Campbell, D. (1969), 'Reforms as Experiments', *American Psychologist*, 24: 409–429.

—— and Stanley, J. (1963), *Experimental and Quasi-Experimental Designs for Research*. Chicago, Ill.: Rand McNally & Company.

Carnevale, P. and Pruitt, D. (1992), 'Negotiation and Mediation', *Annual Review of Psychology*, 43: 531–582.

Carrington, F. (1975), *The Victims*. New Rochelle, NY: Arlington House.

—— (1975), 'Victims' Rights Legislation', *University of Richmond Law Review*, 11(3): 447–470.

Cavadino, M. and Dignan, J. (1997), 'Reparation, Retribution and Rights', *International Review of Victimology*, 4: 233–253.

Chesney, S. and Schneider, C. (1981), 'Crime Victims Crisis Centers: The Minnesota Experience' in B. Galaway and J. Hudson (eds.), *Perspectives on Crime Victims*. St Louis, Miss.: Mosby.

Christie, N. (1977), 'Conflicts as Property', *British Journal of Criminology*, 17(1): 1–15.

—— (1986), 'The Ideal Victim' in E. Fattah (ed.), *From Crime Policy to Victim Policy*. London: Macmillan.

Clairmont, D. (1994), 'Alternative Justice Issues for Aboriginal Justice', paper prepared for the Aboriginal Justice Directorate, Department of Justice, Ottawa.

Coates, R. (1990), 'Victim–Offender Reconciliation Programs in North America: An Assessment' in B. Galaway and J. Hudson (eds.), *Criminal Justice, Restitution and Reconciliation*. New York: Criminal Justice Press.

—— and Gehm, J. (1989), *Victim Meets Offender: An Evaluation of Victim–Offender Reconciliation Programs*. Valparaiso, Ind.: PACT Institute of Justice.

Colson, C. and Van Ness, D. (1989), *Convicted: New Hope for Ending America's Crime Crisis*. Westchester, Ill.: Crossway Books.

Cook, R., Roehl, J., and Sheppard, D. (1980), *Neighbourhood Justice Centers Field Test—Final Evaluation Report*. Washington, DC: U.S. Department of Justice,.

Cook, T. and Campbell, D. (1979), *Quasi-Experimentation: Design and Analysis Issues for Field Settings*. Chicago, Ill.: Rand-McNally.

Coulmas, F. (1981), ' "Poison to your Soul", Thanks and

Apologies Contrastively Viewed' in F. Coulmas (ed.), *Conversational Routine*. The Hague: Mouton, 69–91.

Crawford, A. (2000), 'Salient Themes Towards a Victim Perspective and the Limitations of Restorative Justice: Some Concluding Comments' in A. Crawford and J. Goodey (eds.), *Integrating a Victim Perspective within Criminal Justice*. Aldershot: Ashgate.

Daly, K. (2000), 'Revisiting the Relationship between Retributive and Restorative Justice' in H. Strang and J. Braithwaite (eds.), *Restorative Justice: Philosophy to Practice*. Aldershot: Ashgate.

—— and Immarigeon, R. (1998), 'The Past, Present and Future of Restorative Justice: Some Critical Reflections', *Contemporary Justice Review*, 1: 21–45.

Davis, G., Boucherat, J., and Watson, D. (1989), 'Pre-court Decision Making in Juvenile Justice', *British Journal of Criminology*, 29: 219–235.

Davis, R. (1987), *Providing Help to Victims: A Study of Psychological and Material Outcomes*. New York: Victim Services Agency.

—— Kunreuther, F., and Connick, E. (1984), 'Expanding the Victim's Role in the Criminal Court Dispositional Process', *Journal of Criminal Law and Criminology*, 75(2): 491–505.

—— Lurigio, A., and Skogan, W. (1999), 'Services for Victims: A Market Research Study', *International Review of Victimology*, 6: 101–115.

—— and Smith, B. (1994), 'Victim Impact Statements and Victim Satisfaction: An Unfulfilled Promise?', *Journal of Criminal Justice*, 22(1): 1–12.

—— Tichane, M., and Grayson, D. (n.d.), *Mediation and Arbitration as Alternatives to Prosecution in Felony Arrest Cases: An Evaluation of the Brooklyn Dispute Resolution Center (1st Year)*. New York: Vera Institute of Justice.

Dignan, J. (1992), 'Repairing the Damage: Can Reparation Work in the Service of Diversion?', *British Journal of Criminology*, 32(4): 453–472.

—— and Cavadino, M. (1996), 'Towards a Framework for Conceptualising and Evaluating Models of Criminal Justice from a Victim's Perspective', *International Review of Victimology*, 4: 153–182.

van Dijk, J. (1986), 'Victims' Rights: A Right to Better Service or a Right to "Active Participation?"', in J van Dijk (ed.), *Criminal Law in Action*, Arnhem: Gouda Quint.

van Dijk, J. (1988), 'Victims' Needs or Victims' Rights: Alternative Approaches to Policy-making', in M. Maguire and J. Ponting (eds.), *Victims of Crime: A New Deal?* Milton Keynes: Open University Press.

—— (1994), 'Who is Afraid of the Crime Victim?: Criminal Victimisation, Fear of Crime and Opinions on Crime Control in an International Perspective', Keynote lecture at the VII Symposium of the World Society of Victimology, Adelaide, 21–26 August 1994.

—— (1994), 'Crime and Victim Surveys' in C. Sumner, M. Israel, M. O'Connell, and R. Sarre (eds.), *International Victimology: Selected Papers from the 8th International Symposium 21–26 August 1994 Adelaide.* Canberra: Australian Institute of Criminology.

Dittenhoffer, T. (1981), 'The Victim–Offender Reconciliation Program: A Message to Correctional Reformers', MA thesis, University of Toronto.

Doob, A. and Roberts, J. (1988), 'Public Attitudes towards Sentencing in Canada' in N. Walker and M. Hough (eds.), *Public Attitudes to Sentencing.* Aldershot: Gower.

Edmondson, W. (1981), 'On Saying you're Sorry' in F. Coulmas (ed.), *Conversational Routine.* The Hague: Mouton, 274–288.

Elias, R. (1986), *The Politics of Victimisation: Victims, Victimology and Human Rights.* New York: Oxford University Press.

—— (1990), 'Which Victim Movement? The Politics of Victim Policy' in A. Lurigio, W. Skogan, and R. Davis (eds.), *Victims of Crime: Problems, Policies and Programs.* Newbury Park, Cal.: Sage Publications.

Erez, E. (1990), 'Victim Participation in Sentencing: Rhetoric and Reality', *Journal of Criminal Justice*, 18: 19–31.

—— (1991), 'Victim Impact Statements' in P. Grabosky (ed.), *Trends and Issues in Crime and Criminal Justice*, No. 33, Canberra: Australian Institute of Criminology.

—— (2000), 'Integrating a Victim Perspective in Criminal Justice through Victim Impact Statements' in A. Crawford and J. Goodey (eds.), *Integrating a Victim Perspective within Criminal Justice.* Aldershot: Ashgate.

—— and Roeger, L. (1995), 'The Effects of Victim Impact Statements on Sentencing Patterns and Outcomes: The Australian Experience', *Journal of Criminal Justice*, 23(4): 363–375.

—— —— and Morgan, F. (1994), *Victim Impact Statements in*

South Australia: an Evaluation. Adelaide: South Australian Attorney General's Department.

—— and Tontodonato, P. (1990), 'The Effects of Victim Participation in Sentencing on Sentencing Outcome', *Criminology*, 28(3): 451–474.

—— —— (1992), 'Victim Participation in Sentencing and Satisfaction with Justice', *Justice Quarterly*, 9(3): 393–415.

Estrada-Hollenbeck, M. (1996), 'Forgiving in the Face of Injustice: Victims' and Perpetrators' Perspectives' in B. Galaway and J. Hudson (eds.), *Restorative Justice: International Perspectives*. Amsterdam: Kugler Publications.

Farrington, D. (1983), 'Randomized Experiments on Crime and Justice' in N. Morris and M. Tonry (eds.), *Crime and Justice: An Annual Review of Research*. Chicago, Ill.: University of Chicago Press.

Fattah, E. (1986), 'Prologue: On Some Visible and Hidden Dangers of Victims Movements' in E. Fattah (ed.), *From Crime Policy to Victim Policy*. London: Macmillan.

—— (1993), 'The Rational Choice/Opportunity Perspectives as a Vehicle for Integrating Criminological and Victimological Theories' in R. Clarke and M. Felson (eds.), *Advances in Criminological Theory*, vol. 5. New Brunswick, NJ: Transaction.

Federal Judicial Center (1981), *Experimentation and the Law*. Washington, DC: Federal Judicial Center.

Fisher, B. (1991), 'A Neighbourhood Business Area is Hurting: Crime, Fear of Crime, and Disorders Take their Toll', *Crime and Delinquency*, 37(3): 363–373.

Forst, B. and Hernon, J. (1985), 'The Criminal Justice Response to Victim Harm', *N.I.J. Research in Brief (June)*, Washington, DC: US Department of Justice.

Frank, A. and Fuentes, M. (1990), 'Social Movements' in *New Directions in the Study of Justice, Law and Social Control*, prepared by the School of Justice Studies, Arizona State University. Temple, Arizona, New York: Plenum Press.

Fraser, B. (1981), 'On Apologising' in F. Coulmas (ed.), *Conversational Routine*. The Hague: Mouton, 259–271.

Friedman, L., Bischoff, L., Davis, R., and Person, A. (1982), *Victims and Helpers: Reactions to Crime*. Washington, DC: US Government Printing Office.

Fry, M. (1951), *Arms of the Law*. London: Gollancz.

Galaway, B. and Hudson, J. (1996), *Restorative Justice: International Perspectives*. Monsey, NY: Criminal Justice Press.

Galaway, B. and Rutman, L. (1974), 'Victim Compensation: An Analysis of Substantive Issues', *Social Service Review*, vol. 28, reprinted in J. Hudson and B. Galaway (eds.), *Considering the Victim: Readings in Restitution and Victim Compensation.* Springfield, Ill.: Charles C. Thomas, 421–436.

Gartin, P. (1995), 'Dealing with Design Failures in Randomized Field Experiments: Analytic Issues Regarding the Evaluation of Treatment Effects', *Journal of Research in Crime and Delinquency*, 32(4): 425–445.

Gay, M., Holtom, C., and Thomas, S. (1975), 'Helping the Victims', *International Journal of Offender Therapy and Comparative Criminology*, 19(3): 263–269.

Gehm, J. (1990), 'Mediated Victim–Offender Restitution Agreements: An Exploratory Analysis of Factors Relating to Victim Participation' in B. and J. Hudson (eds.), *Criminal Justice, Restitution and Reconciliation.* New York: Criminal Justice Press.

Geis, G. (1990), 'Crime Victims: Practices and Prospects' in A. Lurigio, W. Skogan, and R. Davis (eds.), *Victims of Crime: Problems, Policies and Programs.* Newbury Park, Cal.: Sage Publications.

George, C. (1999), 'Victim Support's Perspective on Restorative Justice', *Prison Service Journal*, No. 123, May.

Goffman, E. (1971), *Relations in Public: Microstudies of the Public Order.* Harmondsworth: Penguin.

Goodes, T. (1995), 'Victims and Family Conferences: Juvenile Justice in South Australia'. Adelaide: Family Conferencing Team.

Gottfredson, G. (1989), 'The Experience of Violent and Serious Victimization' in N. Weiner and M. Wolfgang (eds.), *Pathways to Criminal Violence.* Newbury Park, Cal.: Sage Publications.

Hagan, J. (1982), 'Victims Before the Law: A Study of Victim Involvement in the Criminal Justice Process', *The Journal of Criminal Law and Criminology*, 73(1): 317–330.

—— (1983), *Victims Before the Law: The Organizational Domination of Criminal Law.* Toronto: Butterworths.

Haley, J. (1986), 'Comment: The Implications of Apology', *Law and Society Review*, 20(4): 499–507.

Harding, J. (1982), *Victims and Offenders*, NCVO Occasional Paper Two. London: Bedford Square Press.

Harris, N. (2000), *Shame and Shaming: An Empirical Analysis*, unpublished PhD thesis, Australian National University, Canberra.

Hayes, H., Prenzler, T., and Wortley, R. (1998), *Making Amends: Final Evaluation of the Queensland Community Conferencing Pilot*. Brisbane: Centre for Crime Policy and Public Safety, School of Justice Administration, Griffith University.

Heinz, A. and Kerstetter, K. (1979), 'Pretrial Settlement Conference: Evaluation of a Reform in Plea Bargaining', *Law and Society Review*, 13: 349–366.

Herman, S. (1999), 'The Search for Parallel Justice', paper presented at the conference 'Restoration for Victims of Crime: Contemporary Challenges', convened by the Australian Institute of Criminology and the Victims Referral and Assistance Service, Melbourne, September.

Hibbert, C. (1966), *The Roots of Evil: A Social History of Crime and Punishment*. Harmondsworth: Penguin.

Hindelang, M. (1976), *Criminal Victimization in Eight American Cities: A Descriptive Analysis of Common Theft and Assault*. Cambridge, Mass.: Ballinger Publishing Company.

von Hirsch, A. (1976), *Doing Justice: The Choice of Punishment*. New York: Hill and Wang.

Holtom, C. and Raynor, P. (1988), 'Origins of Victims Support Policy and Practice' in M. Maguire and J. Pointing (eds.), *Victims of Crime: A New Deal?* Milton Keynes: Open University Press.

Howley, J. (1982), 'Victim–Police Interaction and its Effects on Public Attitudes to the Police', M.Sc. thesis, Cranfield Institute of Technology.

Hudson, J. and Galaway, B. (1975), 'Conclusions' in *Considering the Victim: Readings in Restitution and Victim Compensation*. Springfield, Ill.: Charles C. Thomas.

—— (1980), 'A Review of the Restitution and Community Service Sanctioning Research' in J. Hudson and B. Galaway (eds.), *Victims, Offenders and Alternative Sanctions*. Lexington, Mass.: Lexington Books.

Jeffrey, C. (1957), 'The Development of Crime in Early English Society', *Journal of Criminal Law, Criminology and Police Science*, 47: 647–666.

Joutsen, M. (1994), 'Victim Participation in Proceedings and Sentencing in Europe', *International Review of Victimology*, 3: 57–67.

Kelly, D. (1982), 'Victims' Reactions to the Criminal Justice Response', paper delivered at 1982 Annual Meeting of the Law and Society Association, 6 June 1982, Toronto, Canada.

Kennedy, L. and Sacco, V. (1989), *Crime Victims in Context*. Los Angeles, Cal.: Roxbury Publishing Company.

Kilchling, M. (1991), 'Interests of the Victim and Public Prosecution: First Results of a National Survey' in G. Kaiser, H. Kury, and H.-J. Albrecht (eds.), *Victims and Criminal Justice*, Frieburg i Br: Max Planck Institute for Foreign and International Penal Law.

Kilpatrick, D., Beatty, D., and Howley, S. (1998), 'The Rights of Crime Victims—does Legal Protection make a Difference?', *NIJ Research in Brief*. Washington, DC: National Institute of Justice, US Department of Justice.

Knudten, R., Meade, A., Knudten, M., and Doerner, W. (1976), 'The Victim in the Administration of Criminal Justice: Problems and Perceptions' in W. McDonald (ed.), *Criminal Justice and the Victim*. Beverley Hills, Cal.: Sage Publications, 115–146.

Kuper, L. (1981), *Genocide: Its Political Use in the Twentieth Century*. New Haven, Conn., and London: Yale University Press.

Lacey, N. and Wells, C. (1998), *Reconstructing Criminal Law*. London, Butterworths.

LaPrairie, C. (1995), 'Altering Course: New Directions in Criminal Justice and Corrections: Sentencing Circles and Family Group Conferences', *Australian and New Zealand Journal of Criminology*, Special Issue: Crime, Criminology and Public Policy, December, 78–99.

Levrant, S., Cullen, F., Fulton, B., and Wozniak, J. (1999), 'Reconsidering Restorative Justice: The Corruption of Benevolence Revisited', *Crime and Delinquency*, 45(1), 3–27.

Lind, E. and Tyler, T. (1988), *The Social Psychology of Procedural Justice*. New York: Plenum.

Longclaws, L., Galaway, B., and Barkwell, L. (1996), 'Piloting Family Group Conferences for Young Aboriginal Offenders in Winnipeg, Canada' in J. Hudson, A. Morris, G. Maxwell, and B. Galaway (eds.), *Family Group Conferences: Perspectives on Policy and Practice*. Sydney: The Federation Press.

Lurigio, A. J. and Resnick, P. A. (1990), 'Healing the Psychological Wounds of Criminal Victimization' in A. J. Lurigio, W. G. Skogan, and R. C. Davis (eds.), *Victims of Crime: Problems, Policies and Programs*. Newbury Park, Cal.: Sage Publications.

McBarnett, D. (1988), 'Victim in the Witness Box—Confronting Victimology's Stereotype', *Contemporary Crises*, 7: 279–303.

McCold, P. (1997), 'Restorative Justice Variations on a Theme', paper presented at the Leuven International Conference,

Restorative Justice for Juveniles—Potentialities, Risks and Problems for Research, 12–14 May.

—— and Wachtel, B. (1998), *Restorative Policing Experiment: The Bethlehem Pennsylvania Police Family Group Conferencing Project*. Pipersville, Penn.: Community Service Foundation.

McDonald, J., O'Connell, T., and Thorsborne, M. (1995), *Real Justice Training Manual: Coordinating Family Group Conferences*. Pipersville, Penn: Pipers Press.

Maguire, M. (1982), *Burglary in a Dwelling: the Offence, the Offender and the Victim*. London: Heinemann.

—— (1991), 'The Needs and Rights of Victims of Crime' in M. Tonry (ed.), *Crime and Justice: A Review of Research*, vol. 14, Chicago, Ill., University of Chicago Press.

—— and Corbett, C. (1987), *The Effects of Crime and the Work of Victims Support Schemes*. Aldershot: Gower.

—— and Shapland, J. (1990), 'The "Victims Movement" in Europe', in A. Lurigio, W. Skogan, and R. Davis (eds.), *Victims of Crime: Problems, Policies and Programs*. Newbury Park, Cal.: Sage Publications.

Maitland, F. (1885), *Justice and Police*. London: Macmillan.

Makkai, T. and Braithwaite, J. (1996), 'Procedural Justice and Regulatory Compliance', *Law and Human Behavior*, 20: 83–98.

Marshall, T. (1985), *Alternatives to Criminal Courts*. Aldershot: Gower.

—— (1990), 'Results of Research from British Experiments in Restorative Justice' in B. Galaway and J. Hudson (eds.), *Criminal Justice, Restitution and Reconciliation*. Monsey, NY: Criminal Justice Press.

—— and Merry, S. (1990), *Crime and Accountability: Victim–Offender Mediation in Practice*. London, HMSO.

Martinson, R. (1974), 'What Works?', *Public Interest*, 35: 22–54.

Mason, A. (2000), 'Restorative Justice: Courts and Civil Society' in H. Strang and J. Braithwaite (eds.), *Restorative Justice: Philosophy to Practice*. Aldershot: Ashgate.

Mawby, R. (1988), 'Victims' Needs or Victims' Rights: Alternative Approaches to Policy Making' in R. Maguire and J. Pointing, *A New Deal for Crime Victims?* Milton Keynes: Open University Press.

—— and Gill, M. (1987), *Crime Victims: Needs, Services and the Voluntary Sector*. London: Tavistock.

Maxwell. G. and Morris, A. (1992), *Family Participation, Cultural Diversity and Victim Involvement in Youth Justice: a New Zealand Experiment*. Wellington: Institute of Criminology, Victoria University of Wellington, New Zealand.

Maxwell. G. and Morris, A. (1993), *Family, Victims and Culture: Youth Justice in New Zealand*. Wellington: Social Policy Agency and Institute of Criminology, Victoria University of Wellington, New Zealand.

—— —— (1996), 'Research on Family Group Conferences with Young Offenders in New Zealand' in J. Hudson, A. Morris, G. Maxwell, and B. Galaway (eds.), *Family Group Conferences: Perspectives on Policy and Practice*. Sydney: Federation Press.

Miers, D. (1978), *Responding to Victimisation*. Abingdon: Professional Books.

Miller, W. (1993), *Humiliation and Other Essays on Honor, Social Discomfort and Violence*. Ithaca, NY: Cornell University Press.

Ministry of Justice, New Zealand (1995), *Restorative Justice: A Discussion Paper*. Wellington: Ministry of Justice.

Moore, D. (1993), 'Shame, Forgiveness and Juvenile Justice', in M. C. Braswell, B. R. McCarthy, and B. J. McCarthy (eds.), *Justice, Crime and Ethics*. 2nd edn., Cincinatti, Ohio: Anderson Publishing.

—— Forsythe, L., and O'Connell, T. (1995), *A New Approach to Juvenile Justice: An Evaluation of Family Conferencing in Wagga Wagga*. Wagga Wagga: Charles Sturt University.

—— and O'Connell, T. (1994), 'Family Conferencing in Wagga Wagga: A Communitarian Model of Justice' in C. Alder and J. Wundersitz (eds.), *Family Conferencing and Juvenile Justice*. Canberra: Australian Studies in Law, Crime and Justice, Canberra, Australian Institute of Criminology.

Morgan, J. and Zedner, L. (1992), *Child Victims*. Oxford: Clarendon Press.

Morris, A., Maxwell, G., Hudson, J., and Galaway, B. (1996), 'Concluding Thoughts' in J. Hudson, A. Morris, G. Maxwell, and B. Galaway (eds.), *Family Group Conferences: Perspectives on Policy and Practice*. Sydney: Federation Press.

—— and Young, W. (2000), 'Reforming Criminal Justice: The Potential of Restorative Justice', , in H. Strang and J. Braithwaite (eds.), *Restorative Justice: Philosophy to Practice*. Aldershot: Ashgate.

Morris, N. (1966), 'Impediments to Penal Reform', *University of Chicago Law Review*, 33: 627–656.

—— (1974), *The Future of Imprisonment*: Chicago, Ill: University of Chicago Press.

Mosteller, R. (1998) 'Victims' Rights and the United States Constitution: Moving from Guaranteeing Participatory Rights to Benefiting the Prosecution', *St Mary's Law Journal*, 29: 1053–1065.

Murphy, J. and Hampton, J. (1988), *Forgiveness and Mercy*. Cambridge: Cambridge University Press.

Nelken, D. (1997), 'White Collar Crime' in M. Maguire, R. Morgan, and R. Reiner (eds.), *Oxford Handbook of Criminology*. Oxford: Clarendon Press.

von Neumann, J. and Morganstern, O. (1944), *Theory of Games and Economic Behavior*. Princeton, NJ: Princeton University Press.

Norquay, G. and Weiler, R. (1981), *Services to Victims and Witnesses of Crime in Canada*. Ottawa: Canadian Ministry of the Solicitor General.

O'Connell, T. and Moore, D. (1992), 'A New Juvenile Cautioning Program', *Rural Society*, 22(2): 16–19.

Owen, M. (1980), *Apologies and Remedial Interchanges: A Study of Language Use in Social Interaction*. Berlin: Mouton.

Peachey, D. (1989), 'The Kitchener Experiment' in M. Wright and B. Galaway (eds.), *Mediation and Criminal Justice: Victims, Offenders and Community*. London: Sage Publications.

Peto, R., Pike, M., Armitage, P., *et al.* (1976), 'Design and Analysis of Randomised Clinical Trials Requiring Prolonged Observation of Each Patient, Part 1—Introduction and Design', *British Journal of Cancer*, 34: 585–612.

Pocock, S. (1983), *Clinical Trials: A Practical Approach*. London: John Wiley.

Pollock, Sir F. and Maitland, F. (1898), *The History of the English Criminal Law Before the Time of Edward I*. Cambridge: Cambridge University Press.

Popper, K. (1959), *The Logic of Scientific Discovery*. New York: Basic Books.

President's Task Force on Victims of Crime (1982), *Final Report*. Washington, DC: US Government Printing Office.

Prunier, G. (1995), *The Rwanda Crisis: History of a Genocide*. New York: Columbia University Press.

Reeves, H. and Mulley. K. (2000), 'The New Status of Victims in the UK: Opportunities and Threats' in A. Crawford and J. Goodey (eds.), *Integrating a Victim Perspective within Criminal Justice*. Aldershot: Ashgate.

Reiss, A. (1981), 'Public Safety: Marshalling Crime Statistics', *The Annals of the American Academy of Political and Social Science*, 453: 222–236.

Retzinger, S. and Scheff, T. (1996), 'Strategy for Community Conferences: Emotions and Social Bonds' in B. Galaway and J. Hudson (eds.), *Restorative Justice: International Perspectives.* Monsey, NY: Criminal Justice Press.

Roach, K. (1997), 'Due Process and Victims' Rights', unpublished paper.

Rock, P. (1990), *Helping Victims of Crime: The Home Office and the Rise of Victim Support in England and Wales.* Oxford: Clarendon Press.

Rubel, H. (1986), 'Victim Participation in Sentencing Proceedings', *The Criminal Law Quarterly*, 28: 226–250.

Sandor, D. (1994), 'The Thickening Blue Wedge in Juvenile Justice', in C. Alder and J. Wundersitz (eds.), *Family Conferencing and Juvenile Justice: The Way Forward or Misplaced Optimism?* Australian Studies in Law, Crime and Justice, Canberra, Australian Institute of Criminology.

Schafer, S. (1968), *The Victim and His Criminal: A Study in Functional Responsibility.* New York: Random House.

Scheff, T. (1994), *Bloody Revenge: Emotions, Nationalism and War.* Bolder, Colo.: Westview Press.

—— (1996), 'Crime, Shame and Community: Mediation against Violence', Wellness Foundation Distinguished Lecture, University of California at Santa Barbara, 10 October.

Scheingold, S., Olson, T., and Pershing, J. (1994), 'Sexual Violence, Victim Advocacy and Republican Criminology: Washington State's Community Protection Act', *Law and Society Review*, 28(4): 729–763.

Schluter, M. (1994), 'What is Relational Justice?' in J. Burnside and N. Baker (eds.), *Relational Justice: Repairing the Breach.* Winchester: Waterside Press.

Sebba, L. (1996), *Third Parties: Victims and the Criminal Justice System.* Columbus, Ohio: State University Press.

Shapland, J. (1984), 'Victims, the Criminal Justice System and Compensation', *British Journal of Criminology*, 24: 131–149.

—— (1986), 'Victims and the Criminal Justice System' in E. Fattah (ed.), *From Crime Policy to Victim Policy: Reorienting the Justice System.* London, Macmillan.

—— (1988), 'Fiefs and Peasants: Accomplishing Change for Victims in the Criminal Justice System' in M. Maguire and J. Pointing (eds.), *Victims of Crime: A New Deal?* Milton Keynes: Open University Press.

—— (2000), 'Victims and Criminal Justice: Creating Responsible Criminal Justice Agencies' in A. Crawford and J. Goodey (eds.),

Integrating a Victim Perspective within Criminal Justice. Aldershot: Ashgate.

—— Willmore, J., and Duff, P. (1985), *Victims in the Criminal Justice System.* Cambridge Studies in Criminology, Aldershot: Gower.

Sharpe, J. (1980), 'Enforcing the Law in the Seventeenth Century English Village' in V. Gartrell (ed.), *Crime and the Law.* London: Europa.

Sherman, L. W. (1992), *Policing Domestic Violence: Experiments and Dilemmas.* New York: Free Press.

—— and Berk, R. (1984), 'The Specific Deterrent Effects of Arrest for Domestic Assault', *American Sociological Review*, 49(2): 261–272.

—— Strang, H., Barnes, G., Braithwaite, J., Inkpen, N., and Teh, M. (1998), *Experiments in Restorative Policing: A Progress Report on the Canberra Reintegrative Shaming Experiments*, Law Program, Research School of Social Sciences, Australian National University, Canberra (**www.aic.gov.au/rjustice**).

Skogan, W. (1977), 'Dimensions of the Dark Figure of Unreported Crime', *Crime and Delinquency*, 23(1): 41–50.

—— (1978), *Victimization Surveys and Criminal Justice Planning.* Washington, DC: US National Institute of Law Enforcement and Criminal Justice.

—— (1984), 'Reporting Crimes to the Police: The Status of World Research', *Journal of Research in Crime and Delinquency*, 21: 113–137.

—— Davis, R., and Lurigio, A. (1990), 'Victims' Needs and Victims' Services', Final Report, Washington, DC: National Institute of Justice,

Smith, B. (1983), *Non-Stranger Violence: The Criminal Court's Response.* Washington, DC: Department of Justice.

Stewart, T. (1996), 'Family Group Conferences with Young Offenders in New Zealand' in J. Hudson, A. Morris, G. Maxwell, and B. Galaway (eds.), *Family Group Conferences.* Sydney: Federation Press.

Strang, H. (2001), *Restorative Justice Programs in Australia.* Report to the Criminology Research Council, Canberra. **www. aic.gov.au/rjustice.**

—— and Sherman, L. W. (1997), 'The Victim's Perspective', *RISE Working Papers: Paper No. 2*, **www.aic.gov.au/rjustice.**

—— Barnes, G., Braithwaite, J., and Sherman, L. W. (1999), *Experiments in Restorative Policing: A Progress Report on the Canberra Reintegrative Shaming Experiments (RISE)*, **www.aic.gov.au/rjustice.**

Stuart, B. (1996), 'Circle Sentencing: Turning Swords into Ploughshares' in B. Galaway and J. Hudson (eds.), *Restorative Justice: International Perspectives*. Monsey, NY: Criminal Justice Press.

Stubbs, J. (1995), ' "Communitarian" Conferencing and Violence against Women: A Cautionary Note' in M. Valverde, L. McLeod, and V. Johnson (eds.), *Wife Assault and the Canadian Criminal Justice System*. Toronto: Centre of Criminology, University of Toronto.

—— (2002), 'Domestic Violence and Women's Safety: Feminist Challenges to Restorative Justice' in H. Strang and J. Braithwaite (eds.), *Restorative Justice and Family Violence*. Cambridge: Cambridge University Press.

Tavuchis, N. (1991), *Mea Culpa: A Sociology of Apology and Reconciliation*. Stanford, Cal.: Stanford University Press.

Thibaut, J. and Walker, L. (1975), *Procedural Justice: A Psychological Analysis*. Hillsdale, NJ: Wiley.

Tobolowsky, P. (1993), 'Restitution in the Federal Criminal Justice System', *Judicature*, 77(2): 90–95.

Trimboli, L. (2000), *An Evaluation of the NSW Youth Justice Conferencing Scheme*. Sydney: New South Wales Bureau of Crime Statistics and Research, Attorney General's Department.

Tutu, D. (1999), *No Future Without Forgiveness*. London: Rider.

Tyler, T. (1988), 'What is Procedural Justice?: Criteria Used by Citizens to Assess the Fairness of Legal Procedures', *Law and Society Review*, 22(1): 103–135.

—— (1990), *Why People Obey the Law*. New Haven, Conn.: Yale University Press.

—— and Lind, E. (1992), 'A Relational Model of Authority in Groups' in M. Zanna (ed.), *Advances in Experimental Social Psychology*, vol. 25. San Diego, Cal.: Academic Press.

Umbreit, M. (1985), *Crime and Reconciliation: Creative Options for Victims and Offenders*. Nashville, Tenn.: Abingdon Press.

—— (1989), 'Crime Victims Seeking Fairness, Not Revenge: Toward Restorative Justice', *Federal Probation*, 53(3): 52–57.

—— (1998), 'Restorative Justice through Juvenile Victim–Offender Mediation' in L. Walgrave and G. Bazemore (eds.), *Restoring Juvenile Justice*. Amsterdam: Kugler Publishers.

—— Coates, R., and Kalanj, B. (1994), *Victim Meets Offender: The Impact of Restorative Justice and Mediation*. Monsey, NY: Criminal Justice Press.

US Department of Justice (1986), *Four Years Later: A Report on the President's Task Force on Victims of Crime*. Washington, DC: US Government Printing Office.

Van Ness, D. (1986), *Crime and Its Victims: What We Can Do*. Downers Grove, Ill: Intervarsity Press.

—— (1990), 'Restorative Justice' in B. Galaway and J. Hudson (eds.), *Criminal Justice, Restitution and Reconciliation*. Monsey, NY: Criminal Justice Press.

—— (1993), 'New Wine in Old Wineskins: Four Challenges of Restorative Justice', *Criminal Law Forum*, 4: 251–276.

Viano, E. (1983), 'Violence Victimization and Social Change: A Socio-cultural and Public Policy Analysis', *Victimology: An International Journal*, 8(3)–(4): 54–59.

—— (1987), 'Victims' Rights and the Constitution', *Crime and Delinquency*, 33: 438–451.

—— (1990), *The Victimology Handbook: Research Findings, Treatment and Public Policy*. New York: Garland.

Wagatsuma, H. and Rosett, A. (1986), 'The Implications of Apology: Law and Culture in Japan and the United States', *Law and Society Review*, 20(4): 461–498.

Walgrave, L. and Aertsen, I. (1996), 'Reintegrative Shaming and Restorative Justice: Interchangeable, Complementary or Different?', *European Journal on Criminal Policy and Research*, 4: 67–85.

Walklate, S. (1989), *Victimology: The Victim and the Criminal Justice Process*. London: Unwin Hyman.

Waller, I. (1989), 'The Needs of Crime Victims' in E. Fattah (ed.), *The Plight of Crime Victims in Modern Society*. Basingstoke: Macmillan.

—— and Okihiro, N. (1978), *Burglary: the Victim and the Public*. Toronto: University of Toronto Press.

Watson, D., Boucherat, J., and Davis, D. (1989), 'Reparation for Retributivists' in M. Wright and B. Galaway (eds.), *Mediation and Criminal Justice: Victims, Offenders and Community*. London: Sage Publications.

Weinstein, G. and Levin, B. (1989), 'Effect of Crossover on the Statistical Power of Randomized Studies', *Annals of Thoracic Surgery*, 48: 490–495.

Weisburd, D., Petrosino, A., and Mason, G. (1993), 'Design Sensitivity in Criminal Justice Experiments' in M. Tonry (ed.), *Crime and Justice: A Review of Research*, vol. 17. Chicago, Ill.: University of Chicago.

Weisstub, D. N. (1986), 'Victims of Crime in the Criminal Justice System' in E. A. Fattah (ed.), *From Crime Policy to Victim Policy: Reorienting the Justice System*. Basingstoke: Macmillan.

Weitekamp, E. (1997), 'The History of Restorative Justice', paper to Leuven International Conference, Restorative Justice for Juveniles—potentialities, risks and problems for research, 12–14 May.

Weber, M. (1921), 'Politics as a Vocation' in H. H. Gerth and C. Wright Mills (eds.), *From Max Weber: Essays in Sociology* (1948). London: Routledge Sociology Classics.

Wemmers, J. (1996), *Victims in the Criminal Justice System.* Amsterdam: Kugler Publications.

Wilkins, L. (1991), *Punishment, Crime and Market Forces.* Aldershot: Dartmouth Publishing.

Wolfgang, M. (1965), 'Victim Compensation in Crimes of Personal Violence', *Minnesota Law Review*, 50: 229–241.

—— (1972), 'Making the Criminal Justice System Accountable', *Crime and Delinquency*, January, 15–22.

Wright, M. (1991), *Justice for Victims and Offenders: A Restorative Response to Crime.* Milton Keynes: Open University Press.

Wundersitz, J. (1996), *The South Australian Juvenile Justice System: A Review of its Operation.* Adelaide: Office of Crime Statistics, South Australian Attorney General's Department.

—— (2000), 'Juvenile Justice in Australia: Towards the New Millennium' in D. Chappell and P. Wilson, *Crime and the Criminal Justice System in Australia: 2000 and Beyond.* Sydney: Butterworths.

—— and Hetzel, S. (1996), 'Family Conferencing for Young Offenders: The South Australian Experience' in J. Hudson, A. Morris, G. Maxwell, and B. Galaway (eds.), *Family Group Conferences: Perspectives on Policy and Practice.* Sydney: Federation Press.

Young, R. (2000), 'Integrating a Multi-victim Perspective into Criminal Justice through Restorative Justice Conferences' in A. Crawford and J. Goodey (eds.), *Integrating a Victim Perspective within Criminal Justice.* Aldershot: Ashgate.

Zedner, L. (1994), 'Victims' in M. Maguire, R. Morgan, and R. Reiner (eds.), *The Oxford Handbook of Criminology.* Oxford: Clarendon Press.

Zehr, H. (1985), 'Retributive Justice, Restorative Justice', *New Perspectives on Crime and Justice*, Occasional Papers of the MCC [Mennonite Central Committee] Canada Victim Offender Ministries Program and the MCC U.S. Office of Criminal Justice, September, Issue no. 4.

—— (1990), *Changing Lenses: A New Focus for Criminal Justice.* Scottsdale, Penn.: Herald Press.

—— (1995), 'Rethinking Criminal Justice: Restorative Justice' unpublished paper for a NZ conference entitled 'Rethinking Criminal Justice: Restorative Justice' (Auckland 6/95).

Ziegenhagen, E. (1977), *Victims, Crime and Social Control*. New York: Praeger Publishers.

Index of authors

Subject Index